CCCC STUDIES IN WRITING & I
*Edited by Steve Parks, University (*

The aim of the CCCC Studies in Writing & Rhetoric (SWR) Series is to influence how we think about language in action and especially how writing gets taught at the college level. The methods of studies vary from the critical to historical to linguistic to ethnographic, and their authors draw on work in various fields that inform composition—including rhetoric, communication, education, discourse analysis, psychology, cultural studies, and literature. Their focuses are similarly diverse—ranging from individual writers and teachers, to work on classrooms and communities and curricula, to analyses of the social, political, and material contexts of writing and its teaching.

SWR was one of the first scholarly book series to focus on the teaching of writing. It was established in 1980 by the Conference on College Composition and Communication (CCCC) in order to promote research in the emerging field of writing studies. As our field has grown, the research sponsored by SWR has continued to articulate the commitment of CCCC to supporting the work of writing teachers as reflective practitioners and intellectuals.

We are eager to identify influential work in writing and rhetoric as it emerges. We thus ask authors to send us project proposals that clearly situate their work in the field and show how they aim to redirect our ongoing conversations about writing and its teaching. Proposals should include an overview of the project, a brief annotated table of contents, and a sample chapter. They should not exceed 10,000 words.

To submit a proposal, please register as an author at www.editorialmanager.com/nctebp. Once registered, follow the steps to submit a proposal (be sure to choose SWR Book Proposal from the drop-down list of article submission types).

# SWR Editorial Advisory Board

Steve Parks, SWR Editor, University of Virginia
Kevin Browne, University of the West Indies
Ellen Cushman, Northeastern University
Laura Gonzales, University of Texas-El Paso
Haivan Hoang, University of Massachusetts-Amherst
Carmen Kynard, Texas Christian University
Paula Mathieu, Boston College
Staci M. Perryman-Clark, Western Michigan University
Eric Pritchard, University at Buffalo
Jacqueline Rhodes, Michigan State University
Tiffany Rousculp, Salt Lake Community College
Khirsten Scott, University of Pittsburgh
Jody Shipka, University of Maryland, Baltimore County
Bo Wang, California State University

# Counterstory
## The Rhetoric and Writing of Critical Race Theory

Aja Y. Martinez
*University of North Texas*

Conference on College
Composition and
Communication

National Council of
Teachers of English

National Council of Teachers of English
340 N. Neil St., Suite #104, Champaign, Illinois 61820

Figure 1 (p. 28) by Daniel G. Solórzano and Dolores Delgado Bernal, *Urban Education* (36.3), pp. 308–42, copyright © 2001 by SAGE Publications. Reprinted by permission of SAGE Publications, Inc.

Staff Editor: Bonny Graham
Interior Design: Mary Rohrer
Cover Design: Pat Mayer
Cover Image: Yanira Rodríguez

NCTE Stock Number: 08789; eStock Number: 08796
ISBN 978-0-8141-0878-9; eISBN 978-0-8141-0879-6

Copyright © 2020 by the Conference on College Composition and Communication of the National Council of Teachers of English.

All rights reserved. No part of this publication may be reproduced or transmitted in any form or by any means, electronic or mechanical, including photocopy, or any information storage and retrieval system, without permission from the copyright holder. Printed in the United States of America.

It is the policy of NCTE in its journals and other publications to provide a forum for the open discussion of ideas concerning the content and the teaching of English and the language arts. Publicity accorded to any particular point of view does not imply endorsement by the Executive Committee, the Board of Directors, or the membership at large, except in announcements of policy, where such endorsement is clearly specified.

NCTE provides equal employment opportunity (EEO) to all staff members and applicants for employment without regard to race, color, religion, sex, national origin, age, physical, mental or perceived handicap/disability, sexual orientation including gender identity or expression, ancestry, genetic information, marital status, military status, unfavorable discharge from military service, pregnancy, citizenship status, personal appearance, matriculation or political affiliation, or any other protected status under applicable federal, state, and local laws.

Every effort has been made to provide current URLs and email addresses, but because of the rapidly changing nature of the web, some sites and addresses may no longer be accessible.

**Library of Congress Cataloging-in-Publication Data**

Names: Martinez, Aja Y., 1982- author.
Title: Counterstory : the rhetoric and writing of critical race theory / by Aja. Y. Martinez.
Description: Champaign, Illinois : Conference on College Composition and Communication ; National Council of Teachers of English, [2020] | Series: CCC studies in writing & rhetoric | Includes bibliographical references and index. | Summary: "Makes a case for counterstory as methodology in rhetoric and writing studies through the framework of critical race theory"—Provided by publisher.
Identifiers: LCCN 2020010505 (print) | LCCN 2020010506 (ebook) | ISBN 9780814108789 (trade paperback) | ISBN 9780814108796 (adobe pdf)
Subjects: LCSH: English language—Rhetoric—Study and teaching (Higher)—Social aspects—United States. | Narration (Rhetoric)—Study and teaching (Higher)—United States. | Storytelling in education—United States. | Autobiography—Authorship—Study and teaching (Higher)—United States. | Racism in education—United States. | Discrimination in education—United States.
Classification: LCC PE1405.U6 M373 2020 (print) | LCC PE1405.U6 (ebook) | DDC 808/.042—dc23
LC record available at https://lccn.loc.gov/2020010505
LC ebook record available at https://lccn.loc.gov/2020010506

*To Dr. Maria Teresa Velez (MTV). The bridge was your back. Te amo, mil gracias, que en paz descanse, and I'll see you on the other side.*

The histories that we speak shape the beliefs that we act on.
—Carmen Kynard

Critical race theory writing and lecturing is characterized by frequent use of the first person, storytelling, narrative, allegory, interdisciplinary treatment of law, *and the unapologetic use of creativity.*
—Derrick A. Bell [my emphasis]

# CONTENTS

Foreword xi
*Carmen Kynard*
Acknowledgments xv
Author's Note xxiii
Prologue: Encomium of a Storyteller xxv

1. A Case for Counterstory 1
2. Richard Delgado and Counterstory as Narrated Dialogue 32
   Counterstory: On Storytelling and Perspective, or, The Road Trip 38
3. Derrick Bell and Counterstory as Allegory/Fantasy 53
   Counterstory: The Politics of Historiography, Act 2 64
4. Patricia J. Williams and Counterstory as Autobiographic Reflection 80
   Counterstory: Diary of a Mad Border Crosser 99
5. Counterstory in Education: Pedagogical Implications for CRT Methodology 110
   Counterstory: An Epistolary Email on Pedagogy and Master Narrative Curricula 118

Epilogue: Birth Song 139
Afterword 143
*Jaime Armin Mejía*

Appendix A: Race Critical Theories, Critical Race Rhetorics Syllabus   147

Appendix B: Writing Critical Race Counterstory Syllabus   153

Appendix C: Histories and Theories of Rhetoric(s)—or, Whose Truth Is True? Syllabus   157

Appendix D: Contemporary Rhetorics—Cultural Rhetorics Syllabus   162

Notes   169

Works Cited   179

Index   191

Author   201

## FOREWORD

WAY BACK IN THE EARLY 1990s, I was an undergraduate college student tryna find her way. People in my age group will often talk about these days as the golden age of hip-hop sprinkled with things like *Living Single*-kinda-sitcoms, mixtapes, the electric slide, neo-soul, and the stylings of a hat-2-da-back. All that is true (we was, after all, very fly), but there were new vocabularies and connections to the academy that also played right alongside these soundtracks.

By that time, I knew that race and colonization were intimately connected with every facet of higher education: endowments, land, sorting mechanisms, recruitment, retention, rank, promotion, and tenure. Ironically, I had never used such words before and it never occurred to me that I would someday join the professoriate. Critical race theory (CRT) gave me an ease with this new language and a political lens through Derrick Bell. Bell's *And We Are Not Saved: The Elusive Quest for Racial Justice* (1987) and *Faces at the Bottom of the Well: The Permanence of Racism* (1992) were in heavy rotation though I do not recall anyone ever assigning these texts in my classes. The pages of my original copies are literally scattered across the country from all of the dormitories and apartments where I lived back then.

These two books certainly made me a different kind of reader, but it was a specific 1991 lecture-turned-essay called "Racism Is Here to Stay: Now What?" by Bell published in the *Howard Law Journal* that made me a different kind of writer. When he began arguing for racial realism, namely the idea that race is endemic, with no linear progress available, Bell was often accused of being too pessimistic and hopeless. I was annoyed to no end that somehow it was black people's job to give white folks hope and optimism about racism, but Bell was brilliant in his response: a story that I consider his most compelling message. It's the story of an elder, a Mississippian black woman named Mrs. Biona MacDonald. I tend to talk about Mrs. MacDonald as if I know her, and in some ways I do, not literally but certainly figuratively. Here is what Bell says (please bear with the long quotation for a moment and actually read it):

> The year was 1964. It was a quiet, heat-hushed evening in Harmony, a small black community near the Mississippi Delta. Some Harmony residents, in the face of increasing, white hostility, were organizing to insure the implementation of a court order mandating desegregation of their schools the next September. Walking with Mrs. Biona MacDonald, one of the organizers, up a dusty, unpaved road toward her modest home, I asked where she found the courage to continue working for civil rights in the face of intimidation that included her son losing his job in town, the local bank trying to foreclose on her mortgage, and shots fired through her living room window.
>
> "Derrick," she said slowly, seriously. "I am an old woman. I lives to harass white folks."
>
> You notice, Mrs. MacDonald didn't say she risked everything because she hoped or expected to win out over the whites who, as she well knew, held all the economic and political power, and the guns as well. Rather, she recognized that—powerless as she was—she had and intended to use courage and determination as a weapon, in her words: "to harass white folks." She did not even hint that her harassment would topple whites' well entrenched power. Rather, her goal was defiance and its harassing effect was likely more potent precisely because she placed herself in confrontation with her oppressors with full knowledge of both their power and their willingness to use it.
>
> Mrs. MacDonald avoided discouragement and defeat *because at the point that she determined to resist her oppression, she was triumphant* (92–93; emphasis mine).

Bell closes by telling his readers to remember Mrs. MacDonald and we will understand all that we need to know. That was a defining moment for me. I was clear on whom I walked with as my peeples, ancestors, and soundtracks outside of school, but it was Derrick Bell who gave me the language and attitude to keep them right in the classroom with me in every word, thought, comma, and exclamation point. You see, Mrs. MacDonald is not a source of inspiration, a point of interesting "data," the lines of an interview transcript, the critical subject of an archival research study, a grounding narrative in an oral history project, or a lesson in morality for white folk—those are the frames we are most often offered in white supremacist relationships to language, knowledge, and rhetoric in the academy. Mrs. MacDonald is THE WHOLE STORY. Mrs. MacDonald lived her *counter*story, but if you write/think it like the white academy, you will have no *counter* at all. And if you can't tell that *counter*story in her language, exigency, and race-radical vibe, well, you ain't even really livin right, just livin white.

What Bell saw as the "wellsprings" of CRT—family, ancestors, the everydayness of the struggle and the fight, the long roads home, decentering&messing with white folk—marked CRT as not merely some new theoretically chic concept for university production and consumption. CRT was, as Ella Baker might say: where your people come from (see Charlene Carruthers, Barbara Ransby, and Bob Moses for how I am referencing Baker here). Rooted in deep traditions of everyday protest, resistance, and survivance, CRT grounded its urgency in an alternative intellectual and political legacy, not to the academy and its published scholarship. Today when I think of Mrs. MacDonald, I picture her chopping it up with Professor Martinez's grandfather, Alejandro Ayala Leyva, who is present with us throughout her entire book. I just know that Grampa Alejandro is holding this book in his hands right now and smiling down on us, looking up from time to time to give an upnod to Derrick Bell.

Many of us will read this book and praise the universe as Professor Martinez takes us through the field of rhetoric-composition's race-regimes and assimilationist camps often disguised as publishing, search committees, graduate education, and undergraduate curriculum and instruction. This aspect of Professor Martinez's critique is important here: if we mean CRT as more than just an academic byline claiming expertise on a bourgeois professional CV, then we must direct our analyses at our very institutions, disciplinary canons, fields of study, and sanctioned leaders. Many folk will say that is risky. Yes, that may very well be true. But the radical traditions from which Professor Martinez draws in this book deserve more than the intellectual side-stepping produced by the bullying of institutional racism. Mrs. MacDonald and Grampa Alejandro deserve more than academic subcategories used to mark research and scholarship *about them* but that has never talked *to them*. Professor Martinez's own Huichol people deserve more than the stultifying silences around the ongoing racial violence and retaliations against those of us who speak out. Most important, Professor Martinez's own babygirl, Olivia, deserves a professoriate who will fight to match their pedagogies to the *counter*story of her people.

The risks that Richard Delgado, Derrick Bell, Patricia Williams, and now Aja Martinez took to write themselves into the academy this way require us to take notice and respond with some bravery. These are our CRT teachers, whose presence reminds us that we BIPOC faculty have paid the price over and over again to be here. Yes, white supremacy has always come for us, but it ain't never won. And we got the counterstory right here to prove it!

Carmen Kynard<br>Texas Christian University

## ACKNOWLEDGMENTS

THESE ACKNOWLEDGMENTS ARE in tribute to those who sustain my story. First and foremost, to my families, by birth, and by choice: Mom Pat, dad Ramon, brother Julian, daughter Olivia, nieces Alexis Carmen and Camila Anita, grandparents, godparents, tías, tíos, in-laws, and cousins. You all are my rock-solid foundation and are the reason I do this work. To my friends who are family: Aileen, Lisa, Anna, Mo, Jowell, and Brittany and Jake (who so willingly read my counterstories!). A special thanks to my friends who are my family in the academy: Jaime Armín Mejia, Casie Moreland (#texasforever!), Tom Do, Cruz Medina, Sonia Arellano, Marissa Juarez, Erica Cirillo-McCarthy, Jenna Vinson, Laura Gonzales, Kelly Kinney, Maria P. Chaves, Giovanna Montenegro, Odilka Santiago, Sara Alvarez, and Steve Alvarez—is there anyone whose home I've not yet visited?

To the folks where this PhD story began, University of Arizona RCTE (past and present), particularly: Adela C. Licona, Thomas P. Miller, Roxanne Mountford, Edward M. White, the late Theresa Jarnagin Enos, and Ken McAllister. An especial thanks to Adela.

Although I can say many things about Adela's capacity as a mentor to me within the academy, because I am a storyteller I'd like to zero in on and narrate my personal lived experiences concerning Adela's immense influence on me as a mother, scholar, teacher, colleague, friend, and mentor. During spring 2007, nearly two full years into my graduate studies in Arizona's RCTE program, I had yet to have seen, met, read, or been made aware of scholars or professors of color in rhetoric and writing studies. As far as I was concerned—and as far as my two years of coursework to this point had been concerned—POC did not exist in rhet/writ. And then, within this spring semester, it was announced that *four* POC candidates would visit campus to interview for an assistant professor position with RCTE. The offer went to Adela C. Licona. Two years into my graduate studies, in a grueling and oftentimes cruel MA-PhD program, I was ready to throw in the towel. And then I saw and met Dr. Licona, and to me, someone so desperate for a beacon of hope to sustain me through my studies, Adela Licona appeared to me the way the *Virgen de Guadalupe* is painted—shrouded in a halo of fiery light that surrounds her entire body, communicating her fierce strength, compassion, and power. Adela's hire meant so much at such a critical time for me, and I'll never forget this first encounter. Fast-forward to fall 2007, when Adela offered a graduate seminar titled Rhetorics of Difference/Different Rhetorics, in which the scholarship of queer and/or POC rhetorics was made central to our course inquiry. This was the first time I was ever assigned the work of QPOC, and it was within this course that I first encountered the work of critical race theorists. In this course, Adela modeled for me feminist praxis, including sharing food and fellowship with us, her students. She began class with "checkins"—a good reminder that we are people with bodies and emotions, who are attached to families and partners and communities, and that we should come to her classroom and our academic lives as our whole selves, not just as floating brains, detached from our corporeal realities. Adela has always and continually extended herself beyond any typical role of a teacher-advisor within academic programs and institutions. Adela is a mentor who shares of herself, shares of her life, and shares of her family, and who has modeled for me, and for so many, the truest spirit of feminist praxis, coalition, solidarity, and *comadrismo*. I would not be here as a professor, a scholar, or a mentor/advocate for my own graduate students had Adela not been hired right when she was. I was ready to quit. Yet Adela showed me a path by which I could exist in this life, which she continues to do to this day.

To my colleagues at Binghamton University, Libby Tucker, Bernie Rosenthal, John Havard, and Lisa Yun, and to the students from my first CRT undergrad and grad courses. I cut my R1 teeth at Binghamton, and I am forever grateful for the experience and the opportunity. Y'all took a chance on me. An especial thanks to

Kelly Kinney, who I know fought hard for my "straight outta grad school" hire and who has demonstrated in the most meaningful ways her commitment to allyship, critical self-reflection on privilege, and an activist orientation as a teacher, scholar, and administrator. Thanks for your mentorship and your friendship.

To my continued mentors and inspiration, Victor Villanueva and Carmen Kynard—as can be discerned from the content and style of this project, I have been lifted up and supported by your words, works, and friendships, and I want to be just like y'all when I grow up! To Victor: you were the first person to see my writing and believe there was promise in it, so much so that you reviewed, edited, and published my first ever essay back in that 2009 *College English* special issue. And you're still reading every *papelito guardado* I send your way, with such patience, encouragement, and honesty. I am so grateful to you for the time and energy you've put into this project, I honestly don't know where you find the time for those of us you so generously commit to and support. I can think of no better hands than yours for my project to be in. To Carmen: your words speak to me and through me in ways that make me so brave. When I face situations in this "job" that try me (as is too often the case), I think to myself, "What would Carmen do?" And this refrain keeps me set on path to do the "work" beyond and besides the "job." I model my career on your moves; you clear paths and blaze trails.

To Jaime Armin Mejía, whom I first met at the annual conference of the Council of Writing Program Administration in July 2007 in Tempe, Arizona: Since this initial meeting, we have become family, and I admire and value you so very much. I say this to many people, and often, but I do not send my work to journals and presses without first letting it pass through your copyediting eagle eye (Jaime read and copyedited this manuscript, line by line with a pencil, not once, but TWICE!). The tremendous time and energy you have expended on my writing, all from a place of love and support and of wanting me to do well "out there," is so generous. I count myself very lucky to be one of your mentees, but I am luckier to be your friend. I am so grateful for the hospitality you have shown me, my family, and my cats in your own home, as we've crisscrossed the country on road trips from homes to jobs. I am positive that Texas holds a special place in my heart because it's the place Jaime Mejía hangs his hat. And as you've said, "I owe you a beer or some rum"—how about both over some good barbeque! Thanks so much, Jaime, you really are the backbone of this field in ways I don't think you properly comprehend, but for those of us who know this, you are so loved and honored among us.

To my colleagues at Syracuse University, but particularly: Krista Kennedy (teaching mentor), Eileen Schell (research mentor), Patrick Berry (chair), Brice Nordquist (graduate director), Rebecca Moore-Howard, Collin Brooke, former colleague and SWR editor Steve Parks, and my "*Chingonas por Vida*" partner, Genevieve García de Müeller. An especial thanks to my luminary role models and incredible WOC support, Marcelle Haddix, Gwendolyn Pough, Carol W. N. Fadda, and Dana M. Olwan.

To the students at Syracuse University, particularly students in my CCR 760 and WRT 422 courses, but also, the *buena gente,* students who are colleagues. To Romeo García, who has always treated me like family, but especially when I'm down in the valley. To Vani Kannan and Yanira Rodríguez, who have taught me so much about activism, refusal, and a true feminist spirit of coalition and solidarity. To Karrieann Soto, Telsha Curry, Stephanie Jones, Pritisha Shrestha, André Habet, Camilla Bell, and D. Romo, who have made me feel so welcome and supported as faculty within CCR and CFE. To Noah Wilson, who has shown true critical self-reflection on privilege and who has demonstrated a genuine commitment to allyship. To Alex Hanson, who has reminded me that single parents deserve rights within our institutions and whose project has inspired me in so many ways—Alex, please know that I never wrote about my own experiences as a single mom until your project bolstered my confidence to do so. To B. López and Martín Alberto Gonzalez, who I've had the honor of mentoring and supporting through their own counterstory Independent Studies and projects. I am already thrilled by your work and look forward to what you will teach (and already are teaching!) all of us as your projects develop. And, importantly, to Benesemon Simmons. *Sí se puede*, Bene. We have pushed through so many barriers together, and your resilience, your strength, your brilliance, and your sheer resolve *not* to believe the lies this institution tries to convince you of is proof, is undeniable evidence, of #blackgirlmagic. You are here to do incredible things. I probably say this to all of my students too much, but if not for you all, this work is just a job. I am so honored to be part of your stories.

To the Minnowbrook crew, particularly Mim Readling, Christine Scharf, and Ellen Holzman. K–12 teachers who care about their students the way you all do are so inspiring and encouraging. Thank you all for being my first test audience of students as I crafted a curriculum for the teaching of counterstory. Your feedback and engagement have remained critical to the trajectory of this course but also to the ways this course has featured in this project. I am honored and so lucky to have enjoyed the experience of teaching, yes, but also of learning from such master teachers.

To the extraordinary women, mothers, daughters, and doulas who constitute the "Birth Song" writers workshop. An especial thanks to Marcelle Haddix, Sequoia Kemp (Doula 4 A Queen), and Asteir Bey (Village Birth International). I am not a poet, but I wrote my first and only poem (featured at the conclusion of this book) as part of this incredible experience shared with incredible women who do so much to support moms, babies, and healthy pregnancies and births in the Syracuse community—particularly in service of the BIPOC low-income community.

To the members of the NCTE/CCCC Latinx Caucus, past, present, and future. I am especially grateful to elders who have paved our paths, to my contemporaries who build bridges with our backs, and to the next generation who give me hope and an impetus for this work.

Huge thanks to Texas State University-San Marcos and their Predoctoral Fellowship summer program. Thanks also to my program mentor, Octavio Pimentel, and my unofficial mentor, Charise Pimentel. You all opened your home to me and my Libs for that generative summer back in 2010, and it was under your roof and in the embrace of your mentorship that I was able to write my first ever counterstory, which became the first counterstory for my dissertation, and in turn my first ever published counterstory: "A Plea for Critical Race Theory Counterstory: Stock Story versus Counterstory Dialogues concerning Alejandra's 'Fit' in the Academy."

To my writing groups: Adam J. Banks and the Smitherman/Villanueva Writing Collective, particularly inaugural members Steven Alvarez, Tamika Carey, Rhea Lathan, Gabi Ríos, David Green, Nazera Wright, and Bill Endres, and to Andrea Romero and the AZ Mujeres Writing Group. I think so fondly on the summers we've spent (in various locales all over the country) in food, fellowship, and familial support of one another. I'm so happy to add this book to my bookshelf that proudly displays all of your work. We're doing it!

To Casie Moreland, the Slytherin to my Ravenclaw. You are my sister, and I love you so much. Your enthusiasm and support of my work has always been so important, and I have such a hard time waiting for your feedback on my writing because your opinion matters so much to me. You are a white accomplice in every sense of its meaning, and I'm so honored to be your ride or die. #texasforever!

To my brothers from another mother, Cruz Medina and Tom Do! Cruz, thank you for continually reading and providing feedback on my work, I'm so happy you are part of this project, and I'm glad to have you as a riding partner when it comes to telling ignorant folks how they are and are NOT allowed to talk about our *gente*. Tom, laughing with you is some of the best medicine, and we've had many adventures worth laughing about (reality TV and ice cream, sneaking tiramisu into movie theaters, ridiculous Halloween costumes, and my cat drooling on you!). I know these counterstories and composite characters will continue in your capable hands, and I cannot wait to see Jack's story unfold.

One additional shout-out to Yanira Rodríguez, who so graciously and beautifully provided the cover art for this book. Thank you for sharing your gift with me and the audience for this project. I can think of no better visual representation of my work in counterstory than the stunning art you have created and so generously bestowed.

To Vivian May and the Syracuse University Humanities Center Faculty Fellowship program, without which I would not have had the time and headspace to finish this book! Thanks so much for the full confidence and support of this project, and thanks also for providing a platform to showcase this work to the broader Syracuse campus community in the form of the Humanities Center Faculty Fellows dinner. An especial thanks to Carol N. W. Fadda, without whose encouragement and mentorship I would not be an HC Faculty Fellow. Thanks also to Carol (again!), Dana M. Olwan, and Myrna García Calderón for being my cheering section at the fellows dinner—your support in this capacity means the world to me.

To my fantastic and supportive NCTE and SWR editorial team: Steve Parks, Victor Villanueva, Kurt Austin, and Bonny Graham. Your (in some cases years-long) patience, sheer enthusiasm, and faith in this project have made this process so exciting and enjoyable. I can think of no better hands than all of yours for this work.

To my new colleagues at the University of North Texas, especially Jacqueline Vanhoutte and Matthew Heard, who, as a department of English, have collectively gone above and beyond to make me feel welcome. Y'all have made crystal clear that my work in counterstory is valued as "real" research. I'm so excited about this next adventure in Denton!

And last, but not least—to the folks who impressed on me that I should pursue this path as a storytelling professor: Richard Stoffle and the "Bahama Mamas" (Kathleen Van Vlack, Alex Carroll, Clint Carroll, Fletcher Chmara-Huff, and Nate O'Meara), and Maria Theresa Velez, Andrew Huerta, and Nura Dualeh and the University of Arizona (Bear Down!) McNair Scholars Program. I'd say my story as an academic starts with you all, and I hope you see this project as continuing the story you all so enthusiastically encouraged and generously supported.

## AUTHOR'S NOTE

COMMENTING ON THE NATURE of Latinx rhetorics, Victor Villanueva has said, "Going from experience to theory to reflection and so on will make for a text that cannot be neatly linear" (*Bootstraps* xvii). As such a text, this book, a project composed of a collection of stories and counterstories, does not require a linear read by audiences. In fact, because I imagine a multiplicity of audiences for this project, inside and outside of the academy, I encourage readers to "choose their own adventure." For readers who are unfamiliar with, unsure of, or just plain not sold on critical race theory and counterstory, take a stroll through Chapter 1 and the first parts of each chapter thereafter. But for those who do not need convincing that story is theory and method, for those who know story in their blood and bones, I invite you to engage (and, I hope, enjoy) the variety of stories I tell within. Whatever way you choose to interact with this project, rest assured there is not a wrong path.

## PROLOGUE: ENCOMIUM OF A STORYTELLER

I COME TO THIS PROJECT, this book, as, first and foremost, a storyteller within a legacy and genealogy of storytellers. In his foreword to Richard Delgado's *Rodrigo Chronicles*, Robert A. Williams Jr. details the American Indian tradition of the "Storyteller" as "the one who bears the heavy responsibility for maintaining" the connections of community, "an intricate web of connections: kinship and blood, marriage and friendship, alliance and solidarity" (xi). And, importantly, Williams centralizes the role of the ancestors, "our grandmothers and grandfathers, and their grandmothers and grandfathers"—all of whose stories are held sacred to the Storyteller—they who share all of the stories "so that the next generation will recall these narrative links between generations" (xi). To be a Storyteller, Williams asserts, "is to assume the burden of remembrance for a people," for the Storyteller "is the one who sacrifices everything in the tellings and retellings" of story (xi).

My much-chronicled protagonist, Alejandra Prieto,[1] is inspired in name and spirit by my grandfather, Alejandro Ayala Leyva. After completing an epic journey of ninety-nine years, he passed peacefully into our spiritual *otro lado* on Sunday, December 10, 2017. As a narrative exercise in naming where we came from, how we got here, and where we're going, I have begun this book on counterstory with an encomium to the hero-protagonist of my own stories, my real lived stories, and the imagined alter-egos and hyperrealities this book will explore. In this tribute, I invite my audience to reflect similarly on the narratives of their lives and on the carriers of those stories—the ancestorship of the storytellers in our lives who have illuminated pathways for those of us who would continue the story (Pritchard 1).

## ALEJANDRO

My own grandfather, Alejandro Ayala Leyva, was my first and remains the most prominent storyteller in my life. And with a life such as his, it would be a small tragedy were he not the gifted storyteller that he was. His life spanned nearly one hundred years, and his stories are intricately linked to major events in US history. The link was our own family's histories as they intersected with and were affected by our US and Arizona/Mexico borderlands context. As my grampa's oral histories told, my Leyva family migrated to the US Southwest from Durango, Durango, Mexico, in 1913. At that time, my nana Ignacia—my grampa Alejandro's mother and protagonist heroine for most of his oral histories concerning this generation of our family—was twelve years old. My grampa remembers his mother talking about our heritage as Huichol people, a people indigenous to the Sierra Madre Occidental range that spans several Mexican states, including Durango. Our people are known to outsiders as the Huichol,[2] but we refer to ourselves as Wixáritari, or "the people."

Alejandro Ayala Leyva. (Source: Alex A. Leyva . . . aka Tio Beto)

Somewhere between 1910 and 1912, my nana Ignacia was "given"[3] to my grampa's father, Victoriano Leyva, and in 1913, when my nana was twelve years old, the entire Leyva clan, all the aunts, uncles, siblings, cousins, and many other extended relatives, heeded the call north, entering the United States through El Paso to find construction work on the ever-expanding US railroads. My grampa had many stories relayed to him from family members about their time working on the railroad, ranging from experiences laboring alongside Chinese migrants, to living and setting up households (including stories about women making tortillas and giving birth to children) in boxcars. This particular detail of life in railway boxcars provides a certain foreshadowing for the time spent in boxcars a generation later during the Great Depression, when Franklin Delano Roosevelt deported many Mexican families back to Mexico on rail lines they had built with their own hands.

As contracts involving the railroad drew to a close around 1916 or 1917, the Leyva clan, like many Mexican families of their time, splintered and went in various directions to follow agricultural work contracts to various parts of the United States. Some traveled northeast to Illinois and eventually settled in Chicago; some spread throughout the New Mexico and Texas areas; and others, like Nana Ignacia and Victoriano Leyva, traveled to California. My grampa, Alejandro, the eldest of six siblings, was born May 16, 1918, in Los Angeles, California, and lived the early childhood years of his life in what's now ritzy-ass Marina del Rey, on Howard Street—close enough to the Pacific Ocean to put his toes in the sand and water, to gain a lifelong love of swimming, and to gaze at the horizon with dreams of future travel and adventure.

When the Great Depression hit the United States, many Mexicans were blamed for taking the scarce jobs that white Americans felt entitled to—and if this sounds familiar, it should. If we know anything about racism, rhetorics, and narratives, it's that they are cyclical and repetitive. Also familiar and repetitive are the mass deportations the United States has continually engaged in, which, in terms of nationalist American-benevolence rhetoric, was titled "Mexican Repatriation" during this 1930–1940s era. As NPR's Adrian Florido writes in his essay "Mass Deportation May Sound Unlikely, but It's Happened Before,"

> It was the Great Depression, when up to a quarter of Americans were unemployed and many believed that Mexicans were

taking scarce jobs. In response, federal, state and local officials launched so-called "repatriation" campaigns. They held raids in workplaces and in public places, rounded up Mexicans and Mexican-Americans alike, and deported them. The most famous of these was in downtown Los Angeles' Placita Olvera[, where] one-third of LA's Mexican population was expelled between 1929 and 1944 as a result of these practices. (Para. 5)

My grampa and his family, which included his mother, his father, and now four more siblings, found themselves loaded onto a boxcar on a train headed south of the border and out of the country, the same country in which my grampa and his siblings were born. However, as my grampa told it, his father knew well this detail of the birthright citizenship of his children and complied with this US governmental show of might, but only so far as a final bordertown destination—the very last possible point of departure for the Leyva family if they were to remain in the United States—Nogales, Arizona. In Nogales, my great-grandfather Victoriano Leyva instructed his family to get off the train because, as my grampa put it, "They had no business in Mexico." And in many ways, this was true. The whole of the Leyva clan, extended relations included, traveled north for the railroad contracts, so the likelihood that there was a place or a people to be "repatriated" to was slim to none. But above all, as my great-grandfather logically reasoned, his children were American citizens and effectually had "no business in Mexico."

Thus commenced the legacy of my grampa's life stories and adventures in Nogales, Arizona, on the borderlands and the eventual beyond. And these are the stories I was raised on. My grampa's oral histories fed and nurtured our family's sense of self and place as indigenous-Mexican people in a country that has historically crafted master narratives that would cast us, and people like us, as those who have been conquered—as those who should shoulder a sense of shame at our indigenous status as Mexicans and our minoritized status as US people of color. Yet the sustenance infused in me and my family from my grampa's stories holds an illuminating candle of insight to other narratives, counternarratives to the overarching master tropes that would describe us as "outsiders" to be repatriated in my grampa's generation, "Americanized" in my parents' generation, assimilated in my generation, and victimized yet defiant in the face of colonization in all generations. My grampa's stories always provided us an agency through an alternative narrative: thus, my identity—my very existence and sense of being—has always been tied to counterstory.

So I have come to this project as a storyteller, within a legacy of storytellers, a legacy that I am honored to continue.

*Grampa Alejandro, you are immortal in the beautiful memories and narratives of those who love you—so deeply love you.*

Alejandro Ayala Leyva, on his path. (Source: Alex A. Leyva . . . aka Tio Beto)

# 1

## A Case for Counterstory

> I am a big fan of counterstories. I also appreciate you trying to do something different. One of the first suggestions I have is for you to lay out a much better foundation to what counterstories are. Spend some time here and don't assume that people understand now in the field. This could be done rather easily. Unfortunately, I am willing to bet money that the majority of CCC readers are not too familiar with CRT nor counterstories so lay it out for these people.
> 
> —*CCC* manuscript reader review

> I also think it is important to more explicitly define counterstory in basic terms as a methodology early in the manuscript. While readers steeped in CRT may be familiar with the concept, the journal's generalist audience could likely use more explanation up front.
> 
> —*Composition Studies* manuscript reader review

> Because this essay is a bit different [from] the style usually published in Rhetoric Review, which I love, I have a couple of organizational suggestions for the introduction. . . . I do think that the article would benefit from a more explicit setup of counterstory as a methodology prior to the counterstory itself.
> 
> —*Rhetoric Review* manuscript reader review[1]

A STUDENT ONCE ASKED IF there is ever a point at which we (minoritized folk) will get to stop justifying the methodological choice of telling our stories. I believe that we've *all* been telling stories *all* along, but some stories are elevated to the status of theory, scholarship, and literature, while, too often, minoritized perspectives are relegated to marginalized or overlooked "cultural rhetorics" methods or genres. While I don't know when or if these academic gatekeepers will arrive at a point of admission that all work, especially in the humanities, is story, I do know that narrative has always been theoretical (Cook 185). *Counterstory: The Rhetoric and Writing of Critical Race Theory* makes a case for critical race counterstory as a rhetorical research methodology *and* method by reviewing counterstory through its critical race theory methodological origins and influences, while also analyzing and illustrating the methods of Richard Delgado, Derrick A. Bell, and Patricia J. Williams, whom I term *counterstory exemplars*. Delgado, Bell, and Williams are foundational critical race theorists whose respective counterstory methods (genres) of narrated dialogue, fantasy/allegory, and autobiographic reflection have set a precedent for other scholars (e.g., Gloria Ladson-Billings, Daniel Solórzano, Adrienne Dixson, Dolores Delgado Bernal, Tara J. Yosso, Daniella Ann Cook, Carmen Kynard[2]). Kynard's research is influenced by this methodology and in turn composed by this method. Thus, counterstory as methodology is the verb, the process, the critical race theory–informed justification for the work (Delgado Bernal et al. 364), whereas counterstory as method is the noun, the genre, the research tool. While this entire project is influenced by counterstory as methodology, the individual chapters will review counterstory as method.

Carl Gutiérrez-Jones describes Delgado's *Rodrigo Chronicles,* Bell's *And We Are Not Saved,* and Williams's *The Alchemy of Race and Rights* as some of the more exciting examples of CRT's methodological project. He adds that these contributions engage "very broad questions of consciousness and cultural literacy in the hopes of enabling a broadly conceived political intervention through the reference to, and practice of, certain kinds of storytelling" (71–73). Cook describes counterstory as intentionally blurring the boundaries between theory and method, and she says that stories of/by the minoritized are foundational to both (186). However, Gutiérrez-Jones and Cook agree that greater attention to a methodological mapping of counterstory is necessary to provide a more robust sense of how counterstory's tools shape and are shaped by the rhetoric of CRT's narrative intervention.

As a methodology, critical race counterstory is a theoretically grounded research approach with interdisciplinary roots in ethnic studies, women's studies, sociology, history, legal studies, and the humanities. My engagement in the CRT field builds particularly on the powerful work of critical race theorists (such as the abovementioned Cook, Delgado Bernal, Dixson, Solórzano, and Yosso) who define critical race methodology as a challenge to "majoritarian" stories or "master narratives" of white privilege. This methodology rejects notions of "neutral" research or "objective" research and exposes research that silences and distorts epistemologies of people of color. Importantly, critical race methodology recognizes that experiential knowledge of people of color is legitimate and critical to understanding racism that is often well disguised in the rhetoric of normalized structural values and practices. A critical race methodology includes a range of methods such as family history, biography, autoethnography, *cuentos, testimonios,* and counterstory. Counterstory is methodology that functions through methods that empower the minoritized through the formation of stories that disrupt the erasures embedded in standardized majoritarian methodologies.

*Counterstory: The Rhetoric and Writing of Critical Race Theory* is a methodological contribution to rhetoric and writing studies through the well-established framework of critical race theory (CRT). This project advances counterstory by establishing a humanities-informed intervention in the field for teaching with and composing/publishing counterstory. My scholarship to date has crafted counterstory with central topics of antiracist graduate education and assessment, access to the university, linguistic justice, and institutional diversity. Building on my previously published work, which has been consistently informed by the methodological practice of gathering and shaping data into counterstory contexts and characters, this project further pushes and draws out theoretical specifications of counterstory, inclusive of its histories, tenets, key figures, methods/genres, and pedagogical implications. Shaped by my standpoint as a scholar in the humanities, this project in critical race methodology reviews and analyzes the rich histories and theories of CRT, crediting Delgado, Bell, and Williams for generating a rhetorical intervention through their narrative methods that have come to define CRT as a movement. In an effort toward heeding Gutiérrez-Jones's call to map the rhetorical complexity of counterstory, this project demonstrates how CRT theories and methods inform my—and can inform others'—teaching, research, and writing/publishing of counterstory (Gutiérrez-Jones 71–72).

Considering Kynard's work in *Vernacular Insurrections,* I approach my work in counterstory with the following prompt: As a minoritized voice, with minoritized subjectivities and perspectives, I see it as my task to write my way into the academy through a tracing of a revisionist history of rhetoric and writing studies with critical race theory and counterstory as my guiding forces. I maintain that this process has paved my path into the fields and has made me the rhetoric and writing studies scholar that I am. So, if CRT and counterstory are the work that enables me to frame a revisionist history of rhetoric and writing studies that includes me and people who look like me (Kynard 12) and serves as a guiding force for "where I enter" (Logan), *Counterstory: The Rhetoric and Writing of Critical Race Theory* is my presentation of a methodology and methods that are central to my work, identity, and past/present/future selves in the academy.

### CRITICAL RACE THEORY: A (HI)STORY

> "Life, liberty and the pursuit of happiness" /
> We fought for these ideals; we shouldn't settle for less /
> These are wise words, enterprising men quote 'em /
> Don't act surprised, you guys, cuz I wrote 'em.
> —Thomas Jefferson in
> *Hamilton: An American Musical*

Life. Liberty. The pursuit of happiness. These ideals, as penned by Thomas Jefferson and declared with American independence, set the stage for the United States' Enlightenment-influenced liberal context. Yet from the Declaration's eighteenth-century inception to our present-day raciopolitical climate, these liberal ideals have been and remain color-blind racist abstractions. As Eduardo Bonilla-Silva has asserted, the ideology of color-blind racism relies on four frames that function as Burkean tropes:[3] abstract liberalism, naturalization of race, cultural racism, and minimization of racism (26; Martinez, "The American Way" 588–89). Abstract liberalism involves Jeffersonian ideas associated with political liberalism such as liberty, individualism, and equal opportunity in choice. Applied in an abstract manner, these ideas are used to explain racial matters such as opposition to affirmative action policies because these policies involve supposed preferential treatment, which under the frame of abstract liberalism can be rationalized as a practice opposed to the principle of equal opportunity. However, this claim necessitates ignoring the fact that people of color are and have historically been severely underrepresented in most high-ranking jobs, schools, and universities; hence, it is an abstract utilization of the idea of equal opportunity. Another example involves regarding each person, regardless of social status, as an individual with choices, while ignoring the multiple historical and contemporary structural and state-sponsored practices preventing people of color from the liberty of making individual life choices in pursuit of happiness. This abstract utilization sets the contextual stage for critical race theory's emergence through its critique of American liberalism, specifically as it emerged during the post–Civil Rights era.

In US history courses, students are taught stories about the Civil Rights Movement of the 1960s. Many come away from this experience with the idea that *racism,* as a term, is defined as isolated blatant acts of violence or discrimination toward *individuals* of color. The key word in this equation is *individual,* for racism is still commonly imagined as only visible behavior from one individual toward another (Bonilla-Silva 8). Or as Michael Omi and Howard Winant assert, racism, and the "common sense" surrounding its definition, is "generally understood in a more limited fashion, as a matter of prejudiced attitudes or bigotry . . . and discriminatory practices" (133). This meaning of racism forms the contemporary general understanding of what constitutes racism in the United States, and students in our public institutions are taught the racial progress narrative that the Civil Rights Movement eliminated racism as understood through these forms of derogatory and segregationist behavior (Olson 211). And while it's true that the Civil Rights Movement dismantled racism de jure, the racisms of systemic and institutional prejudice, discrimination, and inequities remain intact and very much inform the lived realities for people of color in the United States. By the 1970s, many legal scholars of color held a deep sense of dissatisfaction with the ways liberal civil rights discourse had lost much of its reformist vision (Mirza 112). Post–Civil Rights era race reform in law, policy, and practice was premised on ideals of assimilation, integration, and color blindness, all of these liberal ideals forming a "new racism" embedded with practices that are subtle, structural, and apparently nonracial (Bonilla-Silva 4).

In their introduction to the collection *Critical Race Theory: Key Writings That Formed the Movement,* CRT scholars Kimberlé Crenshaw, Neil Gotanda, Gary Peller, and Kendall Thomas cite the legal realist movement of the 1920s and 1930s—a body of scholarship that made its case for legal interpretation being political and not neutral or objective—and Oliver Wendell Holmes's 1881 observation of the "hidden and often inarticulate judgements of social policy" as the earliest foundations for what during the Civil Rights era would become critical legal studies (CLS) (xviii). In the 1970s CLS scholars charged that the law is not and cannot be disinterested of the status quo. These scholars declared that the law as established by societal power relationships and court decisions is reflective of bias, though hidden behind a mask of blind justice. As first an extension of CLS, and then a critique, critical race theory arose out of the experiences of students and teachers in US law schools who were witness to CLS and liberal civil rights ideology that failed to address the "constrictive role that racial ideology plays in the composition and culture of American institutions" (xix).

Channeled through the intellectual underpinnings of mid-1970s law professors and legal scholars (oftentimes referred to as "crits" or "the crits")—particularly then-Harvard Law Professor Derrick Bell—CRT worked to focus legal discourse on issues of power, race, and racism to address power imbalances, especially as these are racialized (A. K. Wing 4). Through the lens of this critique of post–Civil Rights liberal race reform, founding crit Mari Matsuda defines CRT as "the work of progressive legal scholars of color who are attempting to develop a jurisprudence that accounts for the role of racism in American law and that works toward the elimination of racism as part of a larger goal of eliminating all forms of subordination" (1331). The body of work by critical race theorists such as Bell, Richard Delgado, and Patricia Williams (among others) addresses the liberal notion of color blindness, arguing that ignoring racial difference maintains and perpetuates the "status quo with all of its deeply institutionalized injustices to racial minorities" (Olson 211). Their work insists that "dismissing the importance of race is a way to guarantee that institutionalized and systematic racism continues and even prospers" (Olson 211).

One of the earliest events cited as contributing to the development of CRT as a movement was the 1981 student protest, boycott, and resulting organization of an alternative course on race and the law at Harvard Law School. This course was organized in reaction to the liberal white Harvard administration's refusal to hire a teacher of color to replace Derrick Bell, who left the institution in 1980. Bell, one of only two African American law professors at Harvard Law following the Civil Rights Movement, developed and taught legal doctrine from a race-conscious viewpoint and used racial politics as the organizing concept for scholarly study. His course textbook, *Race, Racism, and American Law* (1973), and his own opposition to the traditional liberal approach to racism are cited by crits as central to the development of the movement (Crenshaw et al.; Delgado and Stefancic, Introduction). However, when Bell left Harvard to become dean of the University of Oregon Law School, student activists who demanded the hiring of a professor of color were told by the Harvard administration that "there were no qualified black scholars who merited Harvard's interest" (Crenshaw et al. xx). The Alternative Course was the crits' students' response to this administrative assertion. This course encompassed a student-led continuation of Bell's course that focused on US law through the "prism of race" (xxi). It was the first institutionalized expression of CRT and was one of the earliest attempts to bring scholars of color together "to address the law's treatment of race from a self-consciously critical perspective" (xxii). But, more important, the existence of this course challenged the mainstream liberal notion of which subjects were of enough value to include in a standardized core curriculum; it also provided the crits the opportunity to express viewpoints on topics not traditionally privileged by mainstream law schools (xxii).

A second foundational event of CRT history is the 1987 Critical Legal Studies National Conference on silence and race. This conference, as Crenshaw et al. state, "marked the genesis of an intellectually distinctive critical account of race on terms set forth by race-conscious scholars of color, and the terms of contestation and coalition with CLS" (xix). The project of CRT then became the effort to uncover how law constructed race—"the pervasive ways in which law shapes and is shaped by 'race relations' across the social plane" (Crenshaw et al. xxv). However, instead of arguing (as did traditional liberalism) that race was irrelevant to public policy, CLS argued that race simply didn't exist (xxvi). This assertion found its basis in the notion that biological race was a myth; however, scholars of this inclination failed to note the lived material realities of the social construct that are racial formations and racialization (see Omi and Winant; Murji and Solomos). Crenshaw et al. see CLS and CRT "as aligned—in radical left opposition to mainstream legal discourse," but the authors assert that CRT is also different from CLS, stating that their "focus on race means that [they] have addressed quite different concerns, with distinct methodologies and traditions that [are] honored" (xxvi–vii).

Ever evolving, critical race theory scholarship covers a litany of topics, among them a multitude of "energetic crit offshoots" such as critical race feminism (CRF), Latinx CRT (LatCrit), American Indian CRT (TribalCrit), queer CRT (QueerRaceCrit), and disability CRT (DisCrit) (A. K. Wing 5). These various trajectories of CRT can be traced as beginning with Richard Delgado and Jean Stefancic's seminal collection, *Critical Race Theory: The Cutting Edge,* through collections such as Adrien Katherine Wing's *Critical*

*Race Feminism: A Reader* and Marvin Lynn and Adrienne D. Dixson's *Handbook of Critical Race Theory in Education*. Additionally, the professional organization Critical Race Studies in Education Association holds an annual national conference in which crits as an intellectual and organizing community gather to share developing scholarship pursued in directions beyond the black-white binary, critical of whiteness, and informed by feminist, queer, and disability theory.

### THE TENETS OF CRT

Critical race theory is characterized by several major tenets that function as epistemological and ontological premises. According to education scholar Nolan L. Cabrera, these tenets "inform the ways that CRT scholarship is conducted, especially as it relates to its activist orientation, [more than] an overarching framework for how racism operates" (213). While a single framework describing the function of racism is not subscribed to by each of the tenets, I will discuss below the theories of race and racism that intersect with and inform the tenets. The number of tenets varies, depending on how the elements are parsed by CRT legal scholars, and/or scholars in (primarily) education, with the most prominent tenets being

1. Permanence of race and racism
2. Challenge to dominant ideologies
3. Interest convergence
4. Race as social construct
5. Intersectionality and antiessentialism
6. Interdisciplinarity
7. Centrality of experiential knowledge and/or unique voices of color
8. Commitment to social justice (Cabrera 211–13; Delgado and Stefancic, *Critical Race Theory: An Introduction* 8–11; Dixson and Rousseau 4; Kynard, "Teaching While Black" 4; Ladson-Billings, "Critical Race Theory" 37–42; Ladson-Billings, Foreword vii–viii; Solórzano and Yosso 25–27; A. K. Wing 5–6).

Beginning with the "permanence of race and racism": racism is endemic and a central, permanent, and "normal" part of US society (Dixson and Rousseau 4; Kynard "Teaching While Black" 4; Solórzano and Delgado Bernal 312; Taylor 73–77), operating concurrently within multiple forms of social oppression (i.e., intersectionality) (Cabrera 212). As Delgado and Stefancic state, "Because racism is an ingrained feature of our landscape, it looks ordinary and natural to persons in the culture" (*Critical Race Theory: An Introduction* xvi). Edward Taylor asserts that "assumptions of White superiority are so ingrained in political, legal, and educational structures that they are almost unrecognizable" and that "because [they are] all-encompassing and omnipresent, [they] cannot be easily recognized by [their] beneficiaries" (73–74).[4] Ironically, the resulting color blindness and sense of white supremacy mean that whites cannot see or understand the world they've made and are in many cases quick to dismiss or deny the inherited privilege associated with whiteness.[5]

Bell describes a racial realism as a recognition of racism's permanence in addition to its centrality, asserting that "racism lies at the center, not the periphery; in the permanent, not in the fleeting; in the real lives of . . . [people of color] and white people" (*And We Are Not Saved* 198). However, people of color have experiential knowledge from having lived under such systems of racism and oppression. POC have thus developed methods and methodologies that serve as coping mechanisms and navigation strategies, while also serving as ways to raise awareness of issues affecting people of color that are often overlooked, not considered, or otherwise invisible to whites. In other words, we see you, although you do not always (clearly) see us. Further, Gloria Ladson-Billings critiques 1944 Nobel Prize–winning social scientist Gunnar Myrdal's "anomaly thesis" purporting that racism is simply a failure of alignment of liberal democratic practice with theory. She instead offers Arlie Hochschild's "symbiosis thesis," which argues that "liberal democracy and racism in the United States are historically, even inherently, reinforcing; American society as we know it exists only because of its foundation in racially based slavery, and it thrives only because racial discrimination continues" ("Critical Race Theory" 37). It is symbiosis, Ladson-Billings argues, rather than anomaly that distinguishes CRT's theory of race from other race theories (37).

In the effort to end all forms of oppression, CRT "challenges dominant ideologies" and liberal claims of racial neutrality, equal opportunity, objectivity, color blindness, and merit (Dixson and Rousseau 4; Solórzano and Delgado Bernal 313). Concerning educational and institutional injustice, CRT's second tenet questions arguments against policies like affirmative action and interrogates admissions and hiring practices that claim neutrality in their selection of candidates, while justifying a passing over of people of color on the "colorblind" basis of merit and "fit." As stated above in my contextualizing discussion of Bonilla-Silva's theory of color-blind racism, the difficulty of challenging dominant ideologies resides in the resistance met from those who invoke abstract liberal concepts like equal opportunity—a concept not easily examined when the ideology supporting this concept finds its foundation in white supremacist beliefs and practices of meritocracy. Further, as Solórzano and Delgado Bernal argue, racialized ideological "paradigms . . . act as camouflage for the self-interest, power, and privilege of dominant groups in US society" (313). This self-interest informs CRT's third tenet, "interest convergence," and has been most notably discussed by Derrick Bell within the context of racial progress discourses (A. K. Wing 5).

Bell's theory of interest convergence argues that "white elites will tolerate or encourage racial advances for [people of color] only when such advances also promote white self-interest" (Crenshaw et al. xvii), and this form of "racial progress" (and regression) is cyclical, rather than inevitable (Wing 5–6). The most commonly cited example of this theory is the 1954 *Brown v. Board of Education* case, which is generally taught and remembered as a moral victory for African Americans, although, as Bell has pointed out, foreign policy concerns were likely the driving force behind this decision. As Taylor recalls, this case was decided during the Cold War era, when televised images of US racial brutality were more readily available to the world. Communist powers such as the former

Soviet Union and China sparked international sensations by bringing forth stories and images of police brutality unleashed during peaceful protests and Ku Klux Klan lynchings. These stories and images effectively worked toward undermining the United States as a model of democracy just as the country strove to position itself as a leading force of anticommunism. The *Brown* decision then came to represent not a blow to American racism but to communism and was heralded by the Justice Department and the Truman administration as such (Taylor 76).

CRT's fourth tenet, "race as social construct," overlaps with and is informed by another racial theory—most prominently, Michael Omi and Howard Winant's theory of racial formation. Although biologists, geneticists, anthropologists, and sociologists agree that race is not a biological determinant, humans nonetheless have taxonomized and continue to taxonomize human bodies racially (Ladson-Billings, "Critical Race Theory" 38). As social constructs, these categories are the outcome of an unstable and "'decentered' complex of social meanings constantly being transformed by political struggle" (Omi and Winant 123). Further, theories of the social constructs of race assert a permanence of race (see Tenet 1) and describe the dimensions of race as maintained by racial projects that function to secure race as fundamental in the structuring and representing of the social world (124). Racial formation, then, is the theory that explains the "sociohistorical process by which racial categories are created, inhabited, transformed, and destroyed" (124). In terms of racism, Omi and Winant (along with many more race theorists) point to the structural features of racism in US society as a product of "centuries of systemic exclusion, exploitation, and disregard of racially defined minorities" (133; see also Tenet 1, particularly regarding Hochschild's "symbiosis thesis").

Sojourner Truth is one of the earliest US rhetors to describe the first part of CRT's fifth tenet, "intersectionality"—a lived reality expanded upon as a call to action by the Combahee River Collective, and theorized as an analytic framework by crit founding member Kimberlé Crenshaw. As Truth says in her notable 1851 speech, "Ain't I a Woman?":

That man over there says that women need to be helped into carriages, and lifted over ditches, and to have the best place everywhere. Nobody ever helps me into carriages, or over mud-puddles, or gives me any best place! And ain't I a woman? Look at me! Look at my arm! I have ploughed and planted, and gathered into barns, and no man could head me! And ain't I a woman? I could work as much and eat as much as a man—when I could get it—and bear the lash as well! And ain't I a woman? I have borne thirteen children, and seen most all sold off to slavery, and when I cried out with my mother's grief, none but Jesus heard me! And ain't I a woman?

In this earliest US expression of an intersectional consciousness,[6] Truth calls attention to and turns on its head our society's tendency to organize along binaries (Ladson-Billings, "Critical Race Theory" 39). Beyond the black-white and woman-man binaries, Truth's lived reality demonstrates the intersecting aspects of her identities and "how their combinations play out in various settings" (Delgado and Stefancic, *Critical Race Theory: An Introduction* 51).

In their 1977 manifesto, "A Black Feminist Statement," the Combahee River Collective extends awareness of and reflection on identity/status, describing their intersecting "position at the bottom" of racial and gendered hierarchies. They state, "if Black women were free, it would mean that everyone else would have to be free since our freedom would necessitate the destruction of all the systems of oppression" (215). Rounding out this genealogy, in 1989 Crenshaw theorized and named intersectionality in her landmark essay "Demarginalizing the Intersection of Race and Sex." Crenshaw's examination counters the single-axis framework of binaristic racial or gendered analysis and demonstrates how this analytic structure does not accurately account for the intersections of race and gender, thus contributing to the marginalization and exclusion of black women in feminist theory and in antiracist politics. Further, Crenshaw states that "because the intersectional experience is greater than the sum of racism and sexism, any analysis that does not take intersectionality into account cannot sufficiently address the particular manner in which Black women are subordinated" (140).

Twin-skin to "intersectionality" is "antiessentialism," the second half of CRT's fifth tenet. CRT denounces essentialism, countering culturally racist assumptions that attempt to describe or explain socially constructed racial groups as homogenous in the way they think, act, and believe (Bonilla-Silva 76–77). For reasons of navigation, survival, activism, and social justice (none of which are mutually exclusive), there can be a sense of solidarity among cultures or racial groups; however, individuals within groups maintain rights to heterogeneity of perspective, experience, lifestyle, and identity (Ladson Billings, "Critical Race Theory" 40–41). Therefore, the crits caution against essentializing cultures and racial groups and believe an antiessentialist method involves centering experiential knowledge so as to better elucidate lived reality *from* (intersectional) rather than *about* (essentialist) people of color.

Interdisciplinarity, as a sixth tenet, has been historically emphasized primarily by legal and education scholars. Although interdisciplinarity is implicit and assumed in the entirety of this project, and arguably in the field(s) of rhetoric and writing studies as a whole, it is not an assumed premise in other fields, which explains its inclusion and emphasis as a premise for crits from other less disciplinarily porous traditions. Ladson-Billings has traced this history in detail:

> This moving across disciplinary boundaries invokes the strategies proposed by scholars in the 1960s that offered "new studies" that came to be known as Black Studies, Chicano Studies, American Indian Studies, Asian American Studies and Women's Studies. In each of these new scholarly traditions the disciplinary boundaries were made permeable. History, literature, sociology and the arts were tapped as important knowledge sources for documenting and conveying experiences of people. This new approach to scholarship insisted that no one discipline could fully reveal the complexities of human experience and thus amalgamations were deemed necessary. (Foreword vii)

In legal scholarship, Ladson-Billings acknowledges that "the use of other disciplinary traditions was considered heretical," and departures from canon, such as Delgado's, Bell's, and Williams's rule-breaking legal storytelling, were initially rejected. In education, the field where CRT most prominently progressed before branching out to other fields and disciplines, Ladson-Billings recalls a similar battle, stating that "for much of its history, education research and scholarship was moored to psychology. Thus 'real' research was . . . only scholarship that was 'neutral' and 'objective'" (Foreword viii). In all, a premise of interdisciplinarity insists on carving pathways for scholars from disciplines steeped in unyielding commitments to canon. In the spirit of the 1960s activism that resulted in the establishment of ethnic studies, CRT draws on a variety of scholarly traditions toward centralizing and making sense of experiential knowledge.

A commitment to the "centrality of experiential knowledge" is CRT's seventh tenet (Solórzano and Delgado Bernal 314; Taylor 74; Delgado and Stefancic, Introduction 3). Because white people do not often acknowledge the experiences of people of color, the crits recognize and have developed the methodology of counterstory to relate the racial realities of people of color while also providing methods for minoritized people to challenge "the myths, presuppositions, and received wisdoms that make up the common culture about race and that invariably render [minoritized people] one-down" (Delgado and Stefancic, Introduction 3). Further, as Bell has observed, the narrative voice, the teller, "is important to critical race theory in a way not understandable by those whose voices are tacitly deemed legitimate and authoritarian. The voice exposes, tells and retells, signals resistance and caring, and reiterates what kind of power is feared most—the power of commitment to change" ("Who's Afraid" 907).

Of course, people of color can and do reproduce structures, systems, and practices of racism, too, but by incorporating a framework such as "hegemonic whiteness" into writing and speaking against the oftentimes one-sided stories circulating in a white supremacist world, the crits illuminate the fact that the social world is not static but is constructed by people with words, stories, and also silences (Cabrera). As one of the oldest forms of human rhetoric, stories are meant to reflect perspective, and, as should be familiar to rhetoricians, "underscore what the teller, audience, society, and/ or those in power believe to be important, significant, and many times valorizing and ethnocentric" (Ladson-Billings, "Critical Race Theory" 41–42). Although valorizing one's story is common, it is when this valorization and ethnocentrism are named and instituted as objective, universal, and true "history" that the narrative of the group in power is validated while simultaneously the narratives of those with less power are invalidated. As a methodology and method informed by hegemonic whiteness (and in my case by the Sophists), counterstory presents a contrasting description and narrative from a different perspective.

In reflection on what counterstory is and what it is *not,* Ladson-Billings cautions would-be counterstorytellers, citing the crits' use of storytelling as a way to show, reflect on, and analyze legal principles regarding race and social justice. "The point," Ladson-Billings says, "is not to vent or rant or be an exhibitionist regarding one's own racial struggle" ("Critical Race Theory" 42). Narratives constructed with this purpose often fall short of (if they contain this at all) principled argument, and thus a rubric for counterstory resides in whether the story is informed by the tenets toward advancing a better understanding of how law or policy operate. In all, the CRT narrative recognizes experiential knowledge of the nondominant as "legitimate, appropriate, and critical to understanding, and analyzing racial subordination" (Solórzano and Delgado Bernal 314). The crits' aim is to construct counterstory with a deep commitment toward social justice and the elimination of racial oppression as part of the broader goal of ending all forms of oppression (Dixson and Rousseau 4).

CRT's eighth tenet, "commitment to social justice," is arguably the most distinguishing characteristic for CRT's narrative method, counterstory. While there are many stories, and while many data are narrativized, counterstory is distinguished from other forms of storytelling by its transparent commitment to a "liberatory and transformative response to racial, gender, and class oppression" (Mari Matsuda, qtd. in Solórzano and Yosso 26). According to Solórzano and Yosso, CRT and counterstory as its methodology contribute to a vision of social justice research with the goals of

- eliminating racism, sexism, and poverty and
- empowering subordinated minority groups. (26)

CRT, then, and its methodology, counterstory, use a narrative method to theorize racialized experience (framed by any single one or combination of the above-named racial theories: symbiosis, color-blind racism, interest convergence, racial formation, intersectionality, or hegemonic whiteness). And as a necessary function of counterstory, these narratives serve the purpose of exposing stereotypes and injustice and offering additional truths through a narration of the researchers' own experiences.

Through my years of work as a crit researcher/writer of counterstory, I've learned firsthand of counterstory's potential for achieving social justice. A question I often encounter when speaking with audiences about counterstory at various lectures and workshops is, Are *all* marginalized narratives counterstory? While there are indeed many marginal/ized narratives, the measure remains whether the tellers and stories subscribe to CRT's tenets, particularly in their critique of a dominant ideology (e.g., liberalism, whiteness, color blindness) and their sustained focus on social justice as an objective. In other words, what are folks using counterstory to *do?* Expression of minoritized subjectivity is a good starting point, but it is equally important to include the admission of and critical self-reflection on privilege (see particularly the counterstory method in Chapter 4) and to use this privilege to be an accomplice (Martinez, "Responsibility of Privilege" 231). My privilege is that I am a very educated person with the platform of this published project. The question then is, What will I do with this platform and privilege? What kind of project will I craft? What is my contribution and, further, as an audience member once asked me during a campus visit, "What is the political weight of [this] work?" I believe the answer lies in what

I maintain as one additional tenet for CRT—accessibility (Cook 182). Derrick Bell's exemplary counterstories are bestsellers, Patricia Williams's work has been reviewed by mainstream presses as she continues to write her "Diary of a Mad Law Professor" column for the progressive magazine *The Nation*, and Richard Delgado's work is published in law reviews, yes, but has also been reworked as an introductory text for high school students.[7] Their work continues to inspire and resonate across generations and disciplines. My own writing process has included and always will include my family, nonacademics, because the work is for them, is sometimes about them, and is nearly always inspired by them. And if my work in counterstory is inaccessible to the very people it is for—well, then what's the point? Why do the work if it's inaccessible? Thus, in my contribution to defining CRT, I advocate for the premise of accessibility, in the sense that a methodological consideration for counterstory should always envision a multiplicity of audiences beyond the ivory tower so as "to speak with (rather than for and over) others' communities" (NCTE/CCCC Black Caucus et al.).

### WHO'S AFRAID OF CRT (AND COUNTERSTORY)?

> At a time of crisis, critics serve as reminders that we are being heard, if not always appreciated. For those of us for whom history provides the best guide to contemporary understanding, criticism is a reassurance.
>
> —Derrick Bell

As nothing is beyond critique, critical race theory has its share of skeptics, detractors, and naysayers—in a diversity of fields. As Catherine Prendergast has observed, the crits "have often been noted (and often faulted) not so much for their arguments—*what* they are saying—as for their departures from standard legal discourse—*how* they are saying" (46). Prendergast insists critical responses to counterstory demonstrate the crucial place rhetoric occupies in CRT's project, as the crits craft a "new rhetoric" making use of counterstory genres/methods that effectively implicate the limits of a legal system sustained on and by a rhetoric of abstracted liberal inequity (46).

Bell, Delgado, and Matsuda were, for example, famously the subjects of a seventy-six-page *Harvard Law Review* comment by Harvard Law professor Randall L. Kennedy. Dividing his critique into two parts, Kennedy first took aim at CRT for accusing mainstream (i.e., white) scholars of excluding the contributions of writers of color (e.g., rejecting publications, failing to cite, failing to include the work in course syllabi). Relying on a thesis of marketplace dynamics, Kennedy purported that "good" scholarship attracts buyers and thus naturally flows toward inclusion. As follows, within this marketplace rationale, it is not discrimination but a lack of quality that excludes scholarship by people of color from fieldwide recognition (Delgado and Stefancic, *Critical Race Theory: An Introduction* 102–3; Kennedy 1747).

Kennedy's second critique concerns CRT's sixth tenet, the unique voice of scholars of color and the necessity to centralize the experiential knowledge of said scholars. Kennedy argues the writings of critical race theory reveal "significant deficiencies" as these scholars "fail to support persuasively their claims of racial exclusion or their claims that legal academic scholars of color produce a racially distinctive brand of scholarship" (1749). Bell contends Kennedy is perhaps CRT's most politically damaging critic because his blackness lends his critique a "super legitimacy inversely proportional to the illegitimacy bequeathed to critical race theory" (Bell, "Who's Afraid" 908; Delgado and Stefancic, *Critical Race Theory: An Introduction* 102). As Bell astutely observes,

> when a black scholar[8] at a prominent law school tells anyone who will listen that other folks of color are deluded about being excluded on the basis of their race; when a black scholar argues against race-conscious legal remedies or hiring policies; when a black scholar contends that there is no hidden "white" normativity or perspective but rather a meritocratic normativity (the companion claim to the claim that there is no minority perspective); when a black scholar says these things, all who rarely listen to scholars of color sit up and take notice.

And take notes. And turn those notes into more fuel for the legitimacy debate that has always attended renegade movements. ("Who's Afraid" 908)

Extending Kennedy's second critique, Daniel A. Farber and Suzanna Sherry, in their 1993 essay "Telling Stories Out of School: An Essay on Legal Narratives," accuse the crits of hiding behind counterstory to advance their agendas while simultaneously disregarding objective universal truth and merit. Farber and Sherry urge counterstorytellers to tell stories that are more "accurate," that articulate (for mainstream/majoritarian audiences) the relevance of their stories, and that include an analytic dimension by way of more traditional scholarship and dominant social science paradigms (Bell, "Who's Afraid" 907–08; Cabrera 213).

Illustrated through the epigraphs that begin this chapter, reviewers for mainstream journals in rhetoric and writing studies express an interested view of critical race theory and counterstory, yet insist my work must be amenable to mainstream standards. As Bell has said concerning critiques of his own work, these critics

> are not reluctant to tell us what critical race theory ought to be. They question the accuracy of the stories, fail to see their relevance, and want more of an analytical dimension to the work—all this while claiming that their critiques will give this writing a much-needed "legitimacy" in the academic world. ("Who's Afraid" 907)

Throughout my pursuit of this scholarship, beginning as a graduate student and up to my present day "collegial" context, less politically inclined critics have told me (sometimes to my face) that my work "reads like bad fiction," that it's "not real research," and that all I do is write "biased tales of woe." Delgado and Stefancic advise that this kind of response should come as no surprise, as this review of CRT's major[9] critiques demonstrates that this sort of feedback is nothing original, field-specific, or new. Paradigms resist change, and CRT, which seeks to challenge and change reigning paradigms of liberal civil rights thought, has historically sparked stubborn resistance (*Critical Race Theory: An Introduction* 102). It would seem that I'm in good company.

Education scholar and composite counterstory theorist Daniella Ann Cook asserts that an essential challenge to dominant methodological and epistemological research canons is CRT's nuance of explicitly blurring the boundary between theory and method (182). Considering the significance of this research nuance within the context of historically persistent critiques of CRT and counterstory, Cook insists that CRT scholars' rigorous methodological standards matter all the more. Because meaningful race research and high-quality research methods are not mutually exclusive, Cook concludes that composite counterstorytelling serves as a method to build upon "the important dialogue with others seeking to do rigorous, high quality research that draws upon CRT as both a theory and a method" (182), and as I will describe next.

### CRT COUNTERSTORY: A RHETORICAL METHODOLOGY

Counterstory functions as both methodology and method for minoritized people to intervene in research methods that would form "master narratives" based on ignorance and assumptions about minoritized people. Through the formation of counterstories or those stories that document the persistence of racism and other forms of subordination told "from the perspectives of those injured and victimized by its legacy" (Yosso, *Critical Race Counterstories* 10), voices spoken over and buried by racist methods and methodologies become the voices of authority in the researching and relating of our own experiences.

As a theoretical framework, critical race theory made way for the emergence of critical race counterstory, a methodology utilized in scholarly publications, particularly in Richard Delgado's narrative dialogue Rodrigo chronicles (*The Rodrigo Chronicles*, 1995), Derrick A. Bell's landmark allegorical chronicles of Geneva Crenshaw (*And We Are Not Saved*, 1987, and *Faces at the Bottom of the Well*, 1992), and Patricia J. Williams's *Alchemy of Race and Rights: Diary of a Law Professor* (1992). Delgado theorized counterstory as a methodology in his essay "Storytelling for Oppositionists and

Others: A Plea for Narrative" and defines a variety of counterstory methods, including but not limited to chronicles, narratives, allegories, parables, pungent tales, and dialogues (2413, 2438). Latinx critical race theory (LatCrit) scholars Dolores Delgado Bernal, Daniel Solórzano, and Tara J. Yosso further theorized and extended critical race counterstory as a necessary and legitimate methodology of critical inquiry for minoritized scholars, particularly those from cultures where the oral tradition is valued.

As an offshoot of CRT, LatCrit draws on the strengths offered by critical race theory, while also emphasizing "the intersectionality of experience with oppression and resistance and the need to extend the conversation" (Yosso, "Toward a Critical Race Curriculum" 95) beyond the inadequate dualistic conceptual framework offered by the black-white binary. According to Solórzano and Delgado Bernal, LatCrit is

> concerned with a sense of a coalitional Latina/Latino pan-ethnicity and addresses the issues often ignored by critical race theorists such as language, immigration, ethnicity, culture, identity, phenotype, and sexuality[;] [it] is conceived as an antisubordination and antiessentialist project that attempts to link theory with practice, scholarship with teaching, and the academy with the community. . . . LatCrit theory is supplementary [and] complementary to critical race theory [and] at its best should operate as a close cousin—related to [CRT] in real and lasting ways, but not necessarily living under the same roof. (311–12)

LatCrit scholars assert their commitment to intersectionality, with counterstory serving as a natural extension of inquiry for theorists whose research recognizes that the experiential and embodied knowledge of people of color is legitimate and critical to understanding racism, which is often well disguised in the rhetoric of normalized structural values and practices (314).

Solórzano and Yosso assert that "majoritarian" stories are generated from a legacy of racial privilege and are stories in which racial privilege seems "natural" (27). These stories privilege whites, men, the middle and/or upper class, heterosexuals, and the able-bodied by naming these social locations as natural or normative points of reference. A majoritarian story distorts and silences the experiences of people of color and others distanced from the norms such stories reproduce. A standardized majoritarian methodology relies on stock stereotypes that covertly and overtly link people of color, women of color, and poverty with "bad," while emphasizing that white, middle- and/or upper-class people embody all that is "good" (29). Whites (when critically self-reflective of their whiteness) can and do tell counterstories, and people of color, in contrast, can and do tell majoritarian stories (Bonilla-Silva 151; Martinez, "The American Way" 586). The keepers and tellers of either majoritarian (stock) stories or counterstories reveal the intersections of social location of the storyteller as dominant or nondominant, and these locations are always racialized, classed, and gendered. For example, Ward Connerly is African American, from a working-class background, male, and a prominent politician and academic. From his racialized position, Connerly is a member of a minority group, but he speaks and represents himself from dominant gendered and classed locations. From the position of an upper-class male, Connerly crafts stock stories to argue against affirmative action and to deny racial inequities. Alternatively, Frankie Condon's work narrativizes embodied whiteness and individual responsibility as a white ally. Although Condon is white, she is also a woman who speaks from a nondominant social location, while as a white ally she uses her dominant racialized location to craft critical race narratives that disrupt "discourses of transcendence" often responsible for leading audiences of white antiracists to believe they are somehow "absolved from the responsibility of doing whiteness" (13).

## A CAVEAT CONCERNING COMPOSITE COMPOSITIONS

Cook and Dixson argue that composite counterstorytelling (CCS) is a unique innovation of CRT methodology that adds to critical race qualitative research in three ways:

1. CCS provides empirical space for researchers to recount the stories and experiences of people in politically vulnerable positions.
2. CCS as a vehicle to present counterstories necessarily requires descriptions of rich, robust contexts in which to understand those stories and lived experiences while maintaining the complexity of meaning. The use of composite characters turns the focus from individual participants to the larger issues faced by groups and deepens analysis of how race and racism affect the lived experiences of people of color collectively within institutions.
3. CCS is the appeal (ethos, logos, and pathos) of making research accessible beyond academic audiences. (Cook 182)

Victor Villanueva has argued that narratives counter to majoritarian or stock stories provide people of color the opportunity to validate, resonate, and awaken to the realization that we "haven't become clinically paranoid" in our observations and experiences of racism and discrimination within the institution ("*Memoria*" 15). In fact, as Villanueva points out, it is almost shocking to realize that in the academic institution in which the sheer numbers of people of color are as exceptional as they are, "our experiences are in no sense unique but are always analogous to other experiences from among those exceptions" (15). Kynard has theorized that offering her "own personal experiences and stance of bearing-witness" represents more "than just one individual's observations, but an indication of the levels of systemic racism that we do not address" ("Teaching While Black" 4). Cook and Dixson in turn argue that CCS aids in demonstrating the ways people of color have a shared history with racism, discrimination, and white supremacy (1243).

Cook suggests coding potential CCS data[10] for themes informed by CRT tenets to provide the foundation for context and characters. In many cases, composite contexts and characters are abstractions representing cultural or political ideologies, and could mistakenly be read as stereotyped depictions of certain ideologies and politics.

However, in the case of Delgado's, Bell's, Williams's, and my work as well, characters represent more than just a single individual and are intentionally crafted as composites that primarily embody an ideology as informed by a "*trensa*" of personal experiences, the literatures, and hard data.

Beyond the methods/genres of counterstory outlined by Delgado, Yosso also explains these styles as generally composed in the autobiographical, biographical, or composite genre (*Critical Race Counterstories* 10). For this project, I compose my counterstories as composite dialogues, an important feature of which is the composite character. Composite characters are written into "social, historical, and political situations that allow the dialogue to speak to the research findings and creatively challenge racism and other forms of subordination" (Yosso, *Critical Race Counterstories* 11).

Because these characters are written as composites of many individuals, they do not have a one-to-one correspondence to any one individual the author knows (Delgado, *Rodrigo Chronicles* xix). For instance, in "Storytelling for Oppositionists and Others," Delgado crafts a stock story on the topic of rejecting a "black [male] lawyer for a teaching position at a major law school" (2418). The professor in charge of the hiring process, who is featured in the stock story's dialogue, is described as white, male, tenured, midcareer, and "well regarded by his colleagues and students" (2418). The professor, through both his character's description and dialogue, represents more than just a single individual. Delgado crafts a composite character that embodies ideologies of institutional meritocracy and racism in hiring practices. Accordingly, the stock and counterstory characters crafted for my project involve scenarios and dialogues conducted among composite characters who represent university professionals, my chronicled character Alejandra Prieto, her daughter, other family members, her friends/mentors/associates, and her students. Modeled after Delgado's recurring composite character Rodrigo, Bell's Geneva Crenshaw, and Williams's Everyblackwomanlawyer, Alejandra will play a recurring role in all of the counterstories within.

## THE WHAT AND WHY OF COUNTERSTORY: AN ANSWER

In all, it is crucial to use a theory and a methodology that counter theories and methodologies that seek to dismiss or decenter racism and those whose lives are daily affected by it. Counterstory, then, is both method and methodology—it is a method for telling stories of those people whose experiences are not often told, and, as informed by CRT, this methodology serves to expose, analyze, and challenge majoritarian stories of racialized privilege and can help to strengthen traditions of social, political, and cultural survival, resistance, and justice. In rhetoric, composition, and writing studies, Keith Gilyard, Victor Villanueva, Catherine Prendergast, Adam J. Banks, Angela M. Haas, and, most prominently, Carmen Kynard have called for greater attention in the field toward CRT in order to better prepare as teachers-scholars-administrators and activists to be institutionally and pedagogically antiracist. Kynard has astutely observed that "despite everyone's seeming incessant discussion of critical theories from postcolonialism/decolonization to intersectionality[,] theories can become merely the stage for an academic performance, not a way of engaging the world and oppression in it" ("Teaching While Black" 2). Prendergast thus suggests that the tangibility that emerges out of critical race theory for fields beyond legal studies "is not primarily a litigation strategy but a *rhetorical strategy* to revive the struggle for racial justice" (47; emphasis mine). Following Kynard's example, my work suggests counterstory as a methodology and rhetorical method. This approach allows me to incorporate CRT in humanities-oriented fields of study, as a contribution of other(ed) perspectives toward ongoing and crucial conversations about dominant ideology and its influences on the institution, the society, and the very humanity of people of color, a humanity too often denied.

With particular attention to our writing and rhetoric classrooms, John Trimbur has stated that "in a course devoted to rhetorical education, students can learn an ethos of collaborative disagreement that casts their differences as matters of negotiation instead of as fearfully violent" (249). And negotiating this ethos is precisely where CRT finds its place in rhetoric and writing studies. The ideological problem with discussions of racism is that individuals have been socially and politically urged to view race consciousness less favorably than color blindness (Omi and Winant 134), and that bringing attention to difference is a cause for fear, worry, and impending attack. What CRT provides scholars in rhetoric and writing studies is an ability to bring to the foreground the workings of racism in the daily lives of all people, and it further illustrates that we all function within the hegemony of systems of domination and subordination, advantage and disadvantage, structured according to racial categories (Olson 215).

Gary Olson has suggested a race consciousness developed through CRT to be used as an analytical tool with which to examine our own pedagogies, writing programs, and institutions—and, perhaps, to alter them for the better (216). Olson's specific advice is for WPAs to introduce readings and discussions of CRT into pedagogy and training for TAs and adjuncts (208). However, I am dissatisfied with this suggestion, as it first assumes that existing faculty have such issues covered and are not in need of such instruction in the same way newer, more inexperienced teachers (or students!) are. I also agree with Joseph Harris's assertion that the field should focus more on who has access to the writing classroom, both as students and as faculty, and that having a diverse mix of students and instructors of color in our classes is the more pressing task (223). This charge entails a much larger task than simply assigning readings in CRT for TA training, as it involves work at the institutional level regarding access, retention, and success of students *and* faculty from underrepresented backgrounds.

So the question becomes, "How do we change the institution before the classroom?" My suggestion is to have a focus on, an acknowledgment of, and an incorporation of the critical race methodology of counterstory. As part of my ongoing efforts to incorporate CRT into my own pedagogical practice, I have developed curricula (see Chapter 5 and Appendixes A–D) framed by this theory and education's LatCrit. At the societal level, LatCrit can challenge the macro and micro forms of racism sometimes disguised, or even reproduced, by a traditional curriculum, and mindful incorporation of this theory into pedagogy and curriculum development thus holds the potential for a more democratic representation. Additionally, honoring diverse ways of knowing necessarily ensures expanded civic participation to include historically silenced people and communities who can and should be recognized holders and creators of knowledge (Yosso, "Toward" 98).

The work of counterstory as method, including the various genres of counterstory I have composed for this project, illustrate a rhetoric of transformational resistance. According to Solórzano and Delgado Bernal, this form of resistance puts emphasis on "the importance of working toward social justice" (316). The stories and analysis within my project provide a critique of social oppression and are motivated by an interest in social justice that moves toward the possibility of social change (319). Instead of choosing to leave the academy—which at this moment in my career would fall in the quadrant of self-defeating resistance (see Figure 1)—or only offering suggestions pertaining to the ways minoritized peoples can better prepare themselves for assimilationist success in higher education—which would represent conformist resistance—I choose to

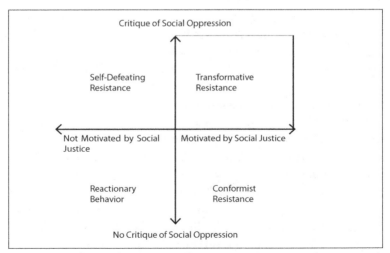

Figure 1. Defining the concept of resistance. (Source: Solórzano and Delgado Bernal [2001])

resist through a project that, through counterstory, critiques the systems in place and is founded on the belief of individual and social change (Solórzano and Delgado Bernal 320).

Likewise, the Latina Feminist Group, a collective of Latina feminists in higher education, found it necessary to gather and "weave *testimonios*, stories of [their] lives, to reveal [their] own complex identities as Latinas" (1). As a collective, they sought to resist "systemic violence and cultural ideologies that continually repositioned [them] at the margins," and this transformational resistance of theirs is pursued through theorizing experience and relying on a methodology that allows them to narrate lived realities otherwise silenced or censured (2, 12). In this pursuit, the Latina Feminist Group created its collection, *Telling to Live*, as a space to resist, but also as a space in which to perform painful and vulnerable disclosure safely. Previous to the creation of *Telling to Live,* and throughout the process of constructing this collection, many of the Latinas involved voiced the fears they felt concerning public storytelling. In particular, Gloria Cuádrez states, "I've been waiting for ten years to feel comfortable enough to say this publicly. I may never say it again, so I am grateful we have created this opportunity" (14).

This collective refers to their writings as *papelitos guardados,* "tucked away, hidden from inquiring eyes" (1). Cuádrez and other contributors pull from these writings to create *testimonios* toward social justice. The Latina Feminist Group adopted the expression "papelitos guardados" because, as they say, it

> evokes the process by which we contemplate thoughts and feelings, often in isolation and through difficult times. We keep them in our memory, write them down, and store them in safe places waiting for the appropriate moment when we can return to them for review and analysis, or speak out and share them with others. Sharing can begin a process of empowerment. (1)

However, if sharing stories of oppression and marginalization "begins a process of empowerment," why do members of the Latina Feminist Group express fear of disclosure? Many of the women in the collective shared stories with one another that they had never shared with anyone before, yet some still opted to publish anonymous *testimonios* because of fear of and vulnerability to the "professional or political consequences for personal disclosures" (20).

Personally, I have been called "*loca*" (literally) for taking on this counterstory project; I have been told to wait until I am no longer in a vulnerable position in the academic power hierarchy. I have also been threatened by senior colleagues who fear I may observe and in turn write about their racist behavior. However, isn't this positionality and perspective exactly what makes my words necessary (Anzaldúa, "To(o) Queer the Writer" 265)? Aren't people with less power precisely those who create *testimonios*? Is there any better moment than now and any greater impetus than social justice for minoritized folk within institutions to propel forward a project such as *Counterstory: The Rhetoric and Writing of Critical Race Theory*?

Thus, what follows is a series of counterstories that weave together a narrative constituted of my own *papelitos guardados* combined with data and literature gathered on each topic. The story of my chronicled character Alejandra Prieto continues[11] as the narratives follow her and her associations through the counterstory methods/genres of narrated dialogue, fantasy/allegory, autobiographic reflection, and dialogic epistolary. The topics covered concern perspective and rhetorical "truth," histories of rhetoric and writing studies, access and navigation in the academy, borderlands rhetorics, and core curricula and pedagogy in rhetoric and writing studies. Taking up Carl Gutiérrez-Jones's call to provide a fuller sense of how the tools (methods) of CRT shape the rhetorical efficacy of counterstory (76), Chapters 2 to 4 analyze the literacies and craft of exemplars Delgado's, Bell's, and Williams's counterstory methods before demonstrating each narrative method. Chapter 5 concludes this project with a discussion of pedagogical implications for CRT and counterstory accompanied by counterstory as epistle, a counterstory form inspired by and modeled on Bell's "An Epistolary Exploration for a Thurgood Marshall Biography," and Daniel Solórzano's "Critical Race Theory's Intellectual Roots: My Email Epistolary with Derrick Bell."[12]

In all, I am satisfied that the counterstory methodology and demonstrated counterstory methods within this project put to rest the field-specific question, "But what is counterstory?" It's high time that the gatekeepers of this profession get out of the way so we as counterstorytellers can get on with the business of writing and sharing our stories without having to repeatedly rationalize the legitimacy of our theoretical and methodological choices. However, this motive is not why I offer this work, and counterstory critics and sceptics are not my audience. As Derrick Bell exhorts us,

> Do not seek to justify. The work, they say, speaks for itself and is its own legitimation. It was written to record experience and insight that are often unique and[,] prior to this new work, too little heard. There is sufficient satisfaction for those who write in the myriad methods of critical race theory that comes from the work itself. ("Who's Afraid" 910)

Thus, this work, above all, is for my fellow counterstorytellers. In the spirit of Bell and the CRT and counterstory genealogies of which I am part, this project is an encouraging nod and a knowing glance exchanged with those who have always known, recognized, and told counterstories. It is my dream that this work holds out an inviting hand and serves as a fortifying reference for those who would continue the story.

# 2

## Richard Delgado and Counterstory as Narrated Dialogue

RICHARD DELGADO WAS BORN in the late 1930s to a family on the move. His father was an immigrant from Mexico and, according to Delgado, "probably undocumented" (TLCP 224). Within the context of this heritage and having lived through the 1960s and 1970s political movements, Delgado states, "I've always been interested in the rights of immigrants and asylees, and . . . I was very much caught up in the ideas students were bringing to the nation" during the Civil Rights era (224).

Particular to the history of critical race theory, in 1989 at the University of Wisconsin–Madison, Delgado was a founding member at a gathering of two dozen critical legal scholars who, according to Delgado, met "to see what we had in common and whether we could plan a joint action in the future, whether we had a scholarly agenda we could share, and perhaps a name for the organization" (TLCP 225). A site well suited to host this event, the University of Wisconsin was a center of leftist legal thought, and over the course of two and a half days this group of legal "Marxists," as described by Delgado, worked out a set of principles that would develop into the major tenets that founded and that still inform critical race theory (see Chapter 1, "The Tenets of CRT"). Most who attended this 1989 meeting have gone on to become prominent critical race theorists, including Kimberlé Crenshaw, Mari Matsuda, Charles Lawrence, Patricia Williams, and Derrick Bell—whom Delgado describes as "an intellectual godfather"[1] for the critical race theory movement (TLCP 225; A. Harris xv).

Comprising more than one hundred journal articles and twenty books, Delgado's work has been reviewed and praised in important mainstream media such as the *Nation*, the *New Republic*, the *New York Times*, the *Washington Post*, and the *Wall Street Journal*. Delgado's books have won a number of national book prizes, including six Gustavus Myers Outstanding Book Awards, given to outstanding books on human rights in North America; the American Library Association's Outstanding Academic Book; and a Pulitzer Prize nomination. Delgado has been prominent and prolific in his writing and theorizing of legal storytelling in both method and methodology, so if Bell is an "intellectual godfather" of critical race theory, Delgado is arguably an "intellectual *padrino*" of counterstory.

### RICHARD DELGADO, PERSPECTIVE,[2] AND COUNTERSTORY VERSUS STOCK STORY

Robert A. Williams Jr.'s foreword to Delgado's *Rodrigo Chronicles* comments on Delgado's stories as outsider stories. Williams says these stories

> help us imagine the outside in America, a place where some of us have never been and some of us have always been, and where a few of us . . . shift-shape, like the trickster, asking the hard questions . . . without answers, questions about what it means to be outside, what it means to be inside, and what it means to be in-between in America. (xii–xiii)

Delgado characterizes counterstory as "a kind of counter-reality" created by/experienced by "outgroups" subordinate to those atop the racial and gendered hierarchy ("Storytelling" 2412–13). While those in power, or as Delgado offers, the "ingroup," craft stock stories to establish a shared sense of identity and reality and to naturalize their superior position, the "outgroup aims to subvert that ingroup reality" ("Storytelling" 2412–13). Delgado describes stock stories as the stories those in positions of dominance collectively form and tell about themselves. These stories choose and pick among available facts and present a picture of the world that best befits and supports their positions of relative power ("Storytelling" 2421). Stock stories feign neutrality and at all costs avoid any blame or responsibility for societal inequality.

Stock stories are powerful because they are often repeated until canonized or normalized, and those who tell them insist that their version of events is indeed reality, and that any stories that counter these standardized tellings are biased and therefore not credible (see also Chapter 1, "Who's Afraid of CRT (and Counterstory)?"). Delgado suggests that counterstory as a methodology intervenes in stock stories told by the "ingroup" that dismiss or decenter racism and those whose lives are daily affected by it. Counterstory then is a method of telling stories by people whose experiences are not often told. Counterstory as methodology serves to expose, analyze, and challenge stock stories of racial privilege and can help to strengthen traditions of social, political, and cultural survival and resistance.

Delgado outlines several forms through which counterstory can rhetorically and methodologically function: chronicles, narratives, allegories, parables, and dialogues ("Storytelling" 2438). In this chapter, I extend my discussion of counterstory as narrated dialogue (Martinez, "A Plea," "Alejandra Writes a Book," and "Core-Coursing Counterstory") through a conversation in which Alejandra and her daughter, Sofia Alejandra, discuss aspects of storytelling and perspective. Dialogue, as a method, is more than common within rhetoric and writing studies, and has been most notably employed by Plato as a function of language to aid philosophical inquiry. As a method, dialogue depicts oral discourse, and, notably, Plato uses dialogue through his crafted version of Socrates to voice his (Plato's) ideas, and in this way develops his ideas through exchanges with surrounding characters. In introducing their selections from Plato, Patricia Bizzell and Bruce Herzberg suggest that Plato values oral exchange because "it responds flexibly to *kairos,* the immediate social situation in which solutions to philosophical problems must be proposed" (81). Likewise, Delgado's specific method of placing characters in narrated dialogue provides him as the author the opportunity to develop his ideas through exchanges between characters that represent and voice contending viewpoints about contemporary issues. The audience is invited to experience the narration of events from the perspective of the status quo, a narrative approach that can appear in the form of stock stories or in the form of stock composite characters. Engaging the stock story, a counterstory or counterperspective is presented to develop the author's minoritized viewpoint and to critique the viewpoint put forth by stock stories and stock characters, while offering alternate possibilities for the audience to consider (see particularly Martinez, "A Plea").

Particular to the narrative in this chapter, counterstory as narrated dialogue involves themes intended to assist learning subjects (i.e., students) in imagining and describing their experience. Counterstory as narrated dialogue also reveals to the most critically conscious of educators that they are and will always be subject to an imperial ideology, and, as Delgado illustrates in his counterstories, particularly in the dialogues between his much-chronicled characters, the professor and Rodrigo, both teacher and student are on the same academic continuum only at different points. The power dynamic represented by the teacher-student exchanges between Delgado's Rodrigo and the professor is not unlike that of Phaedrus and Socrates in Plato's *Phaedrus*. In the way Phaedrus as Socrates's student should "take care to choose a teacher who will raise the student to the teacher's higher level," so Socrates should "take care to choose a student who will not drag the teacher down" (Bizzell and Herzberg 84). Thus, the teacher-student composites represented in Delgado's dialogues are set within contexts in which both teacher and student offer each other insights concerning the thematic focus of the narrative, and both parties generally come away from the discussion enlightened in some way.

Delgado's counterstory as narrated dialogue is pedagogical because of its fundamental features, which involve teacher-student exchanges that lead to learning and instruction for both characters. This form of counterstory consists of stories written to facilitate classroom discussion, while interweaving research data and creative nonfiction. The dialogues employ two characters in particular: a teacher and a student. The teacher is usually a mentor, an established professional in their field and profession, while the student occupies the position of mentee, a less experienced person in the field and profession (Bell, *Faces* xiii). The counterstory usually begins as a dialogue between the mentee and mentor and evolves into either personal narrative or allegory as told by the mentor.

As a teacher, I have crafted curricula on CRT and counterstory, as Appendixes A and B demonstrate. Envisioned and applied as a synergy between a methods course and a creative nonfiction writers workshop, Writing Critical Race Counterstory (Appendix B) breaks down and instructs on the craft of counterstory, and my students and I spend several weeks on counterstory as narrated dialogue. Students begin learning this method through reading Delgado's theorizing of counterstory ("Storytelling") before shifting to crafting their own counterstories as narrated dialogues. Students embark on their research process by brainstorming possible topics. They are then instructed through gathering supporting materials such as literature, statistical data, and social commentary to braid in with their own personal experiences. This research process is foundational toward crafting context and characters for composite counterstories (see Chapter 1, "A Caveat Concerning Composite Compositions") and results in dialogue counterstories that are rigorously researched and then workshopped through several drafts, in-class read-arounds, and peer reviews. While Chapter 5 will discuss specific pedagogical implications for CRT and counterstory, I have found Delgado's method of counterstory as narrated dialogue particularly pedagogically useful, as it readily involves teacher-student exchanges, and it has informed my own curricular endeavors.

The narrative counterstory in this chapter is fashioned specifically after the dialogues in Delgado's *Rodrigo Chronicles*. These particular counterstories are crafted as first-person narratives and are related by the central character, who in Delgado's chronicles is the professor. The dialogues in Delgado's narratives discuss educational and political themes, including affirmative action, graduate school experience, institutional racism, racial microaggressions, and school policy. Speaking on the teacher-student relationship, Delgado says Rodrigo and the professor are similar in that they are both men of color and civil rights scholars and activists but are on different points of the same continuum. Where Rodrigo still occupies the place of a student, he will eventually land at the major law institution where the professor now teaches and where he is in the later stages of his career.

Reminiscent of the Phaedrus-Socrates relationship, Delgado says, because the professor is further along on the academic continuum he has suffered "scars and disappointments from years in the trenches [and] needs Rodrigo's impetuous energy as much as Rodrigo needs his caution and counsel" (xix). This teacher-student dynamic in Delgado's narrative dialogues can be analyzed to represent a conversation between one split into two selves. The professor in these narratives can be interpreted as the mature self in conversation with a student who is literally or figuratively a younger version of himself. The professor is thus able to mentor and teach based on the mistakes and lessons learned through the course of his career. Meanwhile, the student can be read as the professor's younger self, someone the professor still has much to learn from.

An additional, but notable, feature to some of Delgado's narrated dialogues is his establishment of counterstory as book review. Delgado has published book reviews in law journals (see for example "Rodrigo's Roadmap: Is the Marketplace Theory for Eradicating Discrimination a Blind Alley?" or "Locating Latinos in the Field of Civil Rights: Assessing the Neoliberal Case for Radical Exclusion") in which composite characters engage a published book as the focus of the counterstory's conversation. As a feature of counterstory as narrated dialogue, writers are provided explicit opportunity to engage researched literatures to give voice to characters or to influence setting and topics.

As I discuss in Chapter 1, the tenets of CRT are often informed by and intersect with theory. Written in the style of counterstory as narrated dialogue, the following counterstory is framed by (and can be analyzed through) theories of hegemonic whiteness, intersectionality, and neo-Aristotelian rhetorical critique (Cabrera; Crenshaw; Foss 29–36). Because counterstory engages thematic foci concerning the tenets of CRT, the counterstory below subscribes to the following tenets:

- Permanence of race and racism
- Challenge to dominant ideologies
- Race as social construct
- Intersectionality and antiessentialism
- Interdisciplinarity
- Centrality of experiential knowledge and/or unique voices of color

Additionally, Delgado's method of using book review features within this counterstory functions to demonstrate ways of incorporating researched literatures to support dialogue and context, but just as important, to make clear that counterstory is a method that braids together data from the personal, the scholarly, and the literary. As is common with Delgado's counterstories, narration from the perspective of the teacher is combined with dialogue to establish setting, character description, and, if necessary, plot advancement. For the counterstory below, I incorporate a book-review discussion of Octavia Butler's *Kindred* in conversation with Margaret Mitchell's *Gone with the Wind*. Because these texts, when compared, offer divergent perspectives on the same topic, they provide ample opportunity for the teacher, Alejandra, and the student, Sofi, to conduct a pedagogical dialogue on subjectivity, the rhetorical situation, and issues of power.

### COUNTERSTORY: ON STORYTELLING AND PERSPECTIVE, OR, THE ROAD TRIP

"Sofi!" I call up the stairs.

I stretch my neck expectantly. My face is screwed up into the scowl I find myself increasingly wearing while waiting on this teenager to finally be ready so we can get out of the house.

Silence.

So I yell a bit louder, emphasizing every syllable in her name this time.

"So-fi-a A-le-jan-dra! If you don't get your butt down here in two seconds flat, I'm leaving, and you can stay with a sitter this weekend!"

The cat is sitting at my feet, waiting, as we both direct our eyes up the stairs, ears perked for any sound of human activity. And finally, we hear the familiar "click" of the bathroom door unlocking, and the cat bounds his way up the stairs to greet his favorite human in the house. As Sofi emerges, now visible on the upstairs landing, the cat, his purr motor at top volume, is winding and wrapping around her legs, as cats are wont to do.

"What?" she asks, as if she had trouble hearing me, yet continues, "I had to redo the wingtips of my eyeliner; this brush is old and keeps messing up. Can *we* buy a new one when we get to Baltimore?"

Rolling my eyes, I say, "We? You mean *me*, yes?" and flustered I continue, "I don't know; we'll see if we have time to shop before we come home, but we'll never get out of this Philadelphia traffic and into Baltimore if we don't get on the road now!"

"Uggggh okay, calm down, I'm coming," she says, as she begins to lug her overly stuffed suitcase and weekender bag down the wooden stairs.

"Don't you be *una malcriada,* Sofia Alejandra," I say, with parental warning in my voice, the Spanish trill heavy and emphasizing these last words: "You know how I feel about being told to 'calm down.'"

My scowl back in place, I watch as she makes her way down the stairs, head lowered. Then I notice a slightly discernible bratty smile curving the sides of her mouth, and as she meets me on the downstairs landing, she looks up, eyes bright, eyeliner wingtips perfect, and says sweetly,

"I love you, *Mami.* Let's go!" and lands a peck right on my cheek before bounding out the front door and down the stoop steps to our waiting car.

As I watch her go, I can't help smiling to myself, and I call out after her, "I swear to you, my gravestone will read 'Died, waiting for Sofi'!"

Then, shaking my head, I follow her out the door.

More than my daughter, Sofi has been my riding partner. She was born as I began college, when I was still, in many ways, a baby myself. And we joke often that she already has a BA, MA, and PhD because her whole early childhood was contextually set within my pursuit of these degrees. Sofi is an academic's child, through and through, and I find myself reflecting regularly on how quickly a generational shift has occurred between the two of us in terms of race, class, and access to institutions such as the university.

My relationship with Sofi, as her sole parent, has always been more of a mother-daughter partnership than any sort of parental hierarchy, because together, we've endured a lot. As a low-income, brown, teen single mother, who was a college student at that, I was a regular in the state welfare lines throughout the twelve years of my college education, which coincided with the first twelve years of Sofi's life. And although we existed in the poverty bracket through most of Sofi's childhood, I was also attending and eventually teaching at a university. When you're a low-income single mother, the options of sitters and partners to handle the kids are not readily accessible, so Sofi really *did* attend university classes (some that I took, some that I taught). Immersed in the culture of the academy, Sofi's childhood consisted of witnessing visiting guest lectures, department meetings and orientations, dissertation defenses (mine and those of my friends), social gatherings hosted by professors, and even professional conferences. "A paradox" is the only descriptor I can apply to an upbringing like Sofi's. On one hand, we have been considered (and in many ways remain) lowest on the intersectional rung of the sociocultural-economic hierarchies. On the other hand, Sofi has never known the mystification or fear I myself felt as a first-generation student on a college campus. For Sofi, the university as an accessible space has been a constant in her life. A paradox indeed.

Thus, on this day, seventeen years into Sofi's life as the daughter of an academic, we have packed up our car and are heading out on the road for a weekend getaway to Baltimore, where I am scheduled to attend and present at a conference at Towson University. And as for Sofi? Well, our little Sofi will get to see yet another university, in yet another city, and will enjoy the travel perks that are part and parcel of her mother's career.

As I back out of our driveway, I notice in my peripheral vision Sofi making all the necessary adjustments in her seat for optimal travel mode. Being my literal and figurative riding partner in this academic life, Sofi knows how to travel. Conscious of the time, I see that the digital clock on the dashboard reads 2:38 p.m. Having lived in Philadelphia now for nearly four years, I know exactly what this time means: impending 3:00 p.m. traffic that will last clear on until nearly 7:00 p.m., especially on a Friday, as commuters jump onto the I-95 to get home to their suburban weekend lives. The gas gauge hovers worryingly near the quarter-tank mark, and I know this won't be enough fuel to get us all the way to Baltimore, but it should be enough to get us to the Pennsylvania/Delaware border, or, better yet, the Delaware/Maryland border and well clear of city traffic. I make a mental note to stop for gas soon.

"Can I drive after we stop for gas?" Sofi asks, reading my thought process as she so often does. Sofi is a new driver, as many seventeen-year-olds are, and although I've been teaching her the basics since she was about twelve, I still do what Sofi calls "the mom thing" when I'm riding passenger: pumping an imaginary brake pedal and gripping the side door-handle in a bracing-for-impact way.

"Hmm, maybe," I say, "We'll see what traffic looks like at the Maryland line; I'd prefer to get to Baltimore with the same amount of gray hairs I left Philadelphia with."

Sofi snorts a laugh and shrugs as if she expected this response. Reaching for my phone, Sofi starts swiping through apps to cue up our road trip music mix, but then, remembering something, changes her mind and says, "Wait, we didn't finish the audiobook from our road trip to Montreal a couple of months ago! What was it called again?"

"*Kindred,*" I respond. "It's by Octavia Butler, and it should be cued up to the last place we listened to in the app—I don't think we had much left—" and then it dawns on me, "Oh yes, let's finish listening to it now; the route of this road trip is perfect actually, because we're driving the very paths between Pennsylvania and Maryland, between freedom and bondage, that Butler describes in her book!"

"Oh, true," Sofi responds, as she presses play and the car fills with the vocal talents of narrator Kim Staunton.

"I hate Rufus," Sofi says, just over an hour later, as we pull into an Elkton, Maryland, gas station.

"I hate him, and I hate that he gets the benefit of 'well, he was just a man of his time (Butler 25)' as an excuse for his horrible behavior as a slaveowner and a man—if we can even call him a man instead of a beast!"

Sofi is really fuming.

"Well," I start, putting the car into park at a gas stall and searching for words to articulate a fitting response, amused at her youthful fury.

"I'm not really sure that *is* an excuse, so much as an observation. Especially one that is really only possible in hindsight—I mean, in 2019's hindsight you'd be hard-pressed to find anyone who would agree there was a *right* way to be a slaveowner, so I think Butler had the really hard task of trying to give complexity and humanity to a historically vilified and in turn flattened character," I say, exiting the car and stretching my arms up over my head a bit.

"Like that 'Hindsight is 20/20' saying?" Sofi asks, as she walks around the rear of the car and puts her hand out, gesturing for the keys.

"Yeah, sorta like that," I respond, depositing the keys in her outstretched palm and connecting the nozzle of the gas hose to the car, "but deeper, because the 20/20 vision really depends on the perspective of those looking back, I think. Think of the differences in perspective between Butler and Margaret Mitchell, the lady who wrote *Gone with the Wind.*"

"Oh yeah, geez, that long-ass boring book—I can't believe they made us read that whole thing last year in tenth-grade English, and that they have the nerve to call it a 'Great American Classic.' I mean, according to whom? Who makes that call? Especially because in terms of perspective, that Mitchell lady made it seem like everyone in the book, *including the slaves,* were super cool with slavery!"

"Yeah," I agree, "and when we think about Mitchell as an author compared with Butler, there really are a few perspective things to think about."

"Like what?" Sofi prompts.

"Well, first in my mind is when the two books were written. Mitchell wrote *Gone with the Wind* in the 1930s—I just Wikipedia-ed it on my phone—1936 to be exact, and lemme see what it says about *Kindred*—right, 1979. So right off the bat, there's a very different orientation of each author to slavery and the Civil War."

The handle of the gas hose pops to indicate the tank is full, so I close up the tank and beckon for Sofi to follow me into the convenience store for some snacks.

"Okay, I can see that," Sofi says as we walk, "I guess because 1936 is only about seventy years away from the end of the Civil War, Mitchell might have known people or had family who were maybe only a generation away from all of that."

"Yeah, and then if you factor in the fact that Mitchell was a white lady," I say, holding the door open for, as it turns out, two elderly white ladies who exit right as I say "white lady."

They look at me, eyes open wide, possibly mistakenly thinking that I've called them "white ladies"—which they are (why do white people get offended when you call them "white"?). Anyway, once they clear the door, Sofi and I continue into the store and don't skip a beat in our conversation.

"Compared to Butler," I go on, "who was black and writing about slavery from the perspective of having enslaved ancestors; well, there again, puzzle pieces fall into place about how and why their perspectives differ," I finish, as we arrive at the drink coolers in the back of the store.

"It's like that concept you told me about, inter-something—" Sofi starts, as she opens a cooler door to browse the iced teas.

"Intersectionality," I offer, fetching a grapefruit juice out of a cooler for myself.

"Yeah, that," Sofi confirms.

"Yes, intersectionality is a big factor when it comes to perspective because those intersections really do affect how we are able to move through the world—they affect the very way people see us, and that can in turn influence the way we're able to act" (Crenshaw 140–41).

Our drinks selected, we find our way to the chip aisle in silence, and I eventually select my travel favorite, nacho cheese corn chips, while Sofi settles on a small bag of locally made beef jerky. As we walk to the checkout line, I glance around, noticing, as I usually do when stopped at these small-town pit stops, that the store is filled with white patrons, but working the cash register is a black woman. I don't comment on these observations to Sofi, but she knows her mother well, and knows that I, a dark-skinned, sometimes ambiguously ethnic person, almost always perform this mental racial inventory. When we talked about it, earlier in her childhood, I explained to Sofi that it's a certain learned behavior for survival for many people of color. Her upbringing has included countless conversations about this country's tradition of racist and violent behavior toward people of color, and so she well knows that I, her brown mother, consistently calibrate my racial fight-or-flight radar when in unfamiliar surroundings.

Sofi, on the other hand, has another perspective to consider. Having a half-white, half-Mexican light-skinned father, Sofi inherited his hues, but otherwise has many of my facial features. Viewed side-by-side next to me, there is no doubt that she is my daughter. But when she is apart from me, many school peers in our northeastern context have asked if she is Italian, Jewish, or Greek—no one ever arrives at Mexican as the racial/ethnic assumption about Sofi. And because of this and because she has a mother whose line of work centralizes racial observations and analysis, Sofi and I have been discussing, since she was very young, what it means to be white passing, what white privilege is, and the responsibilities of this passing privilege (Martinez, "Responsibility of Privilege"). The reality of Sofi's existence and perspective is that she has access to spaces and conversations from which her own mother would be barred. And Sofi, young as she is, understands her skin-privileged responsibility to disrupt white comfort, white silence, and white complacency (crunkadelic, "Get Your People"; Lorde, "The Transformation of Silence into Language and Action").

Snacks now purchased, we make our way back to the car. The sound of the car keys jangling off Sofi's index finger reminds me I'd handed them to her when we stopped. As we get into the car and make the necessary adjustments to our swapped seats, Sofi brings the conversation back to where we'd left off.

"In *Kindred*," Sofi begins, "I think it was intersectionality that applied to the way people kept telling Dana she didn't talk right or act right for a slave. They kept saying she talked and acted 'white' mostly because she was educated in and from a different time. It was her skin color, tied to the way she spoke, even the way she dressed, as they always made a big deal about her wearing pants instead of a skirt, that got her in trouble so often. So it was all of those things overlapping" (Crenshaw 140–41).

"Yes," I interject, "exactly. And if we think outside the books, back to who wrote them, Mitchell, as a white woman who was a granddaughter of slaveowners and in effect really only a generation removed from people in her own family who fought for the Confederacy during the Civil War—well, there you are again with light shed on why she can be so romantic in her description of this time."

"Yeah," Sofi says thoughtfully, then offers, "and the only real asshole we were supposed to hate in Mitchell's book was Scarlett, because she was a shitty person—not because she and all her friends and family held people in bondage—but because they were all intent on slut-shaming her over the whole Ashley thing. I mean, who cares?! I would much rather have read *Kindred*, or if we had to read *Gone with the Wind*, they should have had us read *Kindred* in the same year so we'd at least get more than just this one racist perspective."

"I agree," I say, swelling internally with parental pride. "Multiple perspectives, especially those from people of color or other minoritized folk, are crucial to get at any sort of truth about racial matters."

As Sofi begins to drive us away from the gas station, I ask, "Did you adjust your mirrors?" I say this more out of habit than because she actually needs the reminder.

Rolling her eyes, as she is already mid–mirror adjustment, she seems to make the choice to withhold her usual "*Mami,* I knoooow" response.

"It's funny," I begin, "how well this conversation on perspective lines up with something so real and tangible as learning to be a safe driver."

"What do you mean?" Sofi asks as she merges back onto the interstate, careful to use her signal and check her blind spot in anticipation of my telling her to do both.

"Well, think about it," I continue, "driving can be a very dangerous activity; you're essentially handling a weapon here. Cars weigh a bunch, and the privilege to drive is so heavily invested in the soundness of your senses, particularly sight."

"Oh yeah, like the way they made me take an eye test with the chart to get my permit in the first place," Sofi offers.

"Yes, exactly," I confirm. "And with a license comes the responsibility of literally staying on top of how your sight, your perspective, influences your driving."

"It's all such a metaphor for whiteness," I think to myself.

Whiteness is heavy, and can be weaponized, and perspectives tied to intersectionality are so much the determinant of how this whiteness will be used. A whiteness perspective most tied to other axes of privilege—gender, ability, sexuality, class, religion—results in a destructive force, a lack of awareness that turns whiteness from vehicle to weapon. Whereas when whiteness is tied to axes of oppression, it seems to result in varying degrees of awareness—an awareness and perspective to keep the potential whiteness-weapon from maiming and injuring others around you (Delgado and Stefancic, *Critical Race Theory: The Cutting Edge* pp. 773–822; C. I. Harris; Haney López).

"Like with the mirrors and checking the blind spots and wearing glasses if you need them, and turning on lights at dusk and watching out for signs and pedestrians, and all that stuff they test you on," Sofi lists, pulling me back from my musings.

"What was that?" I ask.

"We were talking about how sight and driving are related to this idea of perspective," she reminds me, and I can tell she is wondering where I'd wandered off to.

"Oh . . . right," I say, remembering where we've left off. "And think about what sight and perspective have to do with driving when things don't go so well, when there's a car accident," I prompt.

"Oooh," Sofi says, her mouth forming a perfectly round "O" as further insight dawns upon her. "When there's an accident," she begins, "perspective is the most important thing! We just learned about this in my forensic sciences class! My teacher told us that, first of all, there are video cameras at most intersections, so there's the option for a few perspectives there, depending on how many cameras there are. But he also told us that if we witness an accident, we have to stay there until the police come, even if we're not hurt, because the police will want us to tell them what we saw, so there are a few more perspectives there."

"But!" she exclaims, and I can tell she is building toward something, "If the people actually involved in the accident can give statements, they get those two perspectives as well. And my teacher said it's crucial to get what witnesses and cameras saw because the people involved in the accident might be really emotional, or if they're hurt, their memories can be affected, or worse, if they were on drugs or alcohol, their version of events ends up not being trusted at all."

"Right," I respond. "And think about the rhetoric you're learning about in this year's eleventh-grade English. It's easy to see how very rhetorical these perspectives can be, isn't it?

"Yes," Sofi answers. "We learned about logos, ethos, and pathos, and I can definitely see emotions, credibility, and logic are all tied up in these perspectives."

"And at the core of this example," I continue, "what is everybody really in pursuit of?"

"The truth, I guess," says Sofi, uncertainty in her voice—"Why do you sound unsure?" I ask.

"Well—" she begins, "with so many different perspectives about the same event, isn't it sort of impossible for there to be one truth that everyone agrees on? I mean, think about it."

I nod for her to continue.

"Everyone involved, from witnesses to victims, to the person or people who view the video from the intersection cameras, and then even the detectives my teacher told us will be called onto the scene because they're trained to look at tire tracks and stuff—I mean, don't they *all* think their version of events is the truth?"

"I suppose so," I say thoughtfully, and then add, "My guess too is that you could sit four different people down to watch each of the intersection videos from the four possible cameras at the intersection, and you'd probably get four different versions of the accident, from varying angles and perspectives, too!"

"Oh my gosh, yes, exactly!" Sofi says, eyes wide. "So, if these perspectives are endless and if everyone thinks their version of events or reality is the truth, then how does anyone ever agree on what is or isn't true?"

"That, Sofi, is the foundational question for my whole field of study. You've hit the nail on the head. How *does* anyone *really* know what is or isn't true? Or for that matter, if a universal objective truth even exists?"

Sofi expels a sound from her lips much like an explosion with an accompanying exploding gesture of her hand at her temple.

I laugh as this moment reminds me why I love being a parent and why I love teaching first-year students at the university. As with Sofi, there are still things you can tell first-year students that "blow their minds." And it's easy to forget or discount that some of these concepts were ever mind-blowing to you because you, as the professor and adult, have likely been grappling with these subjects for years. As time wears on, your memories grow thin about those childhood learning moments when concepts were new—to you.

We ride on in contemplative silence for a stretch of time, and I look out the window, watching the leafless trees zoom by. I think about Butler's characters in *Kindred,* the enslaved Alice and her husband, Isaac, as they tragically ran away northward to Pennsylvania, in pursuit of happiness and freedom. I think also of the character Kevin, the white male husband to the novel's black female protagonist, Dana. I think of his trek north and south in hopeful and vigilant anticipation of his time-traveling wife's return from 1976 to pre–Civil War Maryland. As I lean my head against the window, I am startled away by the chill absorbed in the glass from the cold air exterior. Since it is mid-March, spring is nowhere in sight, as winter still holds its icy grip on this part of the country. I lean slightly over to Sofi's side of the car to see that the temperature gauge under the car speedometer reads 33 degrees Fahrenheit. As a girl raised in the deserts of the Southwest, I shiver at the thought of this cold. I think also about what these freezing elements mean for anyone attempting outdoor travel, and I remember Butler's description of the journey north for slaves—the way she detailed that if white people didn't get you, the elements and hunger would.

"Hey, *Mami*," Sofi prompts.

"Hmm," I sound jogged from my thoughts.

"I was thinking some more about perspectives, and truly how much cooler our discussions in class would have been if the teacher had assigned both Butler's and Mitchell's books last year."

"Yeah," I say. "I agree."

"And essentially," she continues, "the books take place in a very similar time and place, right? The South, during legal slavery."

"Right," I agree.

"Well, kind of like what we were talking about earlier with the many and various perspectives involved in a car accident, all these perspectives ultimately end up going somewhere to be presented for judgment, right? Like to a judge or a jury but, overall, to an audience, right?"

"Yes," I respond, delighted by where I see her going with this. "Ultimately," I continue, "all perspectives are gathered and presented as stories for the audience to make out their own truth with the various available narratives. Very good, Sofi!"

She hates when I give her these sorts of "teacherly compliments," but I can't help myself; I am truly impressed she is drawing these connections in ways that can take weeks with some of my university students.

"As I said," she continues, pointedly ignoring my praise, "our English teacher this year always makes us think about all your rhetoric stuff: audience, purpose, writer, context, subject—oh, and the pressing issue that makes it urgent to speak up or to write. She says the motivations and thoughts that went into making books or speeches matter just as much as what actually ends up written and said."

"I would say that's true," I agree. "Your teacher is referring to something people in my field call 'kairos' and 'the rhetorical situation,' and, as you just said, exigence and audience are major considerations, in the same way we talked earlier about how important writer and context are as well" (Bizzell and Herzberg 81).

"Right," replies Sofi, "so whether the audience is a judge and jury deciding whose fault a car crash was, or whether it's a class full of high school kids, the only real way we can come to any informed decision on what actually happened is if we're given multiple perspectives, or stories, so we can make up our own minds, right?"

"Right," I confirm.

"So, again, why did my teacher only give us Margaret Mitchell's racist perspective?" Sofi asks.

"That's a great question, Sofi," I begin to answer, "and it has everything to do with the core curriculum and 'standards' in schools that are largely informed by perspective, not very different from the car crash at the intersection that we just talked about. In the way there are so many perspectives involved in the same event, such as a car crash, when you think about whose perspectives get weight in the legal sense, well, that's where we get to questions of power and the ways people with lots of money can pay for a good lawyer who knows how to represent perspectives in a certain way, or where someone like an adult white male's testimony might get more weight than the testimony of a teenage Asian female driver due to stereotypes that are ageist, racist, and sexist. So, although there are many perspectives, a perspective's relation to power is too often what determines whose story gets told, listened to, and believed as truth. But bottom line and above all, there's *always* another story—"

"Keep right at the fork to stay on I-95 South" the weird robotic voice of the GPS interrupts; "use the right two lanes to take exit 64 for Interstate 695 West toward Towson."

"Oops," I say, "we can continue this conversation later so we can pay attention to the GPS."

"Okay, *Mami*," Sofi says, eyes focused forward, both hands on the wheel, attentive to her responsibilities as the driver of a heavy and potentially dangerous vehicle.

As we settle into our Airbnb for the evening, I call across the hall from my room to Sofi's.

"Hey, Sofi."

"Hmm?" she asks.

"What do you think it'd be like if we were suddenly pulled through time, like Dana, to pre–Civil War Maryland?"

She is quiet for a few seconds and then responds, "I don't know, but I know I'd protect you."

Surprise tears well in my eyes, and, doing my best not to let my voice crack, I say, "I know you would. I love you, *Mija*, good night."

"Night, *Mami*," comes her sweet voice in return.

Later, I climb into bed and retrieve my waiting laptop from the bedside table. Opening the PDF window to the several cued-up essays, I decide I'll do some before-bed reading. I am teaching a core-course grad seminar this semester on the histories and theories of rhetoric, so the essays due to be discussed in class the following Tuesday are largely a review of scholarship from my own time as a grad student in a similar course. I glance quickly at my daily reading schedule to be sure the essays cued up on my laptop correspond to those listed. The schedule designates the following:

"Octalog: The Politics of Historiography," 1988
"Octalog II: The (Continuing) Politics of Historiography," 1997
"Octalog III: The Politics of Historiography in 2010," 2010

Satisfied that the cued-up essays match the daily schedule, I begin with the "Octalog," but before realizing it, I startle myself awake to find myself not lying warm and safe in my Towson-area bed, but at the end of a thirty-plus-years' journey into the past, standing in darkness (Bell, *And* 26).

# 3

## Derrick Bell and Counterstory as Allegory/Fantasy

> I am not sure who coined the phrase "critical race theory" to describe this form of writing, and I have received more credit than I deserve for the movement's origins. I rather think that this writing is the response to a need for expressing views that cannot be communicated effectively through existing techniques. In my case, I prefer using stories as a means of communicating views to those who hold very different views on the emotionally charged subject of race. People enjoy stories and will often suspend their beliefs, listen to the story, and then compare their views, not with mine, but with those expressed in the story.
> 
> —Derrick Bell

BORN IN 1930, DERRICK ALBERT BELL JR. was raised in a black Pittsburgh neighborhood known as "the Hill." Bell credits his parents for instilling in him a steadfast work ethic and the will to push against discriminatory and prejudiced authority, and for providing a strategy to navigate a "white man's world . . . of racial discrimination [in which] black people had to be twice as good to get half as much" (Delgado and Stefancic, introduction to *The Derrick Bell Reader* 3). Much of the foundation and many of the major events associated with CRT and counterstory are attributable to Bell, so his biography is as much a history of the development of CRT's tenets as it is a demonstration of his career in and of itself.

Graduating from the University of Pittsburgh Law School in 1957, Bell was the only black student in a class of 120. Embarking on a career defined by professional acts of protest, defiance, and refusal concerning issues of institutional racism (an inspiration and blueprint for CRT as a movement), Bell gained his first professional appointment in 1959 in the Justice Department's Civil Rights Division. Considering Bell's participation in the NAACP a conflict of interest, his superiors demanded he cede membership. Bell refused. Bell was as a result moved off race cases, assigned mundane tasks, and soon resigned (Goldberg 56; Delgado and Stefancic 4). This would not be the last time Bell gave up a prized position for principle. Hired subsequently by Thurgood Marshall, Bell worked from 1960 to 1966 for the NAACP Legal Defense Fund. During this time as a civil rights lawyer, Bell spent a night in a Jackson, Mississippi, jail for refusing to leave a train station's "whites-only" waiting room (Goldberg 56; Delgado and Stefancic 5). In 1969 Bell became Harvard Law School's first tenured African American faculty member, but in 1981 he left over the lack of any black women on the faculty. Bell then became dean of the University of Oregon Law School, but here as well resigned in protest four years later, when the school refused to support his decision to hire an Asian American woman.[1]

Bell was eventually lured back to Harvard, and upon his 1987 return he staged a five-day sit-in inside his office to protest the denial of tenure to two members of the critical legal studies movement. A year later, Bell wrote a scathing indictment of the law school's affirmative action performance, including an allegory in which Harvard increased minority hiring only after all the school's black faculty and the university president were killed in a terrorist bombing ("The Final Report"). By the end of the 1989–90 school year and at the conclusion of yet another faculty search that resulted in the Harvard faculty's passing over *yet another* qualified black woman candidate, Bell announced he would take an unpaid leave of absence until Harvard Law School hired its first woman of color. Two years later, his situation still unresolved with no woman of color appointed, Harvard indicated it would treat his protest as a resignation and would terminate his contract if he failed to return for the 1992–93 academic year (Goldberg 57; Delgado and Stefancic 13). Bell did not return.

Interestingly, this particular moment of protest was brought back into the American consciousness during the 2012 presidential race, when Breitbart[2] released a video of a 1991 demonstration at Harvard Law School in which a young Barack Obama introduces Bell (in that signature Obama timbre), encouraging the crowd of protesters to "open up your hearts and your minds to the words of Professor Derrick Bell" ("Vetting"). Citing this video as supposed evidence of Obama's radical antiwhiteness, even Breitbart cannot deny Bell's impact as a legal scholar, but also, more important, as an activist who broke racial barriers, guided CRT as a movement, and influenced many—even the first black president of the United States (Goldberg 57; Cohen). When interviewed on the *MacNeil/Lehrer Report,* Bell was asked about his motto "I live to harass white people."[3] This was his response:

> As I indicate in the book [*Faces at the Bottom of the Well*], I try to explain that one of the really impressive events in my life was working, back in the '60s, with black people who were challenging discrimination in public facilities or elsewhere at very great risk to themselves and with a hope that they were born to prevail, but surely with no certainty. And I simply quote this woman, Mrs. MacDonald, who had many white friends, but the people who were oppressing her also were white. This is not a hate-filled statement, but I can't sugarcoat it. Harassment is an effort to bring others to see what I see. If there are those who are upset or threatened, good. Because there are plenty of reasons for them to be that way. (qtd. in Goldberg 58)

### BELL'S PEDAGOGICAL "NEW RHETORIC"

In her foreword to the twenty-fifth-anniversary edition of *Faces at the Bottom on the Well,* Michelle Alexander, author of *The New Jim Crow,*[4] cites Bell and his scholarly contributions to the field of critical race theory as foundational and an impetus for her own work (x). As Alexander relates, when reading Bell's words twenty-five years after the book was published, it is "difficult to refute the nuanced argument he weaves so gracefully—and unapologetically—in these pages. I read his words, and chills sweep over me. Something lurks in these pages that is eerily prophetic, almost haunting, and yet at the same time oddly reassuring" (xi). In *Race, Rhetoric, and Technology*, Adam J. Banks zeroes in on Bell's *And We Are Not Saved*, the book that precedes *Faces* in its use of parable, allegory, and science fiction. A series of ten chronicles consisting of Socratic dialogue between Bell and composite character Geneva Crenshaw,[5] the book, Banks maintains, marks the start of the mainstream popularity of CRT and counterstory (93). Further, Banks credits Bell's counterstories as a rhetorical form and genre that engage and intervene in American legal discourse conventions and work toward rewriting "racist code(s) at the root of our legal system" (87, 92). Similar to Alexander's characterization of Bell's words as prophetic, Banks's view is that Bell's allegories invoke the "Black Jeremiad," manipulating and even discarding aspects of this genre. As Banks argues, Bell's counterstories about African Americans in the legal system navigate "America's and Black America's past promise through the myth of a golden age, critique of the nation's fall from that past greatness, and a prophesy that the nation must either fulfill its promise by living up to its ideals or face certain damnation" (88).

Because of Bell's development of and insistence on CRT's tenet of the permanence of race and racism (see Chapter 1)—a framework woven throughout the narratives of both *And* and *Faces*—Alexander acknowledges that audiences may read Bell's work and "find it depressing, disturbing, foolish, or misguided" (xi–xii). But she continues to make the important distinction that accepting the permanence of racism in this country does not mean accepting racism (xvii). Kynard asserts that Bell's racial realism is the "most hopeful and pragmatic theoretical lens and praxis to do antiracist work" ("Teaching While Black" 4), and, in fact, Alexander argues that revisiting Bell's work these twenty-five years later provides occasion to fully (re)examine the tenet of "racial permanence" and insists that we should ask ourselves:

> What if Bell was right? What if justice for the dark faces at "the bottom of the well" can't actually be won in the United States? What if all "progress" toward racial justice is illusory, temporary, and inevitably unstable? What if white supremacy will always rebound, finding new ways to reconstitute itself? (xiv)

And because permanence does not mean acceptance, Alexander concludes her foreword with a call to action, stating,

> Facing the inconvenient truth that America may suffer from an incurable, potentially fatal disease helps to clarify what we're up against. It offers the opportunity to clarify our goals ... [and to] [a]sk yourself if you're willing to commit yourself to the struggle for racial justice even if the battle can't ever be won. (xviii–xix)

Because of the consistently pedagogical intent of his stories,[6] Bell's work in counterstory has bolstered CRT as a movement—and the crits within the movement—in clarifying our goals and affirmative commitment toward racial justice. Bell himself has confirmed that many of his stories were written to facilitate classroom discussion (*Faces* xxvi) and that his use of allegory and fantasy concerning race—and the methodological use of fiction in general—enables him and his audience to separate themselves from the real and perhaps "see things in terms that are less threatening and confrontational."[7] Bell continues, "when the audience reenters reality, messages are left behind that provide a new perspective or set of lenses. It lets them see more clearly what I think I see all the time" (qtd. in Goldberg 57). Specific to rhetoric and writing studies—a field and disciplines virtually obsessed with rhetoric's pedagogical effectiveness and applicability—Prendergast has suggested that Bell's counterstories contribute a "new rhetoric" in the struggle for racial justice (46). She asserts that Bell, through counterstory, enacts literacy practices that not only depart from standard forms of legal analysis—forms valued by the mainstream—but explicitly rejects such practices due to their inadequacies in accurately researching, documenting, and relating the "contradictions and ambiguities faced by people of color in the United States" (46). Likewise, Banks lauds the value of Bell's "new rhetoric" and attributes his strategic "literacy practices" for creating at least the possibility of a genuine rhetorical situation that demands response and forces dialogue (93). Prendergast concludes that crits' "deliberately dissonant rhetorical stance" through counterstory effectively turns a reflective mirror on the academy's inherently and institutionally racist histories and environments, which have marginalized and continue marginalizing people of color (46–48).

## THE CRAFT OF ALLEGORY/FANTASY: A RHETORICAL TRADITION

Allegory as a rhetorical trope is not a foreign concept to writers and scholars in rhetoric and writing studies and is well represented within the Euro-Western rhetorical canon by the work of Parmenides, Anaxagoras, Gorgias of Leontini, Plato, Aristotle, Cicero, Quintilian, Augustine, Boethius, Thomas Aquinas, Christine de Pizan, John Locke, Jean-Jacques Rousseau, Immanuel Kant, Martin Heidegger, Mikhail Bakhtin, Jean-Paul Sartre, and Jacques Derrida, to name a few. The works of many of these same figures are featured in Patricia Bizzell and Bruce Herzberg's tome *The Rhetorical Tradition*. These texts sustain a Euro-Western history of being analyzed for both literal and allegorical meanings, and because this canon is still engaged as foundational in rhetoric and writing studies, allegory as a rhetorical device holds a definitive place. Although contemporary scholars of rhetoric and writing studies do study and interpret allegorical texts, composing allegorical scholarship is not common practice. Thus (at least for me) the questions that surface are: Why does rhetoric and writing studies value allegorical writings as texts for scholarly projects and inquiry alone? Should scholars attempt to compose in an innovative style informed by foundational work? Can we use allegory to convey argument, and are there instances in which allegory conveys meaning and invokes discussion in ways more effective (even affective) than traditional academic prose? I'd wager Derrick Bell would answer "yes."

Derrick Bell has crafted allegorical themes, context, and characters to offer a method of discourse that provides an approach to critique norms "in an ironically contextualized way" (*And* 6). As a readily known referent of allegorical works in rhetoric and writing studies, Plato's works are similarly noted for their dramatic setting, in which he creates philosophical discussions among characters who in many instances can be identified as or associated with historical figures. According to Richard Kraut, Plato did not try to create "a fictional world for the purposes of telling a story, as many literary dramas do; nor do his works invoke an earlier mythical realm" (n.p.). His dialogues often begin with a depiction of the setting/context that forms vivid portraits of a living, breathing social world, and the dialogues are not

> purely intellectual exchanges between characterless and socially unmarked speakers. In *many* of his dialogues . . . Plato is not only attempting to draw his readers into a discussion, but is also commenting on the social milieu that he is depicting, and criticizing the character and ways of life of his interlocutors.

Plato's placement of his dialogues in social contexts achieves two goals, the first being Plato's ability to engage his audience in the topic of discussion because of its cultural relevance. Second, Plato has the opportunity to voice his beliefs about current events through voices of characters that provide him the opportunity to be more candid about his critique while also humanizing the facts and figures to make for a more engaging approach to a discussion of social and political issues.

Drawing from Plato's method of devising a setting reflective of contemporary social issues and depicting characters that can be easily associated with real public figures (but infused with CRT's tenets regarding specific concerns), I have crafted allegorical social contexts that provide an inlet for dramatized dialogue and narrative—evoking imagery and metaphors to address the real problems presented by contemporary racism. For instance, in "Critical Race Theory Counterstory as Allegory: A Rhetorical Trope to Raise Awareness about Arizona's Ban on Ethnic Studies," I argue that the heightened sense of drama accompanied by national media coverage of Arizona's anti-immigrant/anti–ethnic studies legislation provides generative material to craft characters and themes for a discussion placed in a setting reflective of this social context. Within this context, I staged an allegory about immortality, discussing the ferment of American neoconservative ideology that produces legislation rendering some human beings "illegal," all the while dramatizing representation of the power politicians and voters wield toward effectively denying a people the right to a future and, in effect, the right to exist.

As I've discussed throughout this chapter, allegory/fantasy as counterstory is most notably attributed to Bell, who contends that he writes "to uncover enduring truths . . . [and that] allegory employs stories that are not true to explore situations that are real enough but, in their many and contradictory dimensions, defy understanding" (*And* 6–7). Bell's use of this method gets at the "truth" of racism, and his purpose for writing allegorically coincides with my own working definition of allegory. Jane Brown's definition of allegory as "a mode of representation which renders the supernatural visible" (5) is particularly helpful to my analysis of allegory as a method. This definition contributes to Banks's previously discussed characterization of Bell's approach as creating at least the possibility of a genuine rhetorical situation that demands response and forces dialogue within color-blind racist systems and institutions in which racial practices operate in often obscure and invisible ways (Bonilla-Silva 3). In turn, persons not affected by the realities of racism are in a position to minimize or to deny outright the existence of racism altogether (Bonilla-Silva 26). This practice of minimizing or denying racism supports a contemporary racial ideology that renders racism ghostlike, not real, or even "supernatural." Combining the rhetorical understanding of allegory as a trope, Bell's justification for using allegory in his writing, and Brown's definition, I assert allegory as a counterstory method that functions to render visible invisible forms of racism.

Bell succeeds in using imagery and metaphors to address the real problems presented by contemporary racism, particularly in his provocative and well-known story "The Space Traders." Using the historical context of the African slave trade, a setting that allows the audience to connect the allegory's cultural references, "The Space Traders" tells the tale of an offer made by aliens from outer space to the United States: they will ensure enough gold to bail out the nearly bankrupt government, special chemicals to rid the environment of toxic pollutants, and an answer to our fossil fuel energy depletion. In return, the aliens ask for only one thing—that the United States hands over all African Americans to be taken away to an unknown fate when the aliens depart (*Faces* 159–60). In this allegory, African Americans are faced with yet another trade, now the space trade, and the value of the black body is reintroduced as a subject. Bell asks his audience to consider how much an African American life is worth when the rate of exchange involves the ultimate solution for our nation's problems (*Faces* 164). Bell's protagonist, Professor Gleeson Golightly, a conservative black economics professor and member of the president's cabinet (*Faces* 163–64), is the only voice of color represented when the president and his cabinet meet to consider the aliens' offer. Golightly is unsuccessful in his attempt to convince the politicians not to accept the aliens' offer and is instead asked by the president to speak as an African American in favor of the trade (*Faces* 172). In this moment, Golightly comes to consciousness regarding the fact that "black lives are expendable whenever their sacrifice will further or sustain white needs or preferences" (*Faces* 174), in keeping with the CRT tenet of "interest convergence." In the end, African Americans are forced to leave America's shores in the same way they arrived, in chains and on ships (*Faces* 194).

Because Bell weaves his allegories around citations of historical and contemporary American legislation, historical cultural references, and characters that represent existing political and racist ideologies, this method lends itself easily to instruction as a research method. As discussed in my previous chapter, I have crafted curricula on CRT and counterstory (see Appendixes A and B), and when teaching Bell's method of allegory/fantasy in my "Writing Critical Race Counterstory" writers workshop (Appendix B), I've noted the difficulty of this genre for students. Admittedly, this method is the most challenging for me as a counterstory writer as well, and my own first attempt at it, "Critical Race Theory Counterstory as Allegory: A Rhetorical Trope to Raise Awareness about Arizona's Ban on Ethnic Studies," I was told "reads as bad fiction"—by a white male critic, no less. While I can admit this work was not my best,

I can also admit to and empathize with my students that writing allegory is hard—thus making Bell's success with this method all the more impressive. With these method-specific difficulties considered, my students and I spend the necessary time, several weeks, on counterstory as allegory/fantasy. Students begin learning about this method through reading Bell's "The Space Traders" and also have the opportunity to *watch* historic and contemporary forms of allegory, ranging from episodes of "The Twilight Zone" to Netflix's "Black Mirror." In turn, we shift to crafting counterstories as allegory/fantasy, and as with the other CRT methods, students brainstorm and then rigorously research possible topics toward gathering supporting materials to braid in with their own personal experiences. Similar to my instruction with Delgado's method of narrated dialogue, we engage the process of crafting context and characters for composite counterstories;[8] however, during this unit we pay particular attention to the rhetorical strategies of metaphor and fantasy as literary devices (e.g., time travel, mythical creatures, magic, otherworldly contexts). As a class, we progress to workshopping several drafts of allegory/fantasy counterstories, including in-class readarounds and peer review. Although this method is reportedly difficult for students (as is overwhelmingly mentioned in course evaluations), these counterstories are often the most creative and engaging for me, as instructor, to read. In other words, allegories are well worth the collective effort.

As a demonstration of this genre, my own composition within this chapter is inspired by and modeled after Bell's first chapter in his book *And We Are Not Saved*. This allegory involves aspects of time travel, in which Bell's much-chronicled heroine-protagonist, Geneva Crenshaw, travels back in time to the Constitutional Convention of 1787. As a black woman, Geneva speaks to a room full of white "founding father" delegates on the state of black folk in contemporary America because of their inability to make slavery unconstitutional. Banks has commented on the scholarship and data for this method of counterstory, and says, "The delegates respond to her arguments as Bell imagines they would, but he does not leave their responses to whims. He bases them instead on the actual words of some of the delegates to the real convention in 1787, and his historical analysis of the general arguments made at the time" (97). Likewise, my own counterstory as allegory/fantasy travels back in time with Alejandra Prieto to a dramatized version of the 1988 Conference on College Composition and Communication, and places this composite character in conversation with none other than the original Octalog: James Berlin, Robert J. Connors, Sharon Crowley, Richard Leo Enos, Susan C. Jarratt, Nan Johnson, Jan Swearingen, Victor J. Vitanza, and their moderator, James J. Murphy.

As discussed in Chapter 1, the tenets of CRT are often informed by and intersect with theory. The following counterstory, written in the style of counterstory as allegory/fantasy, is framed by (and can be analyzed through) theories of hegemonic whiteness, intersectionality, color-blind racism, interest convergence, and neo-Aristotelian rhetorical critique (Cabrera; Crenshaw; Bonilla-Silva; Bell, *And;* Foss 29–36). Because counterstory engages thematic foci concerning the tenets, the counterstory below subscribes to the following tenets:

- Permanence of race and racism
- Challenge to dominant ideologies
- Intersectionality and antiessentialism
- Centrality of experiential knowledge and/or unique voices of color
- Commitment to social justice

Through the course of Alejandra's engagement with the Octalog, they discuss the contemporary state of rhetoric and writing studies, with a few references to and appearances from voices of the Octalogs[9] subsequent to the 1988 original. As in Bell's work, the Octalog I's contributions to this fictionalized exchange are inspired by their actual words and actions left to us through this published and widely taught and cited document.[10] Although I undoubtedly associate the names of the scholars represented in Octalog I with their quoted words, I do so as an organizing device above all else. I do not deploy these names under the impression (or to suggest) that these scholars as real people are static in the beliefs they espoused in this thirty-plus-year-old text. In fact, I chose allegory/fantasy for Alejandra's engagement with the Octalog (as opposed to other more literal methods such as autobiographic reflection) to better emphasize the allegorical representative nature of each scholar's expressed viewpoint—more so than their name—at a particularly generative moment for the disciplinary and political directions rhetoric and writing studies has splintered into over the past thirty years.

In all, my critique and demonstration of counterstory as allegory/fantasy weave together allegorical citations of historical and contemporary scholarship, historical cultural references, and characters that represent existing political, social, and racial ideologies. Harking back to Bell's pedagogical intent for his narratives, I envision this demonstrated exercise in critical race methodology as serving for histories of rhetoric(s)/rhetorical theories students as an in-class group exercise or a final researched essay in which they creatively enter into imagined conversations with assigned authors. As a whole, this allegory about real topics concerning rhetoric and writing studies' (by some accounts) sanctified foundations/foundational figures and sociocultural motivations/trajectories may evoke many interpretations. I welcome readings and resulting discussions that explore additional meaning in either the themes or characters written herein.

## COUNTERSTORY: THE POLITICS OF HISTORIOGRAPHY, ACT 2

> All the world's a stage, and all the men and women merely players; / They have their exits and their entrances . . .
> —William Shakespeare

At the end of a thirty-plus-years journey into the past, I found myself standing in darkness (Bell, *And* 26). To verify that my eyes were indeed open, I stretched them, feeling them bulge out of my head, the skin of my eye sockets extending to its limits. Yet, still nothing, only darkness. Then, from somewhere above me, I heard a booming voice say: "and, since the Editor[11] views this particular drama as actually Act One of a continuing Brechtean[12] exchange, the reader can interject Self as a character in Act Two by responding to what is spoken here" (Murphy et al. 6). And, snap, a spotlight switched on above me, shrouding me in a yellowish aura. Then, materializing in front of me, under their own individual spotlights and seated on a raised platform, were eight faces.

Gazing up into each of these eight faces, first left to right, then right to left, my eyes adjusted to perceive that the Eight were seated behind a long table with elegantly engraved brass nameplates propped up in front of them: Berlin, Connors, Crowley, Enos, Jarratt, Johnson, Swearingen, and Vitanza. As I continued to gaze at the Eight, I realized, much to my surprise, that their expressions seemed frozen in place and time. Their unblinking visages stared out beyond me into an unseen audience. I turned my back to the Eight so as to squint out into the darkness in an attempt to glean what their collective gazes beheld. Suddenly, a track of gaslights illuminated, one after the other, also left to right, to reveal the edge of a stage, and beyond it, a theater house with rows and balconies of red velvet upholstered seats occupied by dark shadowy figures.[13] Alarmed by this sight, I swiveled back around to face the Eight when once again the loud voice of someone whom I now intuited to be James J. Murphy spoke from above:

"Greetings, Self."

"Self?" I questioned. "No. My name is Alejandra," I corrected.

"Yes," Murphy confirmed. "And today, you will play the role of Self, a character who will act as interlocutor with the Eight.[14] Are there any character details or description the audience should know about you before we commence with Act 2?"

"Hmm," I said, thinking for a bit. "Well, I'm from the future, a little over thirty years in the future."

At this statement, I heard the shadowy figures in the audience behind me "oooh" with interest.

"And, as I mentioned, my name is Alejandra—Alejandra Prieto, I'm Chicana, and I'm an assistant professor of rhetoric and writing studies—oh, but specifically, I examine rhetorics and writing practices of race and racism," I added, thinking this final detail would matter in some way, and it did.

"'Rhetorics and writing of race and racism,'" Murphy's voice from above repeated, as if mulling over the concept in his mind. "Interesting," he surmised, and the audience behind me seemed to agree because I could hear their murmurs of assent.

"And I'm assuming," Murphy continued, "because you've been transported here, that you have some sort of investment in the politics of rhetoric's historiography?"

I nodded.

"And I assume the purpose and position you will take concerns the role that race and racism play in shaping the actions you've taken in your researching of rhetoric and writing?" Murphy asked (5).

"Yes," I began. "I suppose my subjectivities are what have influenced my purpose in rhetoric and writing, and I'd say these same subjectivities shape the actions I've taken to pursue my research interests" (5).

"Excellent," Murphy answered. "And do you pursue your research with the intent to work together with others for the common good?"

"Is there such a thing as a universally agreed upon 'common good'?" I asked in response.

"Ah!" said Murphy in a smiling tone. "Then you're a perfect candidate for the role of Self! Let us tap the ebullient spirits of the Eight to see if, perchance, they have anything they would like to ask or say to you. Let's begin!" (19).

And with Murphy's exclamation, the individual spotlights on the Eight expanded to a fully lit scene of eight professors, dressed in doctoral caps and robes, now fully animated in gesticulating motion and articulation.

Looking down, I now noticed I was standing before this tribunal of eight at a podium. I cleared my throat to begin to speak, but to no discernible notice from the Eight. Then, realizing a gavel had appeared in my hand, I quickly tapped the wooden podium top twice, hard (Bell, *And* 26).

"Esteemed colleagues," I said, "my name is Alejandra Prieto, and I appear here as a representative of rhetoric and writing studies from thirty years into the future. I am here in the role of Self to engage in a 'Brechtian exchange,' from my subject position as a person of color within rhetoric and writing studies, and in response to what you have spoken of together here as the Eight" (Murphy et al. 6; Bell, *And* 26).

At this introduction, all eight faces looked down at me, some with expressions of amused curiosity, some with benign uninterest, others perceptibly pensive, and yet others inscrutable. One of the Eight, with the nameplate saying "Jarratt," spoke first:

"Greetings, Alejandra. We will begin this exchange with you as Self by asking that you first offer us a position statement, a preamble of sorts, to provide us and the audience a general sense of your stance on the issues at hand. So, Self, what is your purpose and method of choice in studying the history of rhetoric?"

"Well," I began, "I suppose I should begin by answering *why* I've chosen to study the histories of rhetoric with race and racism as my centralized frame" (Murphy et al. 5).

Many of the Eight nodded their acquiescence.

"I don't feel there was much choice," I stated bluntly.

I heard a cackle, and I snapped my head in the direction of its source to find myself in direct eye contact with Vitanza, upon which we simply burst into laughter—rolling and uncontrollable laughter. The kind of laughter that makes your sides ache. And when I was finally able to compose myself and stand straight again, I began (Murphy et al. 9, 16).

"Members of the Eight, I am a critical race theorist, what some have called a 'crit.' As such, I hold central beliefs[15] that drive my inquiry and frame the rhetoric and literacy practices I enact in every instance of my work and identity as a teacher-scholar in rhetoric and writing studies. First, I believe race and racism in the United States are permanent, and that it is the responsibility of my privilege to challenge dominant ideologies of white supremacy, but that white self-interest always wins out in matters of perceived racial progress for communities of color. Because 'rhetoric as a discipline engages in practices and politics that require sustained critical attention to race, . . . I will go so far as to argue that rhetorical studies is fundamentally—at its core—the study of race and [that] rhetorical critics must engage' in methods of racial rhetorical criticism (Flores 6). While I believe race is a social construct and that there exists no biological determinant separating 'races' of humans from one another, as a woman of color, I *know* in my bones the lived reality of existing in this skin.

"As such, I believe in the importance of subjective transparency and forthrightness regarding the intersections of our oppressions and privileges, and I believe in pushing against the tendency to essentialize this lived experience among racialized groups. The way to push past essentialism is through centralizing experiential knowledge in critical self-reflective, rhetorically accessible practices of writing and telling in the pursuit of social justice. I am here today to advocate for critical race counterstory as a rhetorical methodology, a methodology that functions as rhetorical criticism reflective of and engaging 'the persistence of racial oppression, logics, voices, and bodies,' a methodology that 'theorizes the very production of race as rhetorical' (Flores 5). I stand here in this moment to urge us as a community of teacher-scholars in rhetoric and writing studies to center race 'in our disciplinary practices, if not because of the fundamental racial-ness of discourse and the art of rhetorical criticism, then because race informs our political possibilities and limitations *and* our critical judgments' of history" (17–18).

At the conclusion of my position statement, I discerned murmurs from the audience, but then a silence formed among them and extended to the Eight. The silence lingered for many moments, causing me to fidget uncomfortably, until Swearingen nodded and offered:

"What I can agree on is there has always been a relationship between literacy and rhetoric, and I can relate to your call for a framing of historiography with race as a lens—as I myself have reviewed the seemingly gender-neutral phenomenon of literacy and its ties to rhetoric through the masculinizing influence of argumentation on both culture and language" (Murphy et al. 19).

"Beyond lenses," Berlin jumped in, "there are also no definitive histories since no historian's ruling perceptual network can ever account for the entire historical field, or even for the field it itself has selected. Thus, there must be multiple histories of rhetoric, each identifying its unique standing place—race, gender, etc.—its grounds for seeing—and the terrain made available from this perspective. Most important, each history endorses an ideology, a conception of economic, social, political, and cultural arrangements that is privileged in its interpretation" (Murphy et al. 6).

"Yes, privileged in its perspective and ideology of whiteness," I blurted.

There was a collective sharp intake of breath from the audience, and Berlin paused, blinked, but then nodded for me to proceed. The audience collectively exhaled.

"Hegemonic whiteness—white supremacy—is pervasive and all-encompassing in its ideological influence on history—even histories—of rhetoric in this country," I began. "As I think you all would agree, history and our rhetorics are bound to context, and there has never existed a context in this nation's history in which white supremacist systems of race and racism did not define economic, social, political, and cultural arrangements which our rhetorics represent and to which they respond."

"I agree," Berlin began, "that our expressed histories 'must be made self-reflexively available to scrutiny and that historians must become aware of the rhetoricity of their own enterprise, rhetoric here being designated the uses of language in the play of power,' but you're claiming white supremacy as the primary terministic screen—" (Murphy et al. 6).

"Isn't it true," interjected Connors, "that 'the teaching of writing is tied in with larger cultural goals, dreams, and fears,' and to be useful, our history 'must show us how this connection has developed and worked in the past?'" (Murphy et al. 7).

"Yes," I agreed, "but then again, when you say 'larger,' you refer to the hegemonic. When you refer to 'us,' I know that has not historically included people of color and I'm not sure it includes people of color now. The past and anything that 'worked' in it were and remain framed by racist assertions of white supremacy, so any cultural goals, dreams, or fears are driven by the desires and interests of whiteness. The inclusive pronouns you invoke can only be analyzed for the color-blind assertions they represent. But if we include race as part of our analysis, I think we can in turn realize and admit that the 'us' in rhetoric and writing studies' past actually primarily concerns white people. Only then, by admitting that the past in this discipline was only for whites, can we move forward with considerations about how to reframe these conversations toward a more inclusive future."

"But 'history cannot exist in a narrow valley of [the] history of ideas,'" Connors responded. "Isn't narrowing your scope to race alone limiting—I mean, '*all* of our disciplinary ideas have been based in people's struggle for a better life[; thus,] meaningful historical writing must teach us what people in the past have wanted from literacy so that we may come to understand what we want'" (Murphy et al. 7).

"But there again," I said, "you invoke inclusive pronouns that are inclusive in expression alone. There is a racialized hierarchy in struggle when it comes to the histories that have been researched about people for the past thirty years, and unsurprisingly to me as a race theorist, these histories have overwhelmingly privileged white lives and narratives—or when they do concern the lives and struggles of people of color, they do so in a way that speaks for them rather than with or from them. So, I don't disagree that learning from people of the past is helpful toward discerning a way forward, but I maintain that our frame must include a rhetorical lens critical of racism that centralizes experiences of people of color—and yes, of course in conversation with these white lives and narratives—but only this multiplicity of perspectives has the potential to offer us a fuller picture of the past."

"Are all historical accounts equally credible?" asked Enos. "Is there some sort of jurisprudence in our community to arrive at, not truth, but the best reasoned account of what we believe took place in the phenomenon?" (Murphy et al. 21).

"I believe credibility is tied to power," I answered, "and that counterstory as a methodology of critical race theory provides a mode for social justice–oriented analysis of the racialized aspects of this power. . . ."

"But 'Whose Reasons Are Good Reasons?'" Vitanza interrupted, looking pointedly at Enos, "'when 50 percent, or more, of the population (in the West) is systematically suppressed. For whom are these reasons good? Be careful how you answer that trick question," Vitanza continued, now looking from left to right among his fellows, "For you can easily slip into the phallogocentric line. Understand that the warrants or representative anecdotes or grand narratives undergirding these so-called Good Reasons are greatly eroded for many of us. Therefore, the Third Sophistic (Post-Modernism) has eternally returned with a vengeance. Such grand narratives, then, as 'emancipation' and 'consensus' have (in eroding) become an outmoded and suspect value. But justice as a value is neither outmoded nor suspect. We must thus arrive at an idea and practice of justice that is not linked to that of consensus" (Murphy et al. 43).

"Yes! Exactly," I agreed. "In critical race theory, these grand narratives are coded as master narratives or majoritarian stories that distort and silence the experiences of people of color and others distanced from the norms such stories reproduce. A standardized majoritarian methodology relies on stock stereotypes that covertly and overtly link people of color, women of color, and poverty with 'bad,' while emphasizing that white middle- and/or upper-class people embody all that is 'good.' A key tenet of critical race theory, a tenet that arguably separates this theory and its methodology counterstory from other narrative forms, is its investment in and pursuit of justice" (Solórzano and Yosso 29).

"And I think it's important you know," offered Berlin, "I am committed to histories of rhetoric that seek the silenced voices, the defeated remnants in the battles of language and power[;] yours is seemingly a project of exposing the mystifications of the powerful, the appropriations undertaken in the name of transcendental truths" (Murphy et al. 35).

I considered Berlin's words for a moment and then said, "But I think my project is about more than simply *seeking* silenced or appropriated voices. Although some have historically characterized people of color as 'in the margins,' we know that we've never been marginal. We've been here all along and have always practiced our rhetorics (Baca and Villanueva; García and Baca). There is a growing number of projects in rhetoric and writing studies, inclusive of the Octalogs subsequent to this one, that do the work of unearthing buried minoritized rhetorics, and these are vital and necessary projects (Ramírez; Enoch and Ramírez; Agnew et al. 115–16). These projects undoubtedly bring to voice primary texts as artifacts for rhetorical analysis that would otherwise go uncharted on rhetoric's map (Glenn; Enos et al. 28–30), and I am grateful to the scholars pursuing such important work. And while my project seeks to centralize minoritized voices through the presentation of counterstories, I am more concerned with providing theory, methodology, and methods by which to do this work. If anything, critical race theory and its methodology counterstory illuminate and contribute to the histories/genealogies of people of color who have been practicing rhetoric for centuries."

"Ah," Johnson said.

I looked to her, and, pausing a moment in consideration, she then proceeded to say, "I work through the assumption that historical research and writing are archaeological and rhetorical activities. As a historian, I am responsible both to the claims of historical evidence and to the burden of proclaiming my enterprise as an attempt to tell 'true stories'" (Murphy et al. 9–10).

Seeing me about to object, Johnson raised her hand, motioning for me to wait for her to finish. I nodded my consent yet still thought internally that "some characterize archaeology as the studies of garbage—so many opportunities to get it wrong. . . ."

"I submit, however, that a self-consciousness of my role as a narrator [of history] does not prevent me from intending my tale to be accepted as a 'true story' in the sense that, as an act of rhetoric, my history imposes formal shape on the probable or on relative truth, while simultaneously seeking acceptance as a logical explanation of reality. Believing in history as an effort to persuade readers to accept one particular story of the past reminds me of the duplicity and the obligations which attend any rhetorical exchange. Although we can know that the nature of reality of past and present is negotiated. . . ."

"Too often from unequal places of power," I inserted.

Johnson nodded, continuing, "although we can know that what historians do is to compel an act of attention to a text which is itself an act of attention, although we can know that histories are just stories, historians and readers alike tend to believe and subsequently proceed as if some stories were truer than others. It is the energy of this contradiction that fuels the political impact of historiography and makes this business of accounting for the past a baffling responsibility" (Murphy et al. 18).

"Yes," I agreed, "and there is privilege of race, gender, class, and ability in that responsibility. There is a responsibility to consider aspects of privilege we have access to across our subjective intersections, a responsibility toward assessing what measures we can take within the institution to make space, and not just take space, toward the agency of those who get pushed to the margins in master narrative histories" (Martinez, "Responsibility of Privilege" 402).

Jarratt cleared her throat, and, as I looked in her direction, she began:

"When a history changes the way writers behave in the classroom (both instructor and student) in ways that allow for the recognition of inequity and oppression, that give voice to silence, that create the means for just action as well as open negotiation over what constitutes 'justice'—then that history is a good one. These two methods of verification are better named 'experience' than 'fact'" (Murphy et al. 45).

"So then it seems to me that this critical race theory is useful because of its inherently rhetorical nature—by rhetoric, I mean language in its service of power," Berlin reasoned (Murphy et al. 30).

"In *critique* of power is more like it," I offered.

"All of these considerations ineluctably situate the writing of the history of rhetoric squarely within a rhetorical situation, an occasion, which is dictated by the institutional and ideological confines within which composition teachers work," Crowley contributed.

Berlin, seemingly frustrated, countered, "I've been arguing this all along!"

"Yes," Crowley agreed, "but I don't think your neo-Marxist critique of history-writing goes quite far enough, or won't, 'as long as the focus and analysis remains aimed at the larger intellectual dialectics that have characterized our past, and away from the power relations that shape the conditions in which each generation's composition proletariat finds itself. Nor will the work of traditional historians be very helpful to its audience if it loses itself in the minutiae of traditional scholarly debate over the relative claims of this or that piece of evidence[;] the writing of history is a profoundly rhetorical art.' Thanks to the academic and intellectual isolation in which we the Eight are encapsulated as 'The Octalog,' we are more inclined, I think, to forget that our work may have profound effects on our readers, and, through them, on a generation of students" (Murphy et al. 40).

"Many generations of students," I affirmed. "The words and names associated with the Eight, frozen in the time of this publication, have indeed had a profound effect on generations of students in rhetoric and writing studies for the past thirty years. If fact, this work is arguably one of the most widely assigned and read in undergraduate and graduate courses concerning rhetorical theories or histories—this was true when I was a student; this remains true now that I'm a professor who is responsible for crafting my own courses.[16] And Crowley, as you prophesized, in many cases this Octalog is authoritative, as many of the theories of historiography associated with each of the Eight are referred to by your names rather than by the title of your work" (Murphy et al. 39).

"Indeed?" Berlin pondered.

And noticing Crowley considering me for a moment, I paused before answering, "Yes, indeed," to Berlin.

"Jay Dolmage," I continued, "a member of an Octalog subsequent to this one, has said that although he has his own ideas about historiography and his own definitions of rhetoric, he nonetheless does so as he weaves together several earlier perspectives, writing himself into a guiding story that you as the original eight began" ("Circulation" 113).

The Eight nodded, seemingly intrigued.

"But to Crowley's point," I resumed, "Ronald L. Jackson, also a member of the third Octalog, insists that 'the principal questions we must insist on asking every year are what counts as rhetorical scholarship? Whose rhetorical legacies and traditions get to be centered in the curriculum such that students cannot leave without learning them?'" ("When" 118).

At this, there was another pregnant silence as both the Eight and the audience seemed to ponder Jackson's pressing question.

"I must interject," said Murphy's moderating voice from above; "'it should not be surprising . . . that historians can differ widely about the efficient causality of their craft when they clearly differ so widely about the *why* of what they are doing. These historical differences are essentially disagreements about the nature of the common good for the polis, which in turn lead to disagreements about ways and means[,] so let us all therefore bear in mind that what is at stake here is not differings in methodology alone but varying perceptions of what ought to be discovered for the good of the community. Those variations in perception lead inevitably to variations in focus, in choice of data, in mode of presentation'" (Murphy et al. 5).

"Yes," Crowley agreed, "There's no such thing as purely inductive or purely deductive historical research. Your motives are what govern all of your choices from the outset when you even decide to do research in the first place" (Murphy et al. 26).

"Hmm, yes," agreed Jarratt as well, "you never go blind into a project" (Murphy et al. 26).

I made no motion to respond, so Jarratt took this as a cue to continue.

"Self, what you've engaged here—having come to our stage in the role of Self—is more story than fact . . . [that] 'serves a particular moment in the history of our discipline. . . . [T]here have been histories in which the presuppositions were so well accepted, that they were kind of blind, so we got the sense that there was a bunch of fact that we're being delivered. And now we, the Eight, realize more and more through each ensuing exchange with every Self who appears before us what those suppositions are and the kind of economic and political ramifications associated with them. So, with interlocutors in the role of Self, we enjoy the opportunity to stop and consider that stories guide histories as well as historiography."

I was about to interject a question, but Jarratt pressed on, saying, "Sadly, we have come to the end of our allotted moment with you. Would you like to impart a closing statement before we say goodbye?" (Murphy et al. 26).

"I don't disagree with your assertion," I responded, "that these suppositions of which you speak are caused by and intrinsically tied to the privileged and oppressed intersections of our identities as set within economic and political contexts. For instance, when asked earlier *why* I study the histories of rhetoric with race and racism as my centralized frame, my response of not seeing another choice was sincere."

"Go on," Crowley chimed in, intrigued.

"As a graduate student, I was told, in no uncertain terms, that I should 'take the MA and go.'[17] In effect, I was being kicked out of my doctoral program. And within this experience, inclusive of the microcosmic experiences of coursework, office hours, and interactions with my peers and professors within the institution, I *felt* the lived reality of a hyperminoritized person of color. I *felt* my ill 'fit,' my lack of 'merit,' my supposed 'poor choices,' but I did not have a means, a frame, a theory, a methodology by which to understand, document, express, learn from, and, in turn, teach about these experiences—not until my mentor, V, introduced me to critical race theory. And at this crucial fork in my career, I had the option to buy into the hegemonic white pushout, urging me to take the MA and leave, or I had the option to become expert in this racial rhetorical methodology of counterstory so as to research, document, analyze, and in effect finally comprehend what these white supremacist yet color-blind and abstract liberal institutions do to people of color—a comprehension for myself, but also for those coming up behind me who seek more than survival in rhetoric and writing studies.

"As I've progressed in my career, I've begun reviewing these beginnings in rhetoric and writing studies as a graduate student who found my way into identifying professionally in rhetorical studies (Kynard, *Vernacular Insurrections* 11) by way of critical race theory (CRT) and counterstory. Presently, I've found myself surveying my immediate situation as a tenure-track assistant professor within a department and graduate program located centrally in the field, and, in terms of privilege, I am vested with credibility and the responsibility to craft and teach courses in rhetorical histories and theories constituting the core curriculum of my institution's rhetoric and writing studies major and graduate program. And I take seriously the responsibility of a core curriculum—in fact, it weighs heavily on me. And I invoke the words of Jackson yet again to ask, is the goal for core courses to focus on a very particular set of canonized rhetorical figures and theories with sanctioned principles and conventions (Lipson and Binkley 1) 'whose rhetorical legacies and traditions get to be centered in the curriculum such that students cannot leave without learning them' ("When" 118)? In other words, is it more important that we know your names, you, the Eight, or is the goal to offer students methods by which to analyze and critique why your names have been centered, but also *why* and *how* (through historiographies processed through power framed by race, class, gender, and access) *the* rhetorical tradition came to be?

"In closing, I would like to share with you the words of rhetoric and writing studies historiographer Carmen Kynard, who has shaped my own politics of historiography:

> While I am writing a kind of (revisionist) history of composition studies with the Black Freedom Movement as my guiding force, I am doing much more than that. This book was the process that made me a compositionist and rhetorician. I needed a way into this field because very little that I had been shown as the canon, as the key moments, as the critical issues, as the seminal edited collections, as "the" history, as the landmarks and signposts, as the categories, or as the inventive engines seemed to include me. (*Vernacular Insurrections* 11–12)

Kynard has prompted me to think about my own guiding force, and upon reflection I know it's counterstory. Counterstory as a methodology and a method guides the conceptual frameworks with which I very intentionally do research and also craft the courses I teach on the histories and theories of rhetoric.[18] Shoot! Counterstory has provided me the otherworldly ability to time-travel for an engagement with you all! So, my esteemed colleagues of the Eight, I close in a hopeful way, one that acknowledges the role your words here have played in shaping me into the teacher-scholar I am—in terms of agreement and divergence. I thank you all for your time, your work, and your consideration of my contributions discussed here at length."

Effecting a reverential nod to the Eight, which they returned, I turned to face the shadowy figures in the audience, who were now politely applauding. Unsure of what to do, I took an awkward and tilting bow and quickly turned back to face the Eight. I noticed Enos was now standing alone, shrouded in a singular spotlight while the rest of the Eight had faded away into the darkness. Speaking in the fashion of a closing Shakespearean monologue, Enos said,

"It is the burden of the historian of rhetoric to articulate views in a manner that enables readers to participate in, to share in, the making of meaning. In a sense, participants in the Octalog, such as you, Self, are engaging in that activity while here on this stage; that is, you, Alejandra, have now participated in the making of meaning about the events of the original Octalog that occurred so many years ago. Do our statements from 1988 withstand the test of time? Each generation of scholars performing the role of Self will again engage in this Act 2 as they enter into dialogue with us as the Eight and determine whether our words remain 'meaningful.' That phenomenon is, as stated by Jarratt earlier, akin to writing 'good' history, and therefore we, the Eight, engage each Self who comes before us in sharing in the making of meaning about events completed but dynamically understood at the moment that meaning is jointly created between Self and the Eight!" (Murphy et al. 41).

At the conclusion of these parting words, the light above Enos was quickly extinguished, and I was once again surrounded in obscurity. I called out into the dark, "Wait! Am I correct in my understanding that exchanges like this *have* happened before? Others have been pulled through time to play the part of Self in dialogue and response with the Eight?"

"Oh, yes," the disembodied voice of Murphy chuckled from above—not unpleasantly—"yes, many, many times. And I suspect many more will continue to arrive to perform the role of Self for many years to come."

At these final words, I was pulled back through time and space and awoke to find myself lying in bed, the side of my face buried in my pillow, "The Politics of Historiography" frozen onto the screen of my adjacent laptop.

# 4
## Patricia J. Williams and Counterstory as Autobiographic Reflection

PATRICIA JOYCE WILLIAMS WAS BORN in 1951 in the Roxbury section of Boston—a historically black but increasingly white working-class neighborhood during her early childhood years. According to Williams, her black family was accepted because of its long tenure in the area, but Williams remembers there was "always the sense that I was 'the colored kid' in school" (Interview). As Williams entered junior high school, white classmates whispered (audibly enough for her to discern the words), "The coloreds are coming," while white Roxbury parents went door to door, warning their neighbors about declining property values—rumors undoubtedly fostered by "block-busting" realtors (Interview). Williams's parents fought back by instilling in Williams and her sister a sense of their worth through bolstering stories, passed down through several generations, of her enslaved forebearers' perseverance (Mirza 120).

One of "the first crop of affirmative action babies," as Williams put it (Interview), she entered Harvard Law School in 1972. At Harvard, Williams faced no shortage of racial backlash as she navigated higher education within an affirmative action–inflected context, in which cases like the landmark *Regents of the University of California v. Bakke*[1] were being debated. Williams recalls, "I spent a lot of time dealing with people who'd come up and ask your LSAT scores; it was very confrontational" (Interview). After graduating from Harvard in 1975, Williams took a job as deputy city attorney in Los Angeles. Gaining both civil and criminal trial experience, mostly in consumer protection, Williams prosecuted cases involving issues such as sterilization and phony doctors. In 1978,

Williams moved on to a position as staff attorney with the Western Center on Law and Poverty (WCLP), and it was there where she began to focus on her future legal specialty of commercial and contract law. Her enthusiasm for this line of work and the "dry, just-the-facts" practice of law (inclusive of its writing style) eventually soured, and the academy seemed a viable alternative, allowing her to teach and explore her inclination toward creative expressions in prose. Throughout the 1980s, Williams traversed various law school appointments, notably receiving a tenured-teaching offer in 1988 at the University of Wisconsin. Overlapping with her 1988–93 tenure at Wisconsin, in 1992 Williams began a professorship at Columbia University School of Law and has remained in this appointment ever since.

Adrien Katherine Wing, in her introduction to *Critical Race Feminism: A Reader,* describes Williams as a critical race feminism foremother (11), while legal scholar Qudsia Mirza characterizes Williams's work as visionary, with an almost prophetic quality about it, giving the impression of a "latter-day seer, tendering insights into our condition, offering a new vision of a society free of racial animus, a society of racial justice" (118). As Williams has surmised of her own career,

> I first started teaching in 1980[;] I was the first [at Golden Gate University Law School;] I've been just about the first black woman to teach or even just speak at every university—the first black woman to take the podium[;] when you're breaking barriers, when you're the first anything there's going to be disgruntlement. (quoted in Mirza 119)

As a barrier breaker, Williams has played a pivotal role in the development of CRT as a movement and of counterstory as a methodology. Making unabashed use of autobiographic reflection as method, Williams's body of work in counterstory focuses

> on her position as a black woman, bringing attention to the intersection of race and gender, cultural and legal representations of black women, and highlighting the manner in which law, liberal race and gender discourse conceptualise the two

as mutually exclusive. In this way, Williams has developed the broader connection between CRT and feminist theory. (Mirza 114)

Committing herself fully to the feminist call to action "The personal is political," Williams undoubtedly performs what this call demands, all the while bashing "authorized" genres along the way (Gates 768; Prendergast 53).

### WILLIAMS'S FEMINIST POETICS, OR, WILLIAMS, AS A BLACK WOMAN, HAS THE AUDACITY TO SPEAK

> Since you have a very poetic way of writing, you should consider writing short stories. As it is, this piece is far too personal for any legal publication, and furthermore, if you don't mind our saying so, its publication anywhere will risk your being perceived as quite unstable in the public eye.
> —A composite law review reader review/rejection of Williams's work in *Alchemy of Race and Rights*

Critical race counternarratives scholar Carl Gutiérrez-Jones declares Williams one of the most accomplished CRT writers in the field (79), and her critically self-reflective method synthesizes moments in her personal life as allegory, metaphor, and storytelling juxtaposed against more traditional expressions of theory and abstraction (Mirza 119). Williams herself has described her counterstory approach as a method that bridges the traditional gap between theory and praxis, stating that it is not her goal "merely to simplify" but instead to present a text that is "multilayered—that encompasses the straightforwardness of real life *and* reveals complexity of meaning" (*Alchemy* 6). Williams's writing is an intentional departure from what she describes as the "highly stylized, precedential, and deductive reasoning" methodology of legal writing—employing a "model of inductive empiricism, borrowed from—and parodying—systems analysis, in order to enliven thought about complex social problems" (*Alchemy* 7).

Citing Williams's practice of developing narratives at the intersection of legal and cultural issues, Gutiérrez-Jones says Williams's critical autobiographies impose "a certain responsibility for self-criticism, for an awareness of how one's training shapes one's tastes" (85), stemming largely from the CRT tenet–informed belief that form and substance (i.e., reality) are connected. Specifically extending the boundaries of the CRT tenet "centrality of experiential knowledge and/or unique voices of color" and largely eschewing the conventional genres of legal writing, Williams's counterstories illuminate the everyday "small aggressions of unconscious racism" (Williams, "An Ordinary Brilliance" 1), revealing layers of history and illuminating the racial permanence of long-past racial iniquity (Mirza 114). Williams's emphasis on the everyday recognizes that

> transformations need not be instantaneous and all-encompassing to still be of value; that such change does not necessarily manifest itself in monumental events conspicuous in the great sweep of history but can be found in the small, the seemingly insignificant and mundane. (114–15)

These seemingly minuscule fragments of one's life are woven together through Williams's rich anecdotes, in which methodological questions form to engage fully a politically invested analysis that illustrates the complexity of racism (Gutiérrez-Jones 87, 89).

However, as Gutiérrez-Jones notes, one risk of Williams's "autobiographical gesture is that the exhilaration [she] describes may fail to resonate in different contexts," chiefly among white male audiences (87). This is especially true because the reality Williams pulls from is that of a black woman—a reality marred by what Angela Davis has characterized as the age-old "blaming the victim" racism (106). When it comes to the testimony of black women, Davis draws our attention to the historic tradition of challenging the credibility of black women and ties this practice to a historical myopia involving the "fictional image of the Black man as rapist" (106). Davis continues that this mythology of the black man rapist "has always strengthened its inseparable companion: the image of the Black woman as chronically promiscuous . . . [since they were] viewed as 'loose women' and whores, Black women's cries of rape [at the hands of white men] would necessarily lack legitimacy" (106). Hence, the slavery-deep racist and sexist practice of challenging and dismissing the experiences of black women contemporaneously exists in legal and narrative genealogies—and short of opening their mouths, black women need do little at all to be accused as liars, crazy, or hysterical. "The problem," reasons Prendergast, is not that Williams "is telling stories or even that she is telling different stories but that she, an African American woman, is the teller" (54).

As discussed in Chapter 1, both CRT theory and methodology have experienced their fair share of critique and attempts at dismissal. This disparagement is true for each of my identified exemplars, but the level of scorn aimed at Delgado and Bell pales in comparison to what can be described as nothing short of an attack, not just on Williams's work, but on her character as well. While Bell has discussed the demi-erasure of his work, due to its perceived "generic ambiguity" (Prendergast 50), Williams's work in *Alchemy* received a reaction from audiences that erupted in a whopping sixty-two reviews of her book in both law reviews and the popular press—an unprecedented feat for an academic publication (*Masader*). As Prendergast has put it, "critics of *Alchemy* have suggested that [Williams] might be [stupid and crazy] and have mused that perhaps Williams is unhinged, or playing at being unhinged, but that either way her style is at odds with her credibility" (53). "It has been charged that her inclusion of 'personal irrelevancies' invites readers to dismiss her" (Jost, qtd. in Prendergast 53). Also, "Williams has been accused of self-indulgence, paranoia, and—perhaps worse—'methodological nonchalance' and 'principled genre-blurring'" (Rieder 41, qtd. in Prendergast 53). Critical race feminist Deborah Waire Post (as a black woman), has reflected on credibility and confirms that critics attribute deficiencies to her own scholarship and teaching. "This is not just some individual psychosis," she says, "some form of paranoia—unless it is a collective paranoia. Far too many Black women . . . have confirmed my experience. Patricia Williams' stories are probably the best known" (132).

As Prendergast has mused, what can these accusations and fear of genre-blurring (genre-bashing according to Williams) reveal? The threat inherent in Williams's work is best characterized by Sara Ahmed's description of the "feminist killjoy":

Let's take this figure of the feminist killjoy seriously. Does the feminist kill other people's joy by pointing out moments of sexism? Or does she expose the bad feelings that get hidden, displaced, or negated under public signs of joy? Does bad feeling enter the room when somebody expresses anger about things, or could anger be the moment when the bad feelings that circulate through objects get brought to the surface in a certain way? (par. 12)

Williams, it would seem, is a feminist killjoy whose genre-bashing "exposes the interested parties hiding behind authorized genres who make up those institutions the nation has invested with great power" (Prendergast 53). Even Henry Louis Gates Jr., who delivered a lauding review of *Alchemy*, admits that Williams's work illustrates the ways experiential knowledge is slighted and "'children's, women's, and blacks' power is actually reduced to the 'intuitive' rather than to the 'real'" (766). Yet Gates believes that Williams "validates her technique in the practice of it," stating that, though Williams offers original insights on "familiar controversies," "some of the most magical turns of argument flow from far less public events" where Williams narrates sometimes as witness, sometimes as participant, sometimes as defendant (768).

Speaking in defense of her counterstory method, Williams reflects on a certain isolation she experienced as a woman, let alone a feminist, in her discipline, which, she says, "is not to say I wrote out of a vacuum but I remember reading Toni Morrison's description of why she started writing and she said: 'I didn't see anybody in what I read who resembled me so I had to invent myself'" (Mirza 120). *The Alchemy of Race and Rights* began as a set of journal notes Williams wrote to herself, jottings, *papelitos guardados* if you will, to keep herself "sane." And although she was stylistically influenced by French and American feminists, "but also less obvious influences that are as diverse as Italo Calvino, Bentham, Rousseau, James Baldwin and the Book of Common Prayer," she states that she was ultimately enacting an African American rhetoric by mimicking certain traditions of storytelling. Contrary to what critics may think, Williams was conscious, intentional, and deliberate in contrasting her methods to more formal legal styles of writing. Finally, invoking what Pritchard calls "ancestorship" (1), Williams says, "I actively played throughout the book with images of my great-great grandfather who was a white Southern lawyer who would have written in a very particular way. Then there were chapters in which I tried to tell the same story in a voice more marked by traditions of orality and African-American speech so that you could hear what my great-great grandmother[2] could not write down" (120). Perhaps what is most threatening about Williams's method of autobiographic reflection is that this approach is very practical in its handling of theory. Williams sees her narratives as an attempt at translating theory or making "visible some of the consequences of theory," which, beyond genre bashing, is a project and body of scholarship that has made legal doctrine accessible[3] to the masses— and we can't have that (118). As Gates says, although *Alchemy* is an invitingly personal, even vulnerable, book, what traditionalists in the legal community cannot forgive is that "Williams has also produced a work at the cutting edge of legal theory" (766). However, making theory accessible through narrative methods is not an uncommon practice in rhetoric, writing, and literacy studies. My study here of Williams, including my own attempts at writing and publishing autobiographic reflection, contributes to a field-specific genealogy—a genealogy to which I am proud to belong.

### AUTOBIOGRAPHIC REFLECTION: A RHETORIC, WRITING, AND LITERACY STUDIES GENEALOGY

Likely the most recognizable method of counterstory among rhetoric, writing, and literacy studies audiences (albeit still not as readily accepted as it should be), autobiographic narrative has been theorized and practiced as long as there have been minoritized people speaking, writing, and sharing our stories in these fields. As a demonstration of this history and genealogy, I offer below a sort of precounterstory to the counterstory within this chapter. In it, an autobiographic reflection octalog of my own composition, another Eight fictionally gather to share visions for and applications of narrative in their own work. This counterstory octalog engages field-specific narrative theorists: Frankie Condon, Keith Gilyard, Carmen Kynard, Eric Pritchard, Elaine Richardson, Victor Villanueva, Vershawn Ashanti Young, and me, Aja Martinez. In this octalog, I serve in two capacities:[4] (1) as a student, because I have honed my own narrative methodology taught by and inspired by these storytellers/narrative theorists, and (2) as a moderator to the discussion, offering guiding questions and prompts.

### AN AUTOBIOGRAPHIC REFLECTION OCTALOG: A PRACTICE IN ANCESTORSHIP

MARTINEZ: Thank you all for agreeing to gather here in my book on counterstory. I want you each to know how fundamental your theorizing of narrative has been to the inspiration and development of my own work, so I'm very honored to feature each of your voices in my own project.

[Nods and smiles all around]

MARTINEZ [continuing]: Now, I'll keep it brief because I know you all are busy folks, and I do have a chapter to finish, so I'd like to open up the floor for just a sort of general discussion about narrative. Why did you go this route in your work? If you had to discuss your rhetorical situation as a writer when it comes to narrative as a method, what might that be?

KYNARD [jumping right in]: I'll start. General discussions about moral and philosophical principles of equity, equality, or diversity are no longer good enough, so I take up the tools of story, metaphor, history, and philosophy, leavened with empirical claims, all of which are as integral to truth-telling and policymaking as field experiments and meta-analyses. I take up these tools in the context of myself as a writer and researcher of black language, education, and literacies and use narratives to offer stories of institutional racism that compositionists—and thereby, our field—have maintained. These narratives offer a place to decode the symbolic violence encoded into our disciplinary sense-making and move towards what a theory of Racial Realism might entail for our classrooms and discipline ("Teaching While Black" 4).

GILYARD [leaning forward, raising a finger]: I know that I, had I been asked, could have told someone something about this clash between cultures, this problem of being Black and attempting to cope with the instruction offered in a school controlled by those of another background. But of course I was never asked by anyone in authority to speak about the conflict. I was just asked to survive it. Years later . . . I finally got around to discussing that earlier period. . . . [W]ith my first child on the way, I decided to fashion a gift of experience, of my education. I began to write a story of my life (10–11).

RICHARDSON [nodding affirmatively in Gilyard's direction]: Speaking of children, I never wanted anyone to hurt my daughters or hold anything over them, so I told them about myself from the time they were very young. Some of the stories were funny. Some were sad. It wasn't long before they began asking me to tell my stories to their friends. My daughters' acceptance of me gave me the courage to tell the truth about my life (*PHD to PhD* vii), [so] I've written a memoir and produced an album based on my life, and I think they have a lot in common, at least for me, my process, the way my brain works. I remember when I was writing [*PHD to PhD*], I used to go back to Cleveland a lot and ride around in the neighborhoods I hung around in, and that helped me remember a lot of stuff. But I think songwriting is memory too. They're both memory and imagination ("Local Music Limelight").

VILLANUEVA [smiling]: Yes, *memoria* is a friend of ours (*"Memoria"* 19).

[Catching the reference, everyone laughs.]

VILLANUEVA [continuing]: So many have said this so well about the connections between narratives of people of color and the need to reclaim a memory, [and] memory simply cannot be adequately portrayed in the conventional discourse of the academy ("*Memoria*" 12).

CONDON [raising her hand, directing her gaze at Villanueva]: May I?

[Villanueva genially nods.]

CONDON: If white participation in the production of resisting stories of racialized experience is to be meaningful, the stories [whites] tell must be conceived of as opportunities to learn, to revise, to reconstruct. [Whites] will need to learn the practice of excavating memories of our own racialization, but also learn to connect those memories to the crucible of history in which the idea of race was forged and the practices of racism, of white supremacy in particular, were justified, legitimated, and reproduced (37).

MARTINEZ: So the place for white folk within the method of narrative is in critical self-reflection on their own whiteness?

CONDON: Yes! Perhaps most of all, we whites will need to learn the ways and degrees to which our stories are troubled and, perhaps, contradicted by the stories of peoples of color.

[Nods and affirmative murmurs all around]

CONDON [continuing, passionately]: We will need to be willing to revise and resubmit without an end in sight, letting go of our conviction that to tell our stories might confer transcendence of our whiteness upon us. To tell our stories should shift us from the ground we believe we know to that which we cannot know, where error is a virtual certainty and failure might be as well. To proceed with narrative in this way requires telling without certifying those strands of the story with which we are most comfortable, that please us in some sense, but also giving voice to those strands that discomfort, that mortify, that disrupt our sense of goodness and righteousness. The purpose of the telling, in this context, can never be the achievement of absolution or of transcendence, but the excavation and critical examination of that history, long suppressed and far more powerful for its silence (37–38).

MARTINEZ [pausing to think for a moment]: Okay, I think that offers some solid inroads for white people who often ask me if they too can craft counterstories.

[Condon nods.]

MARTINEZ: Critical race theorist Patricia Williams is particularly noted for her autobiographic approach to counterstory. Can you all speak a bit more about the connection between your realities and your writing?

PRITCHARD: My work is a story [that] flows from life stories by black lesbian, gay, bisexual, transgender, and queer people to theorize the myriad ways individuals have learned and employed literacy in their quests to build a life on their own terms and, more specifically, toward the goals of self- and communal love, healing, care, and other modes of survival (1).

RICHARDSON [nodding appreciatively at Pritchard]: I went from hiding in the academy, seeking to gain a new identity, to becoming more and more okay with who I am becoming, knowing that none of it was in vain. The education I was learning in the university caused me to interrogate my experiences and the experiences of people in my community. It was definitely a struggle of growing in knowledge of myself. I realized that many things that happened to me weren't my fault. There are a lot of socially sanctioned ways of devaluing poor black people . . . ("Thirteen Questions").

YOUNG [gesturing excitedly with his hands]: Yes, Dr. E., say that! It's true I'm writing about my own racial performance, but it certainly isn't true that what I'm writing concerns only me (3).

MARTINEZ: Wait, so are you saying that the personal can represent the collective?
[Young nods as Kynard begins.]
KYNARD: Right. I [offer] my own personal experiences and stance of bearing-witness as more than just one individual's observations, but as an indication of the levels of systemic racism that we do not address ("Teaching While Black" 4).
GILYARD: I have chosen to write about the various voices I have come to possess . . . using my autobiographical narrative as a focal point. . . . (11).
VILLANUEVA: [And] the narratives of people of color jog our memories as a collective in a scattered world and within an ideology that praises individualism ("*Memoria*" 16).
MARTINEZ: Ah yes, that abstract liberal ideology of individualism; yes, I see. Okay, so this collective voice can speak for a group but can also represent varying/diverse/divergent viewpoints within groups?—similar to what Patricia Williams has done in her autobiographic reflections—she narrates sometimes as a witness, sometimes a participant, sometimes as the defendant (Gates 768).
[Nods all around]
MARTINEZ: When and how did you all come to the realization that this was the method you would engage in your scholarship?
RICHARDSON: When I was an undergraduate, I read a book called *Talkin and Testifyin: The Language of Black America,* by Geneva Smitherman. Dr. G!
[Many nods, smiles, and affirming exclamations from the group at Richardson's mention of this book and praise of this name]
RICHARDSON [continuing with a smile]: That book woke me up to the miseducation of black America and all Americans about language—how precious it is, no matter if it was borne of slavery and oppression or whatever the history of its coming into being. So learning from scholars

like Dr. G has helped me to become who I am becoming. I am continuing to learn so many things about the struggle for Black lives and Black women and girls' lives and the knowledge that we must learn to navigate this place called the world. People are reading our bodies and everything about us, and we must know who we are, fight for our futures, and not be slaves to anyone's evaluation of us ("Thirteen Questions").

KYNARD: That's right, and there is a discursive and pragmatic power in the counternarratives and counterepistemologies that color-conscious compositionist-rhetoricians can use to rupture this horizon of desires; the most dispossessed amongst us must turn the tide and become the intellectuals who (re)write the sociogenic codes of the discipline that currently bind us ("Teaching While Black" 8).

[Nods all around]

YOUNG: You see, by performing my argument [as narrative], I am deliberately shattering the decorum of the scholarly monograph; this writing tension mirrors everyday tension I live. I also follow the examples set by Keith Gilyard and Victor Villanueva in using racial narrative as the vehicle for making conceptual arguments (11).

CONDON: I believe personal narrative is necessary and integral to the creation and sustenance of community and solidarity, not merely produced and then gawked at; [white people] need to learn to read, to engage with one another's stories, not as voyeurs but as players in a dramatic sense . . . and as actors who may be changed not only by the telling of our own stories but also by the practices of listening, attending, acknowledging, and honoring the stories of our students and our colleagues of color as well. Those of us [white folk] who are academics and who hope to join in the work of antiracism will need to stop minimizing the complexity and significance of narrative, stop depoliticizing the personal, and start studying the rich epistemological and rhetorical traditions that inform the narratives of people of color. Further, [acknowledging, with a laugh, Young's "wrap it up, Frankie" face and gesture] those of us who are white may need to admit that we have not yet begun, really, to craft epistemological and rhetorical practices of a performative antiracist tradition; we will need to admit our limit—and indeed the limits whiteness places on us—as philosophers and rhetors (31–33) [making a "There, I'm finished" gesture with her hands].

[Everyone laughs.]

MARTINEZ [chuckling]: Frankie, you seem to be describing an analytic for a white antiracist approach to narrative. Would the rest of you say you have theorized an analytic for your approaches to narrative?

GILYARD: I developed my analytic approach out of beliefs that, first, autobiographical artifacts serve as fairly accurate historical documents. An autobiographical account, despite its subjectivity, provides an important record of events the author has responded to—in short, what has shaped him or her as a social being. In a quest for such significance, the chronological facts of an individual's existence are not nearly as important as the psychological facts of foraging a life, something autobiographies reveal quite well (12).

KYNARD: The series of stories that I tell are intentionally crafted as method for organizing, presenting, and politicizing textual arrangement in scholarship. Narrative as the form of my telling means that I am conscious of the ways that I use stories to understand and present the lives and literacies of students of color where my own cultural role as a black female storyteller enacts its own critical inquiry ("Teaching While Black" 4).

PRITCHARD: As I investigate[d] the voices, faces, and places that inform[ed] *[Fashioning Lives]*, I [was] drawn over and over again to scenes of literacy within my life story that are crucial to narrativizing my life experience as a Black, queer, feminist, cisgender man who is a learner, teacher, scholar, artist, activist, and advocate, scenes that, when read alongside my analysis, dovetail back to the themes of identity formation and affirmation, literacy concealment, [and] ancestorship (1).

VILLANUEVA: My views are grounded in experience, elaborated upon by theory, and tested in research. Perhaps in narrating, the exception can become the rule—boots for everyone, strong straps!

[Everyone laughs.]

VILLANUEVA [continuing]: But praxis is what I'm attempting to do here, more than providing a self-serving story, either glorious me or woe-is-me. What I'm attempting is to provide a problematic based on sets of experience: an experience which leads to a theory, a theory that recalls experience; reflections on speculations, speculations to polemics to reflections—all with an aim at affecting what might happen in classrooms, the sites of action; I am never *just* emoting, never *just* displaying the free associative workings of a mind; this is autobiography with political, theoretical, pedagogical considerations; and in its inclusions the story suggests how we are—all of us—subject to the systemic. This is the personal made public and the public personalized, not for self-glory nor to point fingers, but to suggest how, maybe, to make the exception the rule (*Bootstraps* xvii–iii).

YOUNG [nodding toward Villanueva, pensively pausing, then starting]: Narrative performance is central to my analysis; in effect, my arguments arise from my integration of "staging" episodes from my life and "studying" them, making my merger of what's often considered academic (and white) with what's considered creative (and raced), itself a performance of my argument. (10).

VILLANUEVA [nodding affirmatively toward Young]: The personal done well is sensorial and intellectual, complete, knowledge known throughout mind and body, even if vicariously ("*Memoria*" 14).

[Nods and affirmative murmurs all around]

VILLANUEVA [continuing]: And for the person of color, it does more. The narrative of the person of color validates. It resonates. It awakens, particularly for those of us who are in institutions where our numbers are few. Our experiences are in no sense unique but are always analogous to other experiences from among those exceptions. So more than narrating the life of one of color, we remember the results of our having realized the possibility, discovered the process, found the opening, while finding that there is in some sense very little change on the other side ("*Memoria*" 15).

MARTINEZ: Well, you all have certainly helped me realize possibilities and discover a process, and have opened so many pathways for me and other narrative scholars in rhetoric, writing, and literacy studies. And speaking of the other side, let me move from this genealogical narrative octalog to a discussion of how counterstory has helped me sort through the madness of borders.

[Applause all around]

### CROSSING BORDERS WITH COUNTERSTORY

Williams' book crisscrosses so many boundaries that you forget where they used to be.
           —Henry Louis Gates Jr.

I have discussed borders and being "reasonably suspicious"[5] as a POC within institutional spaces, narrativized within my essay "The Responsibility of Privilege." Upon considering excerpting the borderlands narrative within that essay for inclusion in this project, I soon realized this counterstory was a vignette, a snapshot, a mere diary entry in a broader meditation I've sustained concerning borders and borderland spaces/rhetorics since I was a graduate student writing counterstories for my dissertation. In fact, this narrative brings full circle a larger tale about beings who are subjected to borders and reminds me of what a man I interviewed in the Bahamas once said about rectangular bordered shapes drawn onto the sea.

These boxes were drawn by marine biologists, who, with a National Science Foundation grant, were hired by the Bahamian government to research and draft a proposal for "marine protected areas": sea parks intended to curb overfishing and promote overall marine health and preservation. But because they were biologists and not anthropologists, these researchers left people—particularly Bahamian subsistence fishers—out of the first phase of the study. Soon realizing that this proposal needed a local perspective, the Bahamian government hired anthropologists to talk to/interview local fishers in the project's second phase. At this time, I was a burgeoning researcher and undergraduate research assistant (URA) to University of Arizona applied anthropologist Dr. Richard Stoffle. As a URA, I had the opportunity to travel with Rich and his team of anthropologists to Exuma, Bahamas, to whet my ethnographic chops.[6] Memorably, one of the first fishermen we talked to, Mr. Rolle, took one look at the aerial mapping we possessed of the proposed marine parks—a map that illustrated a strikingly turquoise sea with prominently visible yellow rectangular boxes designating the borders of the parks—and, laughing, Mr. Rolle promptly and definitively informed us nonlocal/nonfisher researchers: "Fish don't stay in a box."

I think often of Mr. Rolle's bluntly stated truth, especially as a metaphor applied to nation-state borders, imperialistically drawn to dictate where beings should stay. As Marta Maria Maldonado, Adela C. Licona, and Sarah Hendricks have asserted, nation-states have their own histories "of relations with other nation-states and . . . in large part, such histories provide the ideological content, the *storylines* that justify who is authorized entry into national space and under what conditions, who is more or less free to move, and who must be removed" (321; emphasis mine). These master narrative storylines inform "border/land security" legislation, and, as crits have been arguing all along, the law is not disinterested or disconnected from the lived realities of its subjects—especially those whose citizenship, rights, and belonging are of "reasonable suspicion" of being "illegal." Yet analysis and engagement with such legislation too often lack a crucial humanized framework. Cruz Medina and I have published responses (more than once)[7] to white authors who found the rhetorical situation of the US/Mexico border/lands interesting artifacts for analysis—completely disregarding the realities of peoples who are vulnerable and affected within this borderlands space. Many Latinx rhetoric and writing scholars such as Victor Villanueva, Jaime Armin Mejía, Adela C. Licona, Karma Chávez, Lisa Flores, Steven Alvarez, Laura Gonzales, Genevieve García de Müeller, Romeo García, Sonia Arellano, and all contributors represented in Iris D. Ruiz and Raúl Sánchez's collection *Decolonizing Rhetoric and Composition Studies* have laid down their bodies toward the vision of bridging gaps between their Latinx and bordered/borderlands home communities and the institution; the bridge, as Cherríe Moraga and Gloria Anzaldúa have memorably affirmed, is our backs.[8] Licona expresses the conviction that "having grown up on the Mexico/US border, [my] own understanding of the concept of borderlands is embodied, intuitive, psychic, and learned" (104). Likewise, I am native to the borderlands of Arizona, and I feel the necessity to speak about borderlands issues of racism and racialized violence in the multiple borderland spaces I occupy—the US/Mexico borderlands, the borderlands of/within academic institutions, and even the US/Canada borderlands. And, like Williams, I cobble together the fragments of my personal experience to speak sometimes as witness, sometimes as participant, sometimes as defendant (Gates 768).

Crossing borders into the academy, I have instructed students in Williams's method of autobiographic reflection as part of my "Writing Critical Race Counterstory" (Appendix B) writers workshop. When learning Williams's method, students themselves have noted their affinity for her approach, stating in teacher-course evaluations that "Williams's counterstories were essential" to their work. As reviewed above in the section "An Autobiographic Reflection Octalog: A Practice in Ancestorship," the method of autobiographic reflection is familiar and even comforting to people whose cultures value oral traditions and storytelling. Happily, during my initial years at Syracuse University, I had the pleasure of working with fellow counterstory writer Martín Alberto Gonzalez—a doctoral candidate in my affiliate graduate program, Cultural Foundations of Education.

Through an independent study I directed, Gonzalez wrote *and* self-published his book of autobiographic reflection counterstories: *21 Miles of Scenic Beauty . . . and Then Oxnard: Counterstories and Testimonies*. Intended as a series of stories to teach with, Gonzalez's highly popular and accessible collection of stories serves as a great companion to Williams's work, and my students and I spend class time learning about this method by first readings these works. In turn, we shift to crafting our own counterstories as autobiographic reflection, and, as is pursued with the other CRT methods, students brainstorm and then rigorously research possible topics toward gathering supporting materials to braid in with their own personal experiences. Not deviating from my instruction with Delgado's and Bell's methods, we engage the process of crafting context and characters; however, during this unit we pay particular attention to the rhetorical appeals of pathos and ethos and feminist rhetorical strategies of developing the personal as evidence and critical self-reflection. As a class, we progress to workshopping several drafts of autobiographic reflection counterstories, inclusive of in-class readarounds and peer review.

In demonstration of Williams's genre, I offer next three vignettes as autobiographic reflection counterstory collectively titled "Diary of a Mad Border Crosser"; as the title suggests, these narratives are united by a common theme of borders. Through the lens of Flores's rhetorical criticism frame, "bounding race," and in line with Williams's discussion of property values and human rights (particularly in her *Alchemy* chapter "Teleology on the Rocks"), these vignettes trace Alejandra's path through three separate borderlands contexts in which territorial lines have been drawn to distinguish and enforce who does and does not belong within the borders of occupied white-space. As discussed in Chapter 1, the tenets of CRT are often informed by and intersect with theory.

The following counterstory, written in the style of counterstory as autobiographic reflection, is framed by (and can be analyzed through) theories of hegemonic whiteness, intersectionality, racial permanence, and color-blind racism (Cabrera; Crenshaw; Bonilla-Silva; Bell, *And*). Because counterstory engages thematic foci concerning the tenets, the counterstory below subscribes to the following tenets:

- Permanence of race and racism
- Challenge to dominant ideologies
- Intersectionality and antiessentialism
- Centrality of experiential knowledge and/or unique voices of color
- Commitment to social justice
- Accessibility

Through the course of Alejandra's journey, I demonstrate through counterstory critique the lived reality of a borderlands subject, woven from my own personal experiences and documented to represent existing political, social, and racial ideologies. As a whole, this diary concerns real topics which, when boiled down to the sum of their parts, are about belonging and the power possessed by those who would draw boxes in the sea.

### COUNTERSTORY: DIARY OF A MAD BORDER CROSSER
Diary Entry 1: The School "Peace" Officer
The high school I attended sits nestled behind a small mountain range and is down the street from the city jail. The same public bus route that transports work-release inmates to their daily jobs also delivers the predominantly POC and low-income students to this school. When I attended high school, there were details I missed or rather overlooked because back then they were part of the "everyday" and not really worth noting because I didn't know any different. For example, this school was and remains in a constant state of lockdown. The wrought-iron fence surrounding the school perimeter is eight feet tall and has curved edges pointing inward. The apparent message to students? "Do not attempt escape."[9]

This school's fenced perimeter is guarded by armed police officers paid to monitor the grounds and "keep the peace."[10] Driving onto campus, no longer as a high school student but as a visiting grad student from the local university, I find myself in immediate contact with a "peace" officer (as these cops are titled) stationed in a guard's shack at the entrance to the school's visitor parking lot. She promptly asks my business on campus, and when I say I am a representative from the university, the "peace" officer's eyes narrow as she takes in my casual appearance paired with my brown skin. Internally I recoil. She's a big and tough-looking Chicana who certainly appears able to handle any out-of-hand situation that might occur at the school's entrance—plus, she's armed with a visibly holstered gun at her hip. I think to myself, "Dress like a grown-up next time." She then requests identification, and I provide both my driver's license *and* my university ID so as to dispel any "reasonable suspicion"[11] she may have concerning my identity and business on campus. She records all my information in a visitor's log and asks what teacher I'll be meeting with and whether I know where the classroom is. When I answer to her satisfaction, she assigns me a visitor's permit, tells me "make *sure* you lock your car" (emphasis hers), and waves me through to the parking lot.

As I drive through the unpaved and pothole-riddled parking lot in pursuit of a parking spot, I notice in my rearview mirror a young Chicanx on foot, approaching the "peace" officer's booth from the sidewalk outside the school. They are androgynous in appearance, wearing long, baggy, khaki-colored Dickies shorts, a loose-fitting white t-shirt, black Converse Chucks, and long white socks pulled up to their knees, which are invisible under the hem of the baggy and sagging shorts. Their long dark hair is held back in a slick low ponytail, and they are holding a balloon bouquet in one hand. After a brief exchange, I see the "peace" officer shake her head at the young Chicanx and point with a dismissive flick of her wrist back to the street in the direction opposite the school. After leaving my car and on my way toward the school building, I pass another "peace" officer and overhear the gate "peace" officer's voice on this new "peace" officer's walkie-talkie: "Yeah *she*—I guess *it* was a *she*, maybe a *he*—was trying to get on campus to give balloons to a student, but I was like 'no way; you can see your friend after school.'" The receiving "peace" officer chuckles appreciatively.

Walking around campus, I come across one closed door after another, and many of these doors do not have knobs on the outside. Most doors are locked, and as I have been informed by the teacher I work with at this school, there are many doors to which even teachers do not have keys. I soon turn a corner and find myself facing the football field. There on the track, students run laps and wear the same PE uniforms I distinctly remember once donning myself: oversized orange t-shirts and navy-blue shorts. From this vantage point, I can see both the football field and the city jail no more than a half mile away in the distance. If I squint, I can just make out some city inmates in the yard running laps—they also wear orange.

**Diary Entry 2: The Security Guard**
It's 6:30 a.m., still dark outside, with a winter chill in the desert air. As I turn the ignition switch to my dad's sleek Mercedes E class, I increase the heat to a cozy 76, and my dad, in the passenger seat, teases, "What, you're cold? I thought those northeast winters made you tough. A badass." I laugh and rub my eyes, sleepy. It's the holidays, and I'm in the Southwest, my borderlands home of thirty years. Working as an assistant professor, I now live in the Northeast, and I've missed my Southwest home. I've romanticized it, written about it, and taught about its incendiary policies on immigration[12] and ethnic studies[13] to my mostly horrified and unknowing northeastern borderlands (think Canada in this case) students. From that safe distance I've critiqued the seemingly endless affronts by my home state's legislature toward its populace, and I've grown more sensitive to, yet less experienced, in the everyday effects of living in this space.

As I round the curved roads near the historic Catholic mission—a church built in the 1700s on indigenous land, land that would become reservation land about 150 years later (see "Jesuit Missionaries")—my dad says, "Rides real smooth, huh?" He's referring to his new Mercedes, a car he worked hard his whole life to buy, a car he is proud of and that he wants me to drive so I can share in his accomplishment. My dad was born in a US Southwest border town and grew up in a predominantly Mexican American barrio (see *Barrio Historico Tucson*), one of ten siblings. His mother was born in the cotton fields of the US Southwest to a family of migrant farmworkers; his father was *Mexicano* but became a US citizen in the 1990s. After serving in the US Marine Corps during Vietnam, my father earned two associate's degrees, in digital electronics and business management, and went directly to work as an electronic technician for a local defense contractor. He has spent more than thirty years working alongside and training recent graduates with BAs in engineering to do a job he knows by experience and by heart, but which he can't officially perform because of his having no four-year degree. For more than thirty years, my dad has supported my academic pursuits—acutely aware of the second-class citizenship his community college degrees have afforded him. He has steadily worked to provide his family with a comfortable life and opportunities. So on this winter morning, with his daughter, the PhD and professor, driving him to work in a car he's worked a lifetime to afford, he's proud.

As I make the left-hand turn onto the company facility, I fumble with my wallet and state driver's license. From years of dropping off my dad, I know that an ID is required for entry. I am prepared for the usual exchange with the guard:

Guard: Where you headed?
Me: Building 501.
Guard: You know the way?
Me: Yes, thank you.
Guard: Have a nice day.

However, this guard, a young rosy-cheeked white male, mid-to-late twenties, wearing a guard's coat and skull cap against the chilly morning air, instead says,

"Are you two US citizens?"[14]

At first my dad and I laugh, both out of surprise and I think because we really did believe the guard was telling a joke. But the guard does not laugh. He does not crack a smile. "Oh, God, he's serious," I realize. As my stomach drops, I look to my dad in the passenger seat, and his face is confused and defiant. Much as I had my state ID extended toward the guard, my dad has his company badge held out in plain sight. You see, because this company is a national defense contractor, you must be a citizen to be hired. You must be a citizen to hold a badge.

Embarrassed and flustered, I answer, "Yes, we're citizens." The guard looks at my dad, who says in an annoyed tone, "Yes, I'm a citizen." The guard holds our gazes for a few moments more, and I hold my breath. He finally says, "Okay, have a nice day." He waves us through, and I exhale.

"What an asshole," my dad mutters.

As I drove back toward my parents' home, I racked my brain for answers to this upsetting experience. Being that it was so early in the morning, I noted that I was still in my pajamas, with my hair, a frizzy tangled mess, tied into a quick ponytail. Was that why? I thought about my dad's Mercedes, my state ID, my dad's badge, and his dismissive "asshole" response about the guard. When and how did this security gate become a border checkpoint? What was it about me that prompted this question? Why do I feel so ashamed? Why was my dad so numb?

**Diary Entry 3: The Human Resources Clerk**
It was the toughest teaching semester I've experienced in my career. Aside from the sociopolitical contextual difficulties associated with the election of Forty-Five,[15] I also signed myself up for a few daunting things: a position as faculty at a new university, an hour-long commute (each way) from my home to work, and my daughter very rudely deciding to stop being my baby and turning, in what seemed like overnight, into a teenager and a first-year student in high school. Needless to say, I began the academic year with a *lot* on my plate. Now, as is the case with any new job, there is bureaucratic hoop after hoop to jump through as your employment at a new institution becomes legitimate. And as is the case when you're human, there is probably a hoop or two you'll forget or will overlook in the whirl of getting started.

In the flurry of the new job whirlwind of orientations, welcome events, and general newness, I forgot to fill out my I-9.[16] Admittedly, I didn't know the intricate details about this form or that it was instituted with and tied to Reagan-era immigration reform in this country, and, honestly, I feel like a privileged shit because before now it's just not something I've had to think about. The details associated with this form weren't part of my own awareness until the form became a problem of access for me—which is pretty much how privilege and oppression works, isn't it? Whereas privilege is the stuff we generally don't think about—because with privilege, access is open, and the world is open (here I think of Julie Andrews on her *Sound of Music* hilltop, running, singing, and smiling, arms wide open and free)—oppressive structures present themselves as barriers—barriers to the access you didn't know you were barred from until the bars are figuratively and sometimes literally blocking your way.[17]

These oppressive barriers remind me of one of the more poignant moments in Stokely Carmichael's 1966 speech on Black Power at Berkeley that I think is worth reviewing as I reflect here on issues of access. Carmichael states:

> Now, then, in order to understand white supremacy we must dismiss the fallacious notion that white people can give anybody their freedom. No man can give anybody his freedom. A man is born free. You may enslave a man after he is born free, and that is in fact what this country does. It enslaves black people after they're born, so that the only acts that white people can do is to stop denying black people their freedom; that is, they must stop denying freedom. They never give it to anyone.
>
> Now we want to take that to its logical extension, so that we could understand, then, what its relevancy would be in terms of new civil rights bills. I maintain that every civil rights bill in this country was passed for white people, not for black people. For example, I am black. I know that. I also know that while I am black I am a human being, and therefore I have the right to go into any public place. White people

didn't know that. Every time I tried to go into a place they stopped me. So some boys had to write a bill to tell that white man, "He's a human being; don't stop him." That bill was for that white man, not for me. I knew it all the time. I knew it all the time. (par. 7–8)

Now, in the pile of paperwork we're usually required to fill out when beginning a new job, I never really paid the I-9 much mind; in fact, because of the "9" in its name, I admittedly didn't distinguish it much from the W-9—what a silly, uninformed, and *privileged* mistake. Thus, within my first week on campus, Human (emphasis on that word here) Resources called this form to my attention with the following email:

Dear Employee,

Employers in the United States are required by law to verify the employment authorization of all workers they hire within three days of the hire date. **Our records indicate that you have not yet completed your I-9. Unfortunately, because you are not in compliance, we are required to temporarily suspend your employment, effective immediately.** You are not to perform any work-related duties until your I-9 has been completed.

You may complete the I-9 at the Office of Human Resources. For the list of eligible documentation that needs to be presented when completing the I-9 please visit the Human Resources Service Center website. If you have any questions, feel free to contact the Human Resources Service Center.

Regards,
Human Resources Service Center

So think about the composition and rhetorical message of an email such as this. I was within my first week on campus, orienting and preparing to start this job. I think another important detail to note is that this email was sent at 4:38 p.m. Admittedly, I am the kind of person who has my email linked to my phone, and I suppose I should also admit I am the sort of person who has my phone in hand during most waking hours of the day. Thus I received this email, in all its boldface glory, pretty much as soon as it was sent. And I assume it can be inferred that when reading language such as "[W]e are required to temporarily suspend your employment, effective immediately," I reacted pretty much as Macaulay Culkin did in *Home Alone:* shocked and yelling with my hands slapped against my cheeks.

It was a new job, it was a form I had overlooked (in an admittedly privileged way, which I'll get into further in a minute), and, oh, here's the real kicker: As I noted, the email was sent at 4:38 p.m., and come to find out, the Human Resources Service Center had closed at 4:30 that day. And I know I already mentioned my hour-long commute, so add distance as salt to this increasingly deep wound. So yes, Culkin's shocked and yelling face accurately captures how I felt in that moment. Luckily, this all occurred on a Thursday, so I still had the opportunity to drive back up the next day to right this apparent wrong.

Returning to the emphasis on the concept of being *human*, in this body that is societally raced, gendered, and aged, among other things, and when thinking about access for this body in university spaces with buildings that, for all intents and purposes, look like Hogwarts, I believed—and my use of the past tense here is intentional—I believed that on the days I want to be treated like the PhD and professor that I am, I needed to "dress the part" (and see my reference to this in Diary Entry 1). As the old adage says, "dress for the job you want . . . ," right? But can this adage be applied equally to all humans occupying the intersections that our bodies represent, especially in spaces marked explicitly or implicitly as traditionally accessible for whites, males, the able-bodied, and cisgender folk? Yes, this adds a dimension to the thought of "dressing the part" when other factors of outward appearance beyond clothes matter in our societal context as well. And this is where this diary about border checkpoints comes to a point of convergence. I guess the theme of these entries begins and ends with my optimism that clothing choices will protect me—but while we're on the topic of logics associated with clothing choice and public reception/perception, I have to acknowledge the advice given to women in this society that would associate clothing choice with the probability of rape or sexual assault. There has been some very effective discussion within the context of social media spaces concerning rape culture that has done well to debunk the erroneous logics implicit in this "dress the part" advice.[18]

But for what was probably the last time in my life, I still attempted to "dress the part," fully conscious that I am not what folk expect to see when they think of (in a very raced, classed, and gendered way) what a professor looks like. Just Google the word *professor* and check out the white man/white-haired/bespectacled/tweed-wearing search results. Thus, in my attempt to "look" like a professor that day, I took precautions in the selection of my clothing, I drove the hour to campus in the morning, allowing myself plenty of time for possible delays, and I checked and then double-checked that I had my necessary documents of verification for the I-9 on my person: my school-assigned ID and my passport.

Upon arriving at the site of the Human Resources Services Center, I walked into the office and was reassured to hear a person already at the desk asking for his own overlooked I-9 to complete. And I say "reassured" because although I was dressing the part, although this job is the second in my career as a professor, although I made it through the years of what was essentially hazing to obtain a doctorate, and I have the letters after my name to prove it,[19] I still, at times, suffer an acute case of imposter syndrome, not an uncommon affliction to those of us whose bodies are in spaces not traditionally constructed for us.[20] So yes, relief and reassurance are what I felt when I saw and heard a white male requesting the very form I was there to fill out—relief that I was in the right location, relief that I wasn't the only one who had made this oversight, and reassurance that all would be okay. When it was my turn to be greeted by the Human Resources employee at the front desk, I approached with my friendliest smile and requested the form.

However, the HR employee, a middle-aged white woman, did not return my smile. If anything, my smile was met with a puzzled look from her before she asked,

"Are you employed here?"

Now it was my turn to look puzzled, because her question threw me. I paused before I could construct an answer, and stuttering a bit, I said,

"I—yes—I . . .," and then I was finally able to splutter out, "Yes, I'm faculty."

This Human Resources worker leaned back a bit in her chair to make a full appraisal of me, and I felt my brows furrow into a frown that made its way to my mouth as I began to say, "Do I need to produce my school ID?" but she spoke over me, and with a dismissive hand gesture she said, "Okay, here's the form and a pen—fill it out over there," and she waved me away toward the waiting area chairs.

I took the form from her and did as directed, seating myself away from the desk, away from this confusing interaction, and filled out the form completely. When finished, I reapproached the HR worker's desk and handed her my completed form, with the required accompanying passport as evidence of my legal status to work in this country. She took the form without a word and passed her eyes over it briefly, as I hovered midway between the desk and the waiting area, not really sure where to place my body in this increasingly hostile-feeling space. And then I watched her eyes narrow to a point on the form from which she looked up, lips pursed, and asked me: "Is this *your* school ID number?"

Again, she stunned me. And, flustered, but now also with a growing spark of anger in my gut, I reached for my school-assigned ID card, a photo ID card that displays my face directly next to my school-assigned identification number, and offered it to her directly, retorting, "The number is here, right next to the picture of my face." At the same moment that I resolved she was messing with me, she realized I was on to her, and, eyes widened, she waved my card away, saying in a newly high-pitched voice,[21] "No, no, it's fine, I believe you; here, you can take your passport; I'll put the paper in your file; have a nice day."

I left the office, searching my mind for any plausible excuse for her behavior: "It's Friday; maybe she's tired. Maybe she had a bad week. Maybe there are problems at home," but then I remembered the genuine smile and friendly demeanor she had for the white man before me. Then I remembered this is the form employees fill out to prove citizenship and/or legal status to work in this country. Then I remembered we were about to vote on a presidential candidate who described Mexican immigrants as rapists and drug dealers. Then I remembered that my "dressing the part" did not mask or disguise my own Mexicanness to this HR worker. And I remembered my context: a northeastern private and predominantly/historically white university, a space where my existence, even in the borderlands of Canada, is of "reasonable suspicion."

From these experiences I've come to terms with a few things:

1. The experience of people of color in the borderlands of this country—all borderlands—is that we are always subject to scrutiny regarding our legality in the land, so much so that people like the Chicanx school "peace" officers at a predominantly POC high school, my Mexican American father, and even myself become numb to, desensitized to, or simply in denial of the continual assaults on our humanity under the reigning white supremacist anti-immigrant political climate and resulting legislation.
2. In a country such as this, with its white supremacist anti-immigrant political climate and resulting legislation, my titles, my degrees, my clothes, or even the car I drive do not matter when my brown skin is of enough "reasonable suspicion" to the law.
3. Because I teach about, critique, and engage in conversations about race, nation, and citizenship, I must remember, even if this is through painful and humiliating personal assaults, that I have a responsibility to always critically self-reflect on my privilege and tell the stories of the human lives affected under this jurisdiction.

# 5

# Counterstory in Education: Pedagogical Implications for CRT Methodology

Critical race theory arose out of the lived experiences of students *and* teachers in US law schools who were witness and subject to liberal civil rights ideology that failed to address the "constrictive role that racial ideology plays in the composition and culture of American institutions" (Crenshaw et al. xix). Founding crit Angela P. Harris has reflected on her own miseducation as a law student, maintaining that students of color during her generation navigated their legal educations, never finding a place where discourses concerning lived realities and racial critiques entered the legal canon (xv). In fact, Harris recalls, "[N]one of my professors talked about race or ethnicity; it was apparently irrelevant to the law. . . . There was only one Law, a law that in its universal majesty applied to everyone without regard to race, color, gender, or creed" (xiv).

As discussed in Chapter 1 and Chapter 3, Derrick Bell, taking active notice of these erasures and absences in the curriculum, developed and taught legal doctrine from a race-conscious viewpoint and used racial politics as the organizing concept for his students' scholarly study. Bell crafted counterstories with pedagogical intent, meant to facilitate classroom discussion. Additionally, Bell's course textbook, *Race, Racism, and American Law*—developed, published, and centralized within his own curriculum in the early 1970s—served as a foundation and a curriculum plan for The Alternative Course, the student-led course on race and the law at Harvard Law School (Crenshaw et al.; Delgado and Stefancic, Introduction). Resulting from the 1981 student protest and boycott of Harvard

Law's curriculum and its refusal to replace Bell with a teacher of color (Bell departed in 1980 in protest of the school's refusal to hire a woman of color), the course encompassed a student-led continuation of Bell's curriculum, which focused on US law through the "prism of race" (Crenshaw et al. xxi). This course is remembered by crits as the first institutionalized expression of CRT as a movement, as it challenged the mainstream liberal notion of which subject matters were of enough value to include in a standardized core curriculum. Importantly, this student and teacher activism and the existence of this course are evidence that a primary CRT concern has always been a critique of education that moves toward social transformation.

By the mid-1990s CRT was incorporated from legal studies into education. At the 1994 American Educational Research Association meeting, Gloria Ladson-Billings and William F. Tate's presentation identified the tenets of CRT's relevance to the study of race and racism in education. Followed by their landmark 1995 essay, "Toward a Critical Race Theory of Education," Ladson-Billings and Tate have remained at the "forefront of engaging CRT and pushing its boundaries in education," influencing and supporting other prominent crit education scholars such as Daniel Solórzano, Adrienne Dixson, Dolores Delgado Bernal, Tara J. Yosso, and Daniella Ann Cook (Dixson and Rousseau 4–5). Having enjoyed a twenty-five-year tenure in education, CRT as a framework for educational research is no longer contested; however, Nolan Cabrera has remarked that this lack of resistance within the field has misdirected and, in some cases, diluted the rigor and theoretical edge of the critique. Likewise, Marvin Lynn and Adrienne Dixson have observed,

> Despite the push by CRT scholars in education to center race and push the field to consider race as more than just a variable, far too many scholars who have an interest in examining race and racism in education misunderstand and misuse CRT[;] . . . some scholars claim a CRT approach simply because their sample may be primarily composed of people of

color. Far too often, scholars have invoked CRT in the introductory sections of their paper never to revisit the theory or even utilize any of its tenets in their analysis. (3)

Reflecting on her contribution of CRT to education, Ladson-Billings says, "I argued that CRT could serve as a *heuristic* for new understandings of multicultural education . . . [;] CRT scholars were working to deploy 'race and racial theory as a challenge to traditional notions of diversity and social hierarchy'" (Foreword xii, emphasis mine). In light of these critiques, it is imperative to review the heuristics of CRT in education with an eye toward the application of CRT's tenets in forward-facing educational research and pedagogy.

Informed by and overlapping with CRT's tenets (but also, from my perspective as a rhetoric scholar, aspects of the rhetorical situation), CRT's heuristic—as theorized by scholars in education—offers the following guidelines to educators who aim to frame their pedagogy and the crafting of curricula with CRT:

- Educators should work from a premise that racism is prevalent in American society in general, and in education in particular (tenet alignment: permanence of race and racism).
- Educators should question the dominant claims and discourses of their field(s) (tenet alignment: challenge to dominant ideologies).
- Educators should historically ground their coursework, acknowledging the importance of context (tenets alignment: permanence of race and racism, interest convergence, race as social construct).
- Educators should aim for interdisciplinarity, drawing from a range of literatures (tenet alignment: interdisciplinarity).
- Educators should centralize the experiences and perspectives of the minoritized, as a focal point—not a passing glance for a day or week's thematic focus (tenet alignment: centrality of experiential knowledge).

- As a follow-up to centralizing the experiences and perspectives of the minoritized, educators should acknowledge and make themselves aware that there is diversity within experience (tenet alignment: intersectionality and antiessentialism).

Ultimately, the goal of CRT is social transformation, and the heuristic of CRT in education is aimed at the social transformation of educational research, classrooms, curricula, policy, the study of knowledge (epistemology), and teaching (pedagogy) (Yosso, *Critical Race Counterstories* 8). As Cook observes, CRT's maintained focus on the centrality of race "elucidates the fluid, shifting, yet consistent message of white supremacy and how it operates in the policies, practices, and everyday schooling experiences of students, teachers, and the larger community" (183). Further, counterstory, as a methodological frame that centers the stories and lived experiences of people of color, embodies an "epistemology for how and why particular methods are chosen" (183). A social transformation of education insists that educational researchers change the structures that prevent all students from receiving the same opportunities to learn and succeed. As Dixson and Rousseau argue, "just as the 'new' song of the spirituals was a call for freedom and justice in an unjust world, CRT not only puts in front of us the image of a 'heaven' in which *all* God's children are able to sing their song. It also demands that we find a way to get there" (7–8)—and for me, that way is methodology—that way is counterstory.

Yosso asserts that counterstory is crucial to CRT scholarly inquiry as it supports scholars and practitioners in understanding how minoritized communities (primarily of color) "experience and respond to racism as it intersects with other forms of subordination in the United States educational system" (*Critical Race Counterstories* 8). Counterstory as a methodology is fundamental in CRT educators' development of a critical race praxis, a praxis that works toward the goal of social transformation inside and outside the classroom (*Critical Race Counterstories* 8, 14). Specific to counterstory as methodology, Yosso has outlined a supplementary praxis to the heuristic of CRT in education:

- Counterstories build community among those who have been marginalized within society, and communicate that we do not struggle alone.
- Counterstories challenge the perceived wisdom of those at society's center, and provide a context to understand and transform established belief systems.
- Counterstories nurture community cultural wealth, memory, and resistance. In affirming pedagogies and knowledges cultivated in minoritized communities, counterstories preserve community memory of the history of resistance to oppression.
- Counterstories facilitate transformation in education. (*Critical Race Counterstories* 14–15)

Yosso argues that stories move us to action, action that informs praxis, and so critical concepts and theory presented through counterstory are an accessible form for both teachers and students. Whether presented as primary texts within class or applied as a framework by teachers to transform curricula, counterstories teach us that "construction of another world—a socially and racially just world—is possible" (*Critical Race Counterstories* 14–15).

### WHERE THIS STORY ENDS AND ANOTHER BEGINS

At the core of my academic identity, I am a teacher-scholar who centralizes the theories and methodology of critical race theory within my writing practices but also within my classroom. This book has reviewed the histories and theories of CRT, with close readings and analyses of three CRT counterstory exemplars, Richard Delgado, Derrick Bell, and Patricia J. Williams. I make a distinct case for counterstory as a viable research methodology and a writing method in public and academic spheres. And while this final chapter is the explicit "pedagogy chapter," all the previous chapters are arguably pedagogy chapters as well because CRT has always held central its critique of education toward social transformation. Thus, this project—while inherently concerned with the rhetoric and writing of CRT—is also intrinsically invested in arguing for CRT's pedagogical potential in rhetoric and writing studies.

As this project has demonstrated, exemplars Delgado, Bell, and Williams consistently speak (through counterstory and other methods of critical self-reflection) regarding their roles as teachers in relation to students. Delgado crafted a chronicle's worth of composite dialogues among composite student-teacher characters, Rodrigo and the professor. Bell, a self-proclaimed student to Geneva Crenshaw, crafted counterstories to teach in the classroom as supplementary to the textbook he wrote for his Harvard seminar—a book students took upon themselves to keep teaching in their own seminar after he left. Likewise, Delgado, along with Stefancic, produced the accessible *Critical Race Theory: An Introduction*, a book Harris describes as "a primer for nonlawyers that makes the now sprawling literature of critical race theory easily accessible to the beginner" (xvi). Intended for a new generation of critical race scholars, Delgado and Stefancic's book employs "reader-friendly language," absent of buzzwords and jargon, covering CRT's central themes, critiques, and implications.[1] Within this important educational text,[2] the authors offer teachers and students classroom exercises for practical application and a glossary of key terms, and the conclusion of each chapter provides discussion questions and short lists of suggested readings. Last, Deborah Waire Post has commented that Williams's narratives are fundamentally reflections on her experiences as a teacher (132), and in Williams's *Alchemy* chapter, "Crimes without Passion," she provides particular inspiration and counterstory modeling for the exchange within this chapter's counterstory between Alejandra and her students Kyle and Connor (Williams 92–97).

While this chapter serves the function of a conclusion, it is also a call to action for educators, particularly those in rhetoric and writing studies, to consider CRT's implications and application in their own educational research and teaching practices. CRT has always been concerned with the colonizing functions of education, which act as a conveyor of hegemonic whiteness—and crits have always aimed to disrupt this hegemony with transformative educational heuristics and praxes. Beyond crafting curricula with CRT and counterstories as primary texts (Appendixes A and B), the theory and methodology of CRT and counterstory can also inform a transformational education that can be employed as a frame to revise, re-envision, and recraft core curricula in many disciplines (Appendixes C and D).

Because I am a teacher-scholar situated in, yes, rhetoric and writing studies, but also very much influenced by literacy studies, my work in this chapter makes space for a synergy of CRT scholarship, histories, and theories that are located primarily in legal studies and education. In light of and as a contribution to this genealogy, the next logical step in CRT's interdisciplinary journey is making a case for the methodology of counterstory in the framing of rhetoric and writing studies pedagogy and curriculum development. This concluding chapter thus reviews the ways CRT and counterstory have informed and influenced my teaching practice and my crafting and teaching of courses within the context of rhetoric and writing studies departments and programs. Specifically discussed within, by way of counterstory as an epistolary email exchange between Alejandra and her teacher-mentor, V, are pedagogical materials such as syllabi and course plans, ideologically framed by CRT and counterstory. In all, my goal in this concluding chapter is to extend the conversations about CRT counterstory as research and writing method toward pedagogy and curriculum development for those who wish to put into practice the rich theories and histories of this methodology. Some questions to consider at the conclusion of this chapter, but also forward-facing at the conclusion of this book, are the following: How does CRT and counterstory as frame change the way we build courses? What becomes different? I suggest we begin by looking at core curricula because these constitute the courses in which the already minoritized become marginalized, and nothing is more central to the ideologies and the teachings of disciplines and fields than their core curricula.

The core is where issues like what Sofi discusses in Chapter 2 occur, issues concerning the unquestioned inclusion of Margaret Mitchell's *Gone with the Wind* and the absence of Octavia Butler's *Kindred*. The core is where names like James Berlin, Robert Connors, Sharon Crowley, Richard Leo Enos, Victor Vitanza, Susan

Jarratt, Nan Johnson, and Jan Swearingen are made immortal in their uptake—to the erasure of other(ed) names and voices. The core is where master narratives take root and are reinforced and sanctioned through the institutional racism of rhetoric and writing studies' disciplinary constructs, resulting in classroom-specific racial violence toward students and teachers of color (Kynard, "Teaching While Black" 1). And while I acknowledge and appreciate the work of an elective curricula, I am more than aware of the marginalizing function elective courses serve for already minoritized perspectives. In 2020, minoritized peoples and our perspectives are still not considered core-course material in the (usually white) racist imaginary. And when assessing the master narrative concerning the core curriculum—this hegemonic story, which even POC at times buy into—we are *still* being told, for no less than twelve years in our elementary and secondary school educations, that the core curriculum is by and large the domain of white Euro-Western perspectives and ways of knowing. The core curriculum is the occupied space of white racialized perspectives, while the voices and stories of the racialized "other" are pushed to the margins in elective courses, at best, or footnotes and asides within the core curriculum, at worst. With the above in mind, it is also no surprise that ethnocentric white students only tolerate the work of POC when it comes in the form of electives—so they can elect not to take these courses. Equally unsurprising is when these same students become angry and resistant upon realizing that *my* approach to these core courses—courses they cannot opt out of because of their major-specific degree requirements—centralizes the rhetorics and theories of POC—albeit still in conversation with white folk.

Thus, I conclude this book with a presentation of counterstory as epistle in which Alejandra and V engage in an email exchange about core curricula in rhetoric and writing studies and about the potential for the social transformation of education in their shared field when a CRT frame and methodology are applied. Alejandra's email has been published (in part) in my *Rhetoric Review* essay "Core-Coursing Counterstory," but within this epistolary exchange V has the opportunity to respond to his student/mentee, offering Alejandra encouragement, advice, and closing words about directions for her CRT counterstory pursuits. In all, the direction toward transformative education really is where the work begun in this book travels next. Because I was not able to publish counterstory without first *learning* about it and its methods, because I did not use CRT and counterstory to frame my own curriculum development without first *learning* about its socially transformative roots and implications, I conclude this project with a call to action to embrace our identities as students—students forever in the process of becoming—who are still capable of learning and reframing education in rhetoric and writing studies toward the social transformation called into action by critical race theory and counterstory.

## COUNTERSTORY: AN EPISTOLARY EMAIL ON PEDAGOGY AND MASTER NARRATIVE CURRICULA

Dear V,

Yesterday was a tough day. Being that I arrive early on my teaching days, I made my way to my office and got right into the grading of my Histories of Rhetorics daily reading responses and found myself feeling assaulted—slapped in the face even, as racist interactions are usually received—by one student's racist and disparaging remarks. But a bit of context for you first.

During class a few weeks ago, we were discussing the concept of decolonization because it was brought up by Sonja Foss in her chapter on feminist criticism from her book *Rhetorical Criticism*. In this section, Foss states (mostly quoting from bell hooks's *Sisters of the Yam*), "Feminist criticism deserves the label *feminist* as well because it is marked by a key objective of feminism—to decolonize minds or to disconnect from hegemonic ways of believing, acting, and being. Decolonization is the 'breaking with the ways our reality is defined and shaped by the dominant culture and asserting our understanding of that reality, of our own experience'" (144).

Because I didn't want to assume my students had a working understanding of what colonization was—that would call for decolonization in the first place—I asked my students for their definitions of colonization. After a lengthy and increasingly uncomfortable silence, a white woman,[3] K. C., who had "National Women's March" and "Fuck 45" stickers pasted to the lid of her laptop, raised her hand. I nodded in her direction, and she said, "Colonization is about power. It's about nations and people with power coming into places that are already occupied, finding ways to label those people lesser beings, and then killing, conquering, and stealing from them."

"Okay, let's keep going with that," I said. "Does anyone have something to add?"

A black male student named Byron chimed in: "It's not even always about killing conquered people physically, which is where Foss's discussion of decolonization comes in. It's also about killing their minds and their cultures. Oppressors still need people alive to serve them, so they make the oppressed enough like them to get things done—to get rich off the back of others."

"And how does the colonizer make the colonized 'like them'?" I prompted.

"Through religion and education," a Chicanx nonbinary student named Billie offered.

"Keep going," I said to Billie; "what does that look like, sound like, feel like for the colonized?"

"One approach is through language—stripping colonized people of their language through school and telling them their language is bad, stupid, wrong, then forcing them to speak the colonizer's language—while usually telling the colonized they can't even do that well," Billie said, shaking their head (Martinez, "Alejandra Writes a Book" 58–59).

From my peripheral vision I'd noticed one of my white male students, Kyle, shifting uncomfortably in his seat, perhaps debating with himself whether or not to engage this conversation, but upon hearing Billie's reference to language Kyle decided to jump in. His hand shot in the air, and I nodded in his direction. This is what he had to say:

"I don't understand why 'the colonizer' (he used air quotes) is being cast in such a negative light. Like, what's our purpose here? To villainize those who came to this country with nothing more than a dream, fleeing religious persecution? The founding fathers *had to* establish a new nation, bound by rules and culture. I don't think they had a choice when it came to instituting English as our national language, yet here we are vilifying them."

V, you've been a friend and mentor to me for a long time, so you know it took every grain of patience in my bones not to respond in a less-than-teacherly way. I pulled from my core a compassion that I reserve for fraught situations, and I had to repeat *Mami*'s wise words in my head: "He's someone's *niño*. Somebody loves him. Be kind" (Martinez, "A Plea"). I'm telling you, V, this was hard! Nonetheless, this was my response:

"It's interesting, Kyle, that in our discussion of colonization in general—something that has occurred over the course of many centuries in many various places in the world—you have heard us 'vilifying' the American founding fathers (now it was my turn to use air quotes). Your perspective on this conversation seems in line with Foss's points from the reading about dominant culture shaping our reality and experiences—thus the need to reexamine these realities through the process of decolonization. For instance, in your telling of US history, you assert that English is a national language instituted by the founding fathers. I'm sorry to say, Kyle, but this is false. There is not and has never been a policy on a singular national language, English or otherwise. What I also find interesting about your perspective, Kyle, is that you attribute an ideology of monolingualism to the founding fathers when many of them in their roles as intellectuals, statesmen, and diplomats spoke no fewer than three languages—French, Dutch, and German—and were trained in Latin and Greek at Ivy League institutions. So, my question to you, Kyle, is where does your version of events resonate from? What does this say about *your* perspective and, in effect, *your* reality?"

Although my tone was friendly, it was also firm. On reflection, I don't perceive my delivery as having been antagonistic, but my response was met with another stretch of silence until I prompted the students to discuss Foss some more in small groups. Kyle got up and left the classroom and did not return until the end of class.

On further reflection, I wonder if my response was the teaching moment I'd intended? This week Kyle returned to class after three weeks of nonattendance and had me sign a drop form. He talked about an opportunity to work on a documentary film that my course was in conflict with, so with apologies he said he didn't want to "waste my time anymore." He was nervous and fidgety as he spoke, and after signing his form I watched his receding back leave my class for good, and wondered if I'd failed as a teacher—if this is what pedagogical failure looks and feels like.

This Kyle-situation within a core course on the Histories of Rhetoric presents a specific resistance to an ideological frame for the course, decolonization to be specific. And with this frame, along with other Foss-inspired rhetorical criticism approaches, my students and I have propelled ourselves into an exploration of texts from the classical era, the Enlightenment, the nineteenth and twentieth centuries, and contemporary times. With Foss's guidance and her diverse offerings of tools for critique, my students are presented a choice of lenses, such as neo-Aristotelian, feminist, ideological, and generic criticism, with which to approach their reading and analysis of artifacts. However, a hole in Foss's text is expertly filled by Lisa A. Flores's work "Between Abundance and Marginalization: The Imperative of Racial Rhetorical Criticism." If you haven't read it yet, V, let me know so I can pass it along.

As Flores defines it, racial rhetorical criticism is "rhetorical criticism that is reflective about and engages the persistence of racial oppression, logics, voices, and bodies and that theorizes the very production of race as rhetorical" (5). Further, Flores says that "rhetoric as a discipline engages in practices and politics that require sustained critical attention to race. Indeed, I will go so far as to argue that rhetorical studies is fundamentally—at its core—the study of race and to argue, therefore, [that] rhetorical critics must participate in the expanding area of racial rhetorical criticism" (6).

Now, V, you and I don't need convincing that rhetorical critics must be cognizant of race in their critical endeavors (Flores 17). And although *we* know not everyone talks about race in rhetoric, Flores supports the positions we've both taken in our pursuit to get our colleagues and students to center race "in our disciplinary practices, if not because of the fundamental racial-ness of discourse and the art of rhetorical criticism, then because race informs our political possibilities and limitations *and* our critical judgments" (17–18). Here again is an example.

As mentioned above, this is a core course in Histories of Rhetoric, and I come from a graduate program that centered a very "classical" perspective as canon, so I'm well acquainted with the work Patricia Bizzell and Bruce Herzberg have accomplished in their renowned anthology *The Rhetorical Tradition*. Through self-education, aided by your guidance, I'm now equally acquainted with the call that scholars (e.g., Haas, Driskill, Baca and Villanueva, the Cultural Rhetorics Theory Lab, Ruiz and Sánchez, Cushman, Cobos et al., García and Baca) have issued to disentangle ourselves from this particularly Euro-Western narrative that Bizzell and Herzberg have woven—a narrative many in the field centralize as *the* word on histories of rhetoric. And here again we arrive at decolonization as a framework and my central questions about whose voices and perspectives are centralized, whose voices are nodded to as asides (see Jackson 118).

Damián Baca asks in the introduction to his and Victor Villanueva's *Rhetorics of the Americas:* "Given that no indigenous community is today free from Euro-American influence, what kind of autonomy or self-determination is possible? To the extent that diasporic and other new forms of identity are the product of colonialism, what are the 'identity politics' of decolonial resistance?" (2). And my answer to Baca's prompts, particularly within the context of a Histories of Rhetoric core course, is that counterstory would insist on acknowledging master narratives, if for no other reason than to refute them from the perspective of the colonized.

As a theoretical approach to how I've formed this course, but also my other core courses, such as my first-year writing course and my grad seminar on histories and theories of composition, counterstory offers a multiplicity of perspectives in terms of primary texts and the tools/skill sets for rhetorical criticism that we use to conduct our readings and our analysis of theories and theorists. And thus, the questions—for me—become less about stripping the core curriculum of white Euro-Western perspectives and more about stripping these perspectives of their *centralized power* in relation to the perspectives/rhetorics/stories that have been historically overlooked. And, V, I know you'll have some opinions to offer, and I invite them because this is the quandary I'm stuck in: Is the goal of a decolonial counterstory approach for the core curriculum to supplant the Euro-Western story, in the same way colonizers sought to supplant the knowledges of the colonized? Or is the goal to strip it of its power as monolithic and central to historical narratives? Is the goal to do what Carmen Kynard (invoking Houston Baker Jr. from his *Afro-American Poetics*) has called for in her own historiographic approach: "To treat central texts and figures as 'discursive formations' that have political and social origins that can be traced and whose regularities are discoverable. That such a tracing allows us to unravel the locations and authorities for discourse . . . rather than the motives, intentions, or transcendent subjectivity of individual speakers" (11)?

With this Kynard-inspired frame, braided together with counterstory and the other decolonial historiographic approaches described above, my histories of rhetoric course aims to engage master narratives (*the* Rhetorical Tradition) in dialogue sometimes, critique sometimes, and sometimes by dissociation from the diverse possibilities of overlooked perspectives. This *trensa* course framework presents students with multiple rhetorics/perspectives, but also with skill sets with which to make choices about how they will read and analyze the offered perspectives. And, V, you've seen my syllabus (Appendix C); it most definitely engages white Euro-Western rhetorics *and* instructs in rhetorical criticism methods (neo-Aristotelian and Burke-informed cluster criticism) most associated with white Euro-Western worldviews. But this perspective is not central to the course, and importantly it is identified—*named*.

Let me assure you, V, I make explicit effort to point out that what is generally touted simply as "rhetorical analysis" is in fact informed by and in the tradition of what Aristotle and Cicero, specifically, but other "classical rhetoric" figures, broadly, have defined as the boundaries. This is where Flores's tools for racial rhetorical criticism are useful. Flores identifies three ways to frame the rhetorical critique of an artifact:

1. Hearing race
2. Seeing race
3. Bounding race (11–16)

As I understand it, the first frame, "hearing race," coincides with your own scholarship, V: English language vernacular(s) and literacy. A "hearing race" frame is an articulation that assists students in understanding the English vernacular debate between Vershawn Ashanti Young and Stanley Fish. With an essay like Young's "Should Students Write in They Own English?" as a centralized artifact, students are able to trace Young's tracks through Fish's essay "What Colleges Should Teach? Part 3," which I assign for the same day (Appendix C).

"Seeing race" is where visual rhetorics take center stage, and I apply this frame to the Nick Wing article "When the Media Treat White Suspects and Killers Better than Black Victims." You shared this essay on Twitter a few years back with your own striking visual rhetoric illustration of the #IfTheyGunnedMeDown hashtag. Applying Flores's frame of "seeing race" to the analysis of textual headlines and displayed images, consciously composed and selected by journalists, the influence of racist ideologies on media reporting is undeniable. The best part is that there are a few rhetoric/journalism dual majors in my course, so I'm hopeful this frame made some sort of impression when it comes to takeaways for them.

Flores's third and final frame, "bounding race," definitely applies to border rhetorics of nationalism, citizenship, and belonging—concepts of who's in and who's not. But the more I think about this concept as a framework, the more I realize how directly this frame is in conversation with Kynard's historiographic approach and others' decolonial methodologies and pedagogies. "Bounding race" provides a toolkit for reading *and* crafting counterstory, and as a class, and with the help of Cornel West's razor-sharp observations, we used this rhetorical criticism method to revisit the Enlightenment era as presented by Bizzell and Herzberg (789–813).

In "A Genealogy of Modern Racism," West directs the audience to look again at key Enlightenment figures and concepts—folk like Thomas Jefferson, Francis Bacon, and Carolus Linnaeus, and ideas like "classical aesthetics of beauty" and biological taxonomies—toward a nuanced understanding of how these thinkers were bound by their contexts and thus had power to devise theories as answers to questions about their subjective realities. Best example? Jefferson. "All men are created equal." These are his words. Yet the reality of his context is that he was a slave owner. So how did Jefferson conciliate his ideals to his life? He wrote *Notes on the State of Virginia* and put forth a theory that black people were inherently not quite "men" and were thus not included within the boundaries of his lofty Enlightenment-influenced espousals of freedom.

So, V, Flores's frames of "hearing race," "seeing race," and "bounding race" ushered along conversations, with my students exploring whose version of English has capital in academic institutions. Whose histories are preserved and taught? Whose lives matter? And in all, how do we relate these questions to larger concerns about canon and core curriculum? And this, V, brings us full circle to the student exchange that prompted this email to you in the first place.

Now that I've detailed my theoretical approaches to how I've formed this course, I have to share also where I've painfully run into resistance and backlash from students. I remain pedagogically unsettled by the above-described Kyle situation; however, a recent exchange with a student, Connor, has me pedagogically *and* personally shook. Connor's (perceivably underexplored) identity politics are what he asserts as an answer to the centralized rhetorics of POC, particularly American Indians.

In terms of the bad day I mentioned at the start of this email, I've been privately and individually receiving reader responses (R&Rs) from Connor, a white male student who is boldly asserting his perspective in response to the week's assigned texts:

- Victor Villanueva's "Rhetoric of the First 'Indians'"
- Qwo-Li Driskill's "Decolonial Skillshares: Indigenous Rhetorics as Radical Practice"
- from Ana Castillo's *Massacre of the Dreamers*
- from Gloria Anzaldúa's *Borderlands/La Frontera*

I include below, for your own rhetorical criticism, Connor's and my exchanges regarding this set of course texts:

Connor, R&R 1:
Question: What does this [the above texts] mean for people who don't really worry about Native Americans and the oppression that happened to them a long time ago?
Quotation 1: "And as we enter the influences of the peoples of this hemisphere, we must remember the first people the Europeans met, kidnapped, enslaved, and announced as dead. These are my people" (Villanueva 15).
Reaction: I know that this [is] awful and what happened to this people back then was just wrong. As for me, I am not very interested in this Native American talk.
Quotation 2: "Colonization and genocide in the Americas and elsewhere depend on the destruction of cultural memory through attacks on indigenous rhetorical practices" (Driskill 57).
Reaction: I do agree with what this author said, to how yes many Native American have suffered, but did they really go through genocide? I do not understand why we do not know more about indians rhetoric. Like are they buried under ground or can we not find any of those works[?]
Alejandra, feedback:
Concerning your comments about not being in-

terested in or worried about what happened to Native Americans, I suggest you examine why you maintain this position. What about your own demographic subjectivities and upbringing have led you to feel this way when encountering material that you yourself said you've not encountered before taking this course? Also, as someone pursuing a university degree that includes encountering new information, you should reflect on how or why you find yourself resistant or apathetic toward knowledge you are not previously versed in. Last, these historic issues, related to American Indians and many of the other rhetorics we are exploring this semester, are foundational for contemporary issues, so while we are reviewing things that happened in the past, they very much inform and have built the context in which we all currently exist, so it is in your best interest to be informed as an educated citizen of this country. And, above all, this course is only a semester long, so in the scheme of your entire education at this university, if this is the only time you learn about Native American rhetorics, understand this is a fraction of your time spent. Feel free to come to my office hours to further discuss any of the above.

Connor, R&R 2:
Question: The rhetoric to what I [sic] was reading makes me understand a couple of things. I understand people of color are placed in this world in not great locations, but I do understand that they can get out of what they are placed in. The decisions they make might place them in such a bad place and then they might blame the people above them for their issues. I see so much complaining and hate towards people above them, but I do not see the work being put in.

Quotation 1: Chicanos and other people of color suffer economically for not acculturating. This voluntary (yet forced) alienation makes for psychological conflict, a kind of dual identity—we don't indentify [sic] with the anglo-american cultural values and we don't totally identify with the Mexican cultural values (Anzaldúa 1590). Reaction: Honeslty [sic] i am not a writing major because I love to sit on my butt and write books. I onlu [sic] chose this major because i couldn't get into the business management school here. I learn differently, i do not learn from grades and stuff like that. I want to go into money and the stock market mostly. Selling things are really like to do. I am not like most wrting [sic] majors.

V, my dearest of mentors and advisors, how do I move forward, with resolve to keep teaching a student who has written responses that land as racist slaps on my face? This is admittedly not a student or ideology unique to my course, my campus, or my experience as a professor. I understand implicitly that many of the scholars I've mentioned through the course of this email have been prompted to research, write, and teach if for nothing more than to provide a counterstory to the master narratives crafted by the Kyles and Connors of their worlds. And I know counterstory as a methodology and as a writing method guides my research and the conceptual frameworks with which I very intentionally craft the courses I teach.

With this in mind, I don't want to lose sight of the students who seem to understand and appreciate what I am doing here. There are plenty of students of color and white students alike who, for reasons of representation, locate aspects of their own identities and subjectivities in the words and works of the frames and primary texts in this course. And while I acknowledge that it is not uncommon as teachers to be distracted and discouraged by the few students who actively resist our work, I can't forget the students who are eager to learn—the students I can see myself in. On further reflection, I think we as instructors are prone to make one of two pedagogical choices in course creation: (1) To teach the courses we've taken or (2) to teach the course we wish we had taken and be the teacher we wish we'd had.

So, V, I close this email to you in a hopeful way, one that acknowledges the role you have played in shaping me into the teacher-scholar who would craft a course like this. I am grateful to you for being the advocate and ally who has fostered my own confidence to stay strong and focused through times when this profession tries me. I am indebted to you for being available to me as a sounding board full of wisdom gained from your own turbulent experiences paving the path for *cabronas* like me to follow you down. And most of all, thank you for sticking with this *essay* of an email. It's rare that anyone writes lengthy letters anymore—we are all so enchanted by brevity—but some things are best discussed at length, and the politics of the core curricula in rhetorical studies deserve an extended engagement and ensuing exchange. I look forward to your response.

Your friend and student *por vida*,
Alejandra

**V's Response**

Dear Alé,

Thanks for writing, and I'm really sorry to hear about your tough time with the Kyles and Connors at your institution. Believe me, I've encountered my fair share of Kyles and Connors, and although their expressions of whiteness and masculinity might vary with institutional and temporal context, the privilege they invest in remains the same—and they'll not lightly give an ounce of it up—not without violence. And hey, know this: if you're actively working to dismantle systemic oppression, understand you're going to be the villain in a few folks' stories.[4] *Sigh*.

Thanks also for your detailed discussion about crafting core curricula. This topic has really jogged my memory and transported me back to my own beginnings as a junior professor. I remember well trying my best to get my bearings in a department with a high-profile national reputation for churning out doctoral graduates who become notable scholars in the field. While this reputation of the graduate program is what initially attracted me to this job, it quickly became a major source of anxiety for me once I actually landed the job. I mean, now I would be expected to contribute to the success of said students, and I was under no misconceptions about whether or not these students would be tough and have very high expectations for me as their professor—and after all, what did I know? I was so newly arrived from grad school myself; how would I ever possibly *assert* my authority in such a rigorous space?

Well, that was my first mistake—thinking I had to enter this space as an authority, and attempting to prove this over the course of a semester, was nothing short of a pedagogical fail. And let's face it, while my own graduate program trained me very well (in terms of practical experience and theoretical/methodological coursework) to pedagogically navigate a first-year writing classroom, I was never presented the opportunity to learn how to teach or craft curricula for graduate students. I mean, who teaches grad students how to teach grad students anyhow? How do we learn this vital skill set? Is our instruction and training in graduate-level pedagogy simply our own experiences in graduate courses? Do we simply do unto our grad students what has been done to us? And for a field so concerned with pedagogy, are we satisfied with this?

A lot of questions, I know, but your final thoughts where you say, "I think we as instructors are prone to make one of two pedagogical choices in course creation: (1) To teach the courses we've taken or (2) to teach the course we wish we had taken and be the teacher we wish we'd had," very much prompted me to think hard about what has driven my own pedagogical choices. When you apply these two prompts to teaching graduate students, particularly when tasked with teaching graduate seminars that are part of the core curricula, and considering our field-wide lack of attention to and training in pedagogy at this level—well, then we arrive at issues too reminiscent of the kind you faced in your own graduate school experience (Martinez, "A Plea" and "Alejandra Writes a Book"). In fact, the only revision I'd offer to your first prompt is that not only do some folks make the decision to teach the courses they've taken, but they also enact the same, sometimes violent, pedagogical strategies of their own teachers.

And you know what? While so much of the scholarship in rhetoric and writing studies chronicling "the multiple literate lives of students of color has been embraced, it is not clear that" this same work "has actually been mobilized to change classrooms for students of color in schools and colleges." I think many folks find it much "safer to unfurl the specialized, disciplinary methodologies and vocabularies in which we have been trained rather than turn our analytical gaze onto our institutions and its actors that have maintained calculatingly repressive environments, policies, and climates for students and faculty of color" (Kynard, "Teaching While Black" 2). And you know what else, Alé? Turning the "analytical gaze" inward for some critical self-reflection about our role and actions as educators (and administrators!) is exactly what Sylvia Wynter calls for when she proposes that: "(1) we begin to notice the violence in the classrooms and research that we sustain, and (2) we question the disciplinary apparatus that makes it possible that racially subordinated students of color will experience racial violence at the site where they are supposed to be democratically educated" (qtd. in Kynard, "Teaching While Black" 4).

Answering Wynter's call seems critical to me in a "field where even the texts that address race/anti-racism parade mostly white authors with an obligatory nod to the celebrity minorities of the field, allowing yet another publication of a white text by white authors who have often themselves perpetrated exactly the kinds of white supremacist violence" we've talked about as long as we've known each other (Kynard, "Teaching While Black" 14). What we need is what LaNita Jacobs-Huey has described as the natives *"gazing and talking back"* in ways that *"*explicitly interrogate the *daily operation of white supremacy in our field and on our campuses,"* adding that "this is work that requires you to make people *uncomfortable. Some folk gon need to get called out"* (qtd. in Kynard, "Teaching While Black" 14). And that's where CRT enters rhetoric and writing studies. I know you've read a bunch from the CRT folks out of legal studies, but because your research is so specifically shifting its focus to the classroom and questions of the core curriculum, I have to push you in the direction of the CRT conversations that have been happening in education. Those folks have crafted an entire heuristic and praxis to frame this critical and crucial work. Let me break it down for you.

We've discussed together some of Gloria Ladson-Billings's work before, but as far as CRT is concerned, I'm not sure if you know she's the cited foremother of CRT in education. She, along with William Tate, introduced their field to CRT's tenets because it's a viable "theoretical and conceptual tool that has the possibility of breaking open the frozen conversations and perspectives on race and racial analyses in education" (Ladson-Billings, Foreword vi). And I have to say, Alé, I have not yet worked at any single institution "where I have found as many as even three other colleagues who notice, much less speak out, against . . . everyday racist microaggressions . . . despite everyone's seeming incessant discussion of critical theories from postcolonialism/decolonization to intersectionality" (Kynard, "Teaching While Black" 2). And you see, without an activist-oriented heuristic and praxis, these theories just "become the stage for an academic performance, not a way of engaging the world and oppression in it" (2). As you well know, Alé, some of these well-meaning educators in our field like to think of racism—institutional and structural—as some "kind of general and generic racially divided world somewhere out there over the rainbow" (2). Yet you and I (and our students!) know damn well "there is never any moment when racism is subtle or exists as some kind of fine mist that is out there" on campuses for us! And this field surely needs "to stop talking about racism and institutions this way in our writing and to our students. Oppression could never work if it were invisible, unarticulated, or unfelt by [the folks] it targets. Bonilla-Silva's work on today's college undergraduate students' unwavering reproduction of color-blind racism seems everywhere replicated in our field" (3), and I ardently believe that a "misplaced faith in the progress of the field, shifting demographics at our colleges, or a naturally-occurring expiration of racism have left" too many inert, unconscious, and frozen in the conversations of their own racism-reproducing tendencies (3).

So here we arrive at education's CRT heuristic and praxis. Ultimately, the goal of CRT is social transformation, so education's CRT heuristic targets the social transformation of educational research, classrooms, curricula, policy, the study of knowledge (epistemology), and teaching (pedagogy) (Yosso, *Critical Race Counterstories* 8). Now, social transformation is where the real *work* of education is because this call to action *insists* that educational researchers change the *structures,* Alé, that prevent all students from receiving the same opportunities to learn and succeed. And as I'm sure you'll recognize, this heuristic is informed by and overlaps with CRT's tenets as it offers cogent guidelines to educators willing to traverse the bounds of their comfort and privilege to do the political work we must do that ruptures the "whiteness, racial violence, and the institutional racism of our disciplinary constructs" in rhetoric and writing studies (Kynard, "Teaching While Black" 1). To better illustrate how I myself have used the heuristic to frame my own crafting of curriculum, I'm attaching to this email for reference, my syllabus (Appendix D) for the most recent grad seminar I taught on the core subject of contemporary rhetorics.

Part one of this six-part heuristic states that educators should work from a premise that racism is prevalent in American society in general, and in education in particular. As you can easily infer, this guideline aligns with the CRT tenet asserting the permanence of race and racism. Applying this as a guiding heuristic, my course considers social constructs created by rhetoric(s), as they exist in cultural, historic, economic, and political contexts, and so the curriculum engages the production of knowledge as a raced (but also a gendered and ableist) but ultimately contested process with material consequences that have served to normalize and legitimize some while delegitimizing and even dehumanizing others. This premise that centralizes racism lends itself to the second part of the heuristic that calls on educators to question the dominant claims and discourses of their field(s). Again, in terms of CRT tenet alignment, this heuristic serves as a challenge to dominant ideologies, and my course very explicitly approaches the question of "contemporary rhetorics" with a cultural rhetorics–informed frame that offers students methods by which to analyze and critique whose voices and narratives have been centered, but also *why* and *how* (through processes of power linked to race, class, gender, and access) the rhetorical canon came to be (Cobos et al. 139–41).

Granted, these processes of power are contextually situated, so a CRT heuristic insists that educators historically ground their coursework, acknowledging the importance of context in establishing the permanence of race and racism (our country was founded in it!), interest convergence (whites will never allow progress for people of color if white self-interest is not also secured), and race as social construct, which so many cultural rhetorics account for. The fourth aspect of the heuristic calls on educators to aim for interdisciplinarity, drawing from a range of literatures, and of course this translates to the processes by which we select primary texts for our core courses. Alé, I very much appreciate your discussion concerning how you select and pair texts, and I too gravitate toward culling literatures from a variety of disciplines, especially as I build a frame with my students at the start of the semester that moves across disciplinary boundaries and invokes the strategies proposed by scholars in the 1960s that offered "new studies" that came to be known as black studies, Chicano studies, American Indian studies, Asian American studies, and women's studies. In each of these new scholarly traditions, the disciplinary boundaries were made permeable, and, as you'll see within the schedule of readings for the first few weeks of my course (Appendix D), history, sociology, rhetorical criticism, and the arts are tapped as important knowledge sources for framing analysis of texts and ensuing seminar discussions. This interdisciplinary approach insists that no one discipline can fully reveal the complexities of human experience, and amalgamations in our frames for textual analysis are thus all the more necessary (Ladson-Billings, Foreword vii).

As you've already discussed, I could easily provide primary texts and offer nothing other than directives that graduate students read them and arrive to seminar ready to discuss their interpretations. And this is a verifiable model employed in our undertheorized pedagogical approach to graduate education. But because I am of the same mind as you in wanting to extend (in my case, graduate level) education beyond just textual consumption, I build with students tools/skill sets for rhetorical criticism that I ask they in turn apply to our readings and analysis of theories and theorists. In fact,

I take inspiration from Jay Dolmage's disability studies–informed approach to the same methodological intent when he says,

> We need to search for the meanings hiding in texts and artifacts through submersion and subterfuge—and disability studies offers an ideal set of methodological tools for wading through this rhetoric. Most notably, [we will] channel disability studies methodologies of "reading" sideways, of searching for "crooked" meanings, of continually asking more questions around bodily values, of valuing the meaning that comes from bodily difference even as we recognize the ways that bodily difference is used to stigmatize, remove human rights, and relocate bodies. (*Disabled upon Arrival* 3)

The final guidelines within the heuristic are twin sides to the same coin. First, educators should centralize the experiences and perspectives of the minoritized, as a focal point—not a passing glance for a day's or week's thematic focus (e.g., African American Rhetorics day/week). As you can see (Appendix D), I make explicit selection of texts from minoritized perspectives, but my *arrangement* of said texts around thematic issues rather than race or ethnicity is informed by the final premise of the heuristic: educators should acknowledge and make themselves aware that there is diversity within experience. In the same way that neither you nor I would *ever* title a day or week (or even a whole course) "White Rhetorics"—although this descriptor is certainly warranted for much of what passes as core curriculum in this field—it is equally nonsensical, illogical, and just downright racist to do the same with other racial and ethnically identified authors/theorists. I don't need to tell you this, but not all scholars of color are concerned about the same issues, neither do they research and write about the same things. News flash, *lots* of differently raced folks in this field are concerned with literacy acquisition. So why not a few weeks dedicated to that thematic? Lots of differently raced folks are concerned with language and languaging; how about a week on that? Lots of differently raced folks (and differently gendered and abled too!) are concerned with access to institutions; how about several weeks on that? You get my point, but unfortunately too many in our field are still crafting curricula, especially within the core, with the same old tired-ass "plug-in ____ minoritized folks minimally here" model. And there's no longer an excuse.

But here again we arrive at the CRT praxis of counterstory that holds the potential to actually *move* us toward the social transformation of education. Beyond counterstory's ability to support students and teachers in understanding how minoritized communities experience and respond to racism as it intersects with other forms of subordination (arguably what assigning and reading primary texts from minoritized voices accomplishes), counterstory as a methodology is fundamental to educators' development of a critical race praxis (Yosso, *Critical Race Counterstories* 8, 14). Yosso has outlined this praxis as supplementary to CRT's heuristic, arguing that:

- Counterstories build community among those who have been marginalized within society, and communicate that we do not struggle alone.
- Counterstories challenge the perceived wisdom of those at society's center, and provide a context to understand and transform established belief systems.
- Counterstories nurture community cultural wealth, memory, and resistance. In affirming pedagogies and knowledges cultivated in minoritized communities, counterstories preserve community memory of the history of resistance to oppression.
- Counterstories facilitate transformation in education. (*Critical Race Counterstories* 14–15)

Counterstory, then, provides an active methodology to push back against the pull to "contribute to a kind of 'race-management science' in academia's (our home institutions and our field) embrace of our scholarship on race" that on the flip side of the same coin also attempts to censure or punish us for "speaking or writing against the ways our institutions actively reproduce inequality" (Kynard, "Teaching While Black" 3). Counterstory is a methodology of employing but also applying stories to and within curricula that move us to action. The reframing of our curricula with critical concepts and theory presented through counterstory is accessible for both teachers and students, and whether presented as primary texts within class or applied as a framework by teachers to transform curriculum, counterstories teach us that the "construction of another world—a socially and racially just world—is possible" (Yosso, *Critical Race Counterstories* 14–15).

And here's the thing, Alé—I don't have all the answers; I only have my experiences. "Over the years, I have developed my own definition of good teaching," and if I have learned anything at all, "it has to be that power and politics are not separate and different from teaching. They are the heart of it," and "we simply cannot avoid the nastiness of politics, because schools are the places where ideas are most likely to be contested" (Post 137). Several of my colleagues who identify as activists have confessed to me that they are too tired to fight the classroom- and field-specific battles. And if there's anything I can understand, it's what it feels like to be battered by resistant students and colleagues, yet I still do not understand why one would give up the fight (Post 137). But who knows, maybe we should publish this email exchange as Frankie and Vay did [see Chapter 1 note 13], and perhaps it will spark a broader fieldwide discussion about core curricula and pedagogy, ha! However, "if readers are not willing or able to put aside preconceptions and traditional paradigms and 'hear' the counterstories and challenges to the dominant discourse reflected in this work, they are likely to miss the point" (Dixson and Rousseau 3–4). Needless to say, it's high time we take up the good points you bring up concerning a critical re-envisioning of core curricula and extend this discussion to think through issues of graduate-level pedagogy as well. To quote from a source of my favorite counterstories: The Truth is out there.[5] And, "Yes, I believe in Truth with a capital *T*." As far as I'm concerned, "Truth is found in a perspective that sees both what the dominant discourse would have us see and what those who are outside and underneath see as well. Truth is a vision recorded with a wide-angle lens" (Post 138).

Chew on that for a bit and get back to me with your thoughts later. As for me, my back hurts, and I've already stayed up past my bedtime writing you this "essay of an email." You take good care, keep pushing, and hold your head high—you have no reason to do otherwise. *Adelante, y somos juntxs.*

Your friend,

V—

# Epilogue: Birth Song

> Mommy, tell me my baby story.
> —Olivia Isabel Martinez

### A STORY

IT WAS JANUARY WHEN I found out I was pregnant. I was eighteen and a first-year student in college. My mom didn't speak to me for two weeks. My gramma cried. "Not you," she said. "We wanted more for you."

I turned nineteen that April and thought, "Well, almost twenty, almost not a teen (mother)." And in September, *she* was born.

My pregnancy was harrowing—not because it was physically difficult but because it was emotionally devastating to come to terms with the fact that I would be a single mother. Her father, a boy I loved, a boy with whom I shared so many "firsts," would not be a father at all. He made sure I knew this in the most painful and abusive ways. His communication was clear. So, from January through to her September birth, I lived nine months in a suspended reality. A floating time of pain, torment, and depression—but also wonder. The little human growing inside me was a wonder.

In May, my gramma died, but before she left, she told me she saw my baby. She saw my child and knew this baby would have large eyes and curly dark hair. My baby would look like me. Their paths crossed as they made their way to and from this existence.

During the summer, my mom sent me off to San Diego to escape my daughter's father and the pain he was inflicting on me. I ran from his abuse into the arms of my cousin, who made space for me in her life to nest, to hide, and to heal. I found solace in an exhibit of medieval torture devices at a Balboa Park museum, and I visited it often. It was somehow comforting to walk slowly through the aisles of this twisted and spiked metal, and to know that my pain, my misery, did not compare to the excruciating torment the unlucky souls who were victims to these devices had to endure. It was also somehow a comfort to know the pain her father inflicted on me was not unique when here stood a museum exhibit filled with evidence people have intended harm to others for a very long time. This exhibit illustrated the cruelty humans are capable of. So, in a strange way, my time in San Diego had a healing effect. The distance helped. The sea air helped. The museum of torture helped. The embrace of a queer cousin and her strong womanist friends helped.

By August I returned to my home, and I resumed my life as a pregnant teen who also attended university. I began my second year of college in office hours with my professors, letting them know I would deliver within the next month, and planning for the projected two weeks I would allow myself to take off from courses—should they each agree this was an acceptable amount of time to be absent from class. They agreed.

I attended classes in big lecture halls, with an even bigger belly that made for a difficult time sidling into a seat along the crowded rows. I waddled around campus, my feet painfully swollen, and I endured blatant stares from the campus community. By this point, my ego was of little consideration; however, I could hardly escape noticing the looks people sent my way: fear from the women my age, pity from the women older than me, disgust from the men my age, indifference—if a glance at all—from the men older than me.

On the morning of September 22, I opened my eyes, and my water broke. It was time.

At the hospital, her father showed up; he demanded I give my baby his last name. My mom told him, "This isn't the time or place to discuss that." "Shut up. *You* shut up," he retorted. *Malcriado.* He was sure to squeeze my hand in the spot bruised from attempted IV needle insertions. He wanted me to feel pain because he felt no control. His grip on me was lessening and he knew it. And trickle by trickle—much like the trickle of the pain-relieving medication from the IV—the women of my life arrived: cousins, *tías,* friends, godmothers and grandmothers. Sixteen women filled my delivery room, and soon there was no more space for him; he was "suffocating," he said. They all "made him sick," he said. These women's collective energy pushed him to the margins of this space, snuffing out his assertion and rights to occupation; so he left.

And just like that, as if a pipe had unclogged, my stalled and excruciating labor progressed. The women of my life surrounded my bed and filled my room with prayer, song, energy, and pain relief. These important women held my legs, breathed with me, and gave me their strength. This space, this time, this sense of being was about women, our power and endurance and love, and within this most powerful of moments, she was born. Olivia. My baby girl, my daughter, my love. How could she be anything less than wonderful when she is so loved, so blessed, so empowered by the strength of those sixteen women who ushered her into this world? How could she be anything less?

In two weeks, as promised, I was back in classes, a new momma with a love and a vision. We've not looked back.

### A POEM

My grandmother saw you,
Olivia
The two of you passed each other,
in the darkness of the beyond
—as family often do—
one exiting the world, one entering.
And before she left,
she assured me
beyond my fear,
she assured me
of our love,
of our shared power
as women—
a power beyond hunger or hurt.

And although her time here
was at its end,
she bridged my time with you,
Olivia,
beyond the darkness,
into the light
of our love.

**A very honest declaration. By Olivia Isabel Martinez.**

# Afterword

Originating in legal studies and then moving on to studies in education, critical race theory (CRT) disrupts the racialized status quo through the crucial use of counterstory. Aja Y. Martinez presents the how and why counterstories work; she presents important examples that will help those of us working in rhetoric and writing studies to quit pretending as if the need is and has always been welcomed here. Rather than continuing to pretend that POC haven't always experienced racism, that racism hasn't always existed everywhere in this country, CRT affords us a crucial critical response in places like academia where few POC have been allowed by the dominant group. The core curriculum of many disciplines, like rhetoric and writing studies, has been expanding, becoming more inclusive, in recent decades, more diverse and democratic, but the struggle to open up academia continues. In rhetoric and writing studies, white people need to embrace counterstories and take responsibility for their own complicity in keeping the canon of our discipline narrow. Professors of rhetoric and writing, particularly in dealing with their graduate students, continue lacking the imagination to see counterstories as crucial to having a fuller picture of the past and of how to live in today's multidimensional world. POC have always desired a future where the fuller participation of everyone is respected and dignified, not just of those whose selfish interests are served by inequality and segregation. So while inequalities persist, counterstories represent one of the most important ways of opening up academia and challenging the status quo so as to disrupt the racism that continues keeping us apart.

In this fine work, *Counterstory: The Rhetoric and Writing of Critical Race Theory,* Martinez provides the field of rhetoric and writing studies with an invaluable gift—a deeper and a clearer understanding of how counterstories, based on the tenets of critical race theory, speak truth to power and work toward making the lives of POC more central in a more democratic society. Her work represents an incredible call to action, movingly advancing the idea that unless we rock our field from top to bottom, the inequalities and injustices resulting from racism will continue plaguing our nation and our world. Professor Martinez daringly believes, as do I, that rhetoric, as it currently operates in our field, is thoroughly imbricated and entangled with racism. Placing CRT and counterstories at the center of our field and making this our highest priority will not only eradicate racism but will also teach our students the value counterstories bring to such an important task. Her radical idea, based on the works of current and past CRT crits, is that we as a diverse people need counterstories, not just to tell our side of history, but to present a fuller and deeper story that reveals what has brought us together but, sadly, also what has kept us apart.

My own experience as a POC in this academic field and as a citizen of this country has certainly been significantly marked by racism. My attempts at introducing Chicanx counterstories have been disciplined and sanctioned by academic forces in my school in ways that have sought to protect the dominant group's power over what can be taught and how. In Texas these forces have held significant negative sway over the schooling of POC, infamously so. When we as Texas Mexicans are taught in our schools to remember the Alamo, it remains difficult educating our students, white and Mexican alike, of the racist complexities surrounding what happened in 1836. These complexities continue shaping Texas today, especially all along the borderlands, where we see the construction of a wall and the illegal detention of children in concentration camps. The myth that the United States is a beacon of hope is thus exposed as a lie and demands counterstories, from "your tired, your poor, / Your huddled masses yearning to breathe free," to explain where this country has gone astray because of racism. It's not just that the United States has turned its back on its democratic principles. The truth is that this country has never, ever held them closely. This must change. We as members of rhetoric and writing studies, through the gift Aja Y. Martinez presents here with this volume, have a way to enact—through counterstories—democratizing forces that promise to help bring this country and this academic discipline to be a better, freer land. So let us follow her lead and make of this world what we as deeply cultured human beings are capable of—the kindness that caring for others means by affording all stories a place at the table where all are welcomed, respected, and loved as equals.

Jaime Armin Mejía
Texas State University

## APPENDIX A: RACE CRITICAL THEORIES, CRITICAL RACE RHETORICS SYLLABUS

**Course Description**
"Race" in the United States is defined by societal structure, human representation, and cultural representation to form a "common sense" regarding racial order, meanings, and identity. Race is endemic; it is deeply ingrained in American life through historical consciousness and ideological choices that then influence and shape societal structures such as education. This course will review foundational race critical theories through to the emergence of critical race theory (CRT) from its origins in the field of law and through its development in civil rights scholarship and feminist thought. We will explore CRT's contemporary applications for analyzing overt and colorblind racist rhetorics and practices in academia, in the field of rhetoric and writing studies, and as it applies to identity, national politics, and institutional policy. While this course will clearly be focused on race, it will also—must also—include essays that consider the connections between race, gender, sexuality, and class inequalities. You are encouraged to make these connections, too. In our discussions and in addition to the primary texts, essays, and films we will use for this class, we will also draw from borderlands, Mestiza, feminist, queer, and disability rhetorics. Class will be conducted in a seminar format.

**Required Materials**
Crenshaw, Kimberlé, Neil Gotanda, Gary Peller, and Kendall Thomas, editors. *Critical Race Theory: The Key Writings that Formed the Movement.* New Press, 1995.
Delgado, Richard and Jean Stefancic, editors. *Critical Race Theory: The Cutting Edge,* 3rd ed. Temple UP, 2013.
Essed, Philomena, and David Theo Goldberg, editors. *Race Critical Theories: Text and Context.* Blackwell, 2001.

## Online Materials
Online materials can be found on our course site and are due to be read as indicated on our daily course syllabus.

## Suggested Materials
Bonilla-Silva, Eduardo. *Racism without Racists: Color-Blind Racism and the Persistence of Racial Inequality in America*, 5th edition. Rowman & Littlefield, 2017.

## Course Requirements
Required work [Assignment sheets, if any, will be located on our course website.]

## Reader Response (R&Rs)
This assignment will be due at the beginning of each class period from Week 2 through Week 14. Each week you will submit one question and one quotation from each of the assigned readings (**i.e., if three texts were assigned, you will have, at minimum, three quotations—one from each text**). You should pose open-ended questions that generate conversation and cannot be answered with a "yes" or "no." Your question can address a specific reading or a theme running through several readings. Quotations may be anything from the readings that resonate with you. Along with the quotation you will discuss why you find the quotation significant. Personal reflections that are connected with the readings/discussions are perfectly appropriate for this assignment.

## Rhetorical Précis and Discussion Facilitation of Assigned Reading
You are each expected to facilitate class discussion once in the semester. Signup will be during Week 2. I will provide a detailed assignment sheet on the course website. **You are required to meet with me in my office five days prior to your scheduled facilitation in order to discuss the approaches you are considering and any questions you may have.**
By the time of your scheduled facilitation you should have carefully and critically read through the week's readings. Before the day of your facilitation, you will submit to the course website a handout that includes rhetorical précis for the assigned readings/authors and an accompanying list of discussion questions. Finally, you should feel free to suggest up to twenty pages of additional readings for the class in anticipation of your own facilitation.

**Facilitation Reflection Paper**
A day or two after your facilitation, you will submit a two-page reflection paper about your experience. Include a short summary of the discussion, including the ways it did and did not go according to your plan. Again, I will provide a detailed assignment sheet for this assignment on our course website.

**Seminar Project**
One seminar project in critical race counterstory. Details forthcoming.

**Schedule**

**Week 1: Race Literacy, Race Rhetorics**
- General introductions and course description
- Tenets of rhetoric
- Quiz: Race Literacy
- Handout: Ten Things Everyone Should Know about Race

**Week 2: Foundational Theories, Defining Race and Racism, Part 1**
- Tatum, "Defining Racism: 'Can We Talk?'"
- Omi and Winant, "Racial Formation," with "Reflections on 'Racial Formation'"
- West, "A Genealogy of Modern Racism," with "Reflections on 'A Genealogy of Modern Racism'"
- Davis, "Education and Liberation: Black Woman's Perspective," with "Reflections on 'Education and Liberation'"

**Week 3: Foundational Theories, Defining Race and Racism, Part 2**
- Said, "Imaginative Geography and Its Representations," with "Reflections on 'Imaginative Geography and Its Representations'"
- Bhabha, "Of Mimicry and Man: The Ambivalence of Colonial Discourse," with "Reflections on 'Of Mimicry and Man'"
- Pérez, "Introduction"
- Pérez, "Sexing the Colonial Imaginary: (En)gendering Chicano History, Theory, and Consciousness"
- Mignolo, "Introduction: Coloniality, The Darker Side of Western Modernity"

**Week 4: Foundational Theories, Defining Race and Racism, Part 3**
- Hall, "Race, Articulation, and Societies Structured in Dominance," with "Reflections on 'Race, Articulation, and Societies Structured in Dominance'"
- Balibar, "The Nation Form: History and Ideology," with "Reflections on 'The Nation Form: History and Ideology'"

- Guha, "Preface to *Dominance without Hegemony: History and Power in Colonial India*," with "Reflections on 'Preface to *Dominance without Hegemony*'"
- Stoler, "Racial Histories and Their Regimes of Truth," with "Reflections on 'Racial Histories and Their Regimes of Truth'"

**Week 5: Foundational Theories, Defining Race and Racism, Part 4**
- Essed, "Everyday Racism: A New Approach to the Study of Racism," with "Reflections on 'Everyday Racism'"
- van Dijk, "Denying Racism: Elite Discourse and Racism," with "Reflections on 'Denying Racism'"
- Hill Collins, "Defining Black Feminist Thought," with "Reflections on 'Defining Black Feminist Thought'"
- Roediger, "Whiteness and Ethnicity in the History of 'White Ethnics' in the United States" with "Reflections on 'Whiteness and Ethnicity'"

Suggested Readings:
- Bonilla-Silva, "The Strange Enigma of Race in Contemporary America"
- ———. "The Central Frames of Color-Blind Racism"

**Week 6: Critical Race Theory: Its Origins and Histories**
- Martinez, "Critical Race Theory: Its Origins, History, and Importance to the Discourses and Rhetorics of Race"
- Bell, "Serving Two Masters: Integration Ideals and Client Interests in School Desegregation Litigation"
- Bell, "Brown v. Board of Education and the Interest Convergence Dilemma"
- Bell, "After We're Gone: Prudent Speculations on America in a Post-Racial Epoch"
- Delgado, "Liberal McCarthyism and the Origins of Critical Race Theory"

Suggested Readings:
- Crenshaw et al., foreword and introduction

**Week 7: CRT, an Introduction**
- Bell, "The Space Traders"
- Martinez, "Critical Race Theory Counterstory as Allegory: A Rhetorical Trope to Raise Awareness about Arizona's Ban on Ethnic Studies"
- Olivas, "The Chronicles, My Grandfather's Stories, and Immigration Law: The Slave Traders Chronicle as Racial History"
- Gotanda, "A Critique of 'Our Constitution Is Color-Blind'"

- Freeman, "Legitimizing Racial Discrimination through Antidiscrimination Law: A Critical Review of Supreme Court Doctrine"

**Week 8: Intersectionality**
- Combahee River Collective, "A Black Feminist Statement"
- Anzaldúa, *"La conciencia de la mestiza:* Toward a New Consciousness"
- Crenshaw, "Mapping the Margins: Intersectionality, Identity Politics, and Violence against Women of Color"
- Harris, "Race and Essentialism in Feminist Legal Theory"
- Caldwell, "A Hair Piece: Perspectives on the Intersection of Race and Gender"
- MacKinnon, "From Practice to Theory, or What Is a White Woman Anyway?"

**Week 9: Spring Break**

**Week 10: Critical Race Feminisms**
- Roberts, "Punishing Drug Addicts Who Have Babies: Women of Color, Equality, and the Right of Privacy"
- Evans, "Stealing Away: Black Women, Outlaw Culture, and the Rhetoric of Rights"
- Montoya, *"Máscaras, Trenzas, y Greñas*: (Un)Masking the Self while (Un)Braiding Latina Stories and Legal Discourse"
- Cho, "Converging Stereotypes in Racialized Sexual Harassment: Where the Model Minority Meets Suzie Wong"
- Rosales Arriola, "Of Women Born: Courage and Strength to Survive in the Maquiladoras of Reynosa and Río Bravo, Tamaulipas"

**Week 11: Beyond the Black-White Binary**
- Perea, "The Black/White Binary Paradigm of Race"
- Chang, "Toward an Asian American Legal Scholarship: Critical Race Theory, Post-Structuralism, and Narrative Space"
- Haney López, "Race and Erasure: The Salience of Race to Latinos/as"
- Ahmad, "A Rage Shared by Law: Post-September 11 Racial Violence as Crimes of Passion"
- Brooks and Widner, "In Defense of the Black-White Binary: Reclaiming a Tradition of Civil Rights Scholarship"
- Prewitt, "Racial Classifications in America: Where Do We Go from Here?"

**Week 12: Critical Whiteness Studies**
- Harris, "Whiteness as Property"
- Haney López, "White by Law"
- Ross, "Innocence and Affirmative Action"

- Wildman and Davis, "Language and Silence: Making Systems of Privilege Visible"
- Delgado, "Rodrigo's Portent: California and the Coming Neocolonial Order"
- Bell, "Property Rights in Whiteness: Their Legal Legacy, Their Economic Costs"

**Week 13: Counterstory: A Critical Race Methodology**
- Delgado, "Storytelling for Oppositionists and Others: A Plea for Narrative"
- Williams, "Alchemical Notes: Reconstructing Ideals from Deconstructed Rights"
- Solórzano and Yosso, "Critical Race Methodology: Counterstorytelling as an Analytical Framework for Education Research"
- Baszile, "Rhetorical Revolution: Critical Race Counterstorytelling and the Abolition of White Democracy"
- Martinez, "A Plea for Critical Race Counterstory: Stock Story vs. Counterstory Dialogues concerning Alejandra's 'Fit' in the Academy"
- Martinez, "Alejandra Writes a Book: A Critical Race Counterstory about Writing, Identity, and Being Chicanx in the Academy"

**Week 14: Seminar Project/Paper Workshops**
**Week 15: Writing Day**
**Week 16: Seminar Project/Final Paper Due**

## APPENDIX B: WRITING CRITICAL RACE COUNTERSTORY SYLLABUS

**Course Description**
Counterstory is a writing and research method of critical race theory, founded in creative nonfiction genres of oral history, slave narrative, and *testimonio*. As a narrative form, counterstory illuminates other(ed) perspectives about genre and dominant ideology, and functions as a method for social justice–oriented writers to intervene in and counter practices that dismiss or decenter racism and those whose lives are affected by it daily. Students will craft counterstories in genres of dialogue, autobiographic reflection, and allegory, based on personal experience and supported by data and literatures on their chosen topics.

This course will instruct on and concentrate on three genres of counterstory:
- Counterstory as dialogue
- Counterstory as narration
- Counterstory as allegory

Class sessions will alternate between:
- Discussion of varying examples of the three genres of counterstory, with examples to read by authors writing in these genres;
- Trying our hand at writing counterstory and sharing our drafts with one another through workshops—I am open to incorporating past writing projects into the genre specifications of counterstory.

**Course Materials**
Delgado, Richard, and Jean Stefancic. *Critical Race Theory: An Introduction,* 3rd edition. New York UP, 2017.

Online materials: Online materials can be found on our course site.

## Course Requirements

Required work [Assignment sheets, if any, will be located on our course site.]

## Reader Response (R&Rs)

This assignment will be conducted at the beginning of each class period. Within this assignment you will come up with a question and quotations from the assigned daily reading(s). You should pose open-ended questions that generate conversation and cannot be answered with a "yes" or "no." Your question can address a specific reading or a theme running through several readings. Quotations may be anything from the reading that resonate with you. Along with the quotation, write a paragraph or two explaining why you find the quotation significant. Personal reflections that are connected with the readings/discussions are perfectly appropriate for this assignment. An assignment sheet will be provided on the course site for further details.

## Writing Prompts and Exercises

I will hand out writing prompts each day that we will pursue through our specific writing sessions. I will make sure there are a variety of writing prompts available for you to choose from, and the prompts will tie into what we have been reading and learning about counterstory. However, these are "prompts," not must-do assignments, so you can feel free to depart from what I've suggested and pursue your own directions.

The prompts give you a chance to try your hand at different genres of counterstory and they push you to experiment with different forms and styles (keyed into the readings/examples of counterstory texts). These prompts also give you a body of writing to draw on as you think about your final projects. You will find that during the course of the week you may "hit upon" a rich vein of material or take a new direction in your writing that you did not anticipate.

I will give some time for writing in class (anywhere from 15–25 minutes). When we return from the writing sessions, we will have "read-arounds" (large and small group) where everyone reads a short excerpt or piece and specific workshop sessions where group members present a piece of writing they are developing for discussion and feedback.

**Final Course Project**

For the major course project, you will submit an extended piece or set of shorter pieces of counterstory. I will provide a specific assignment sheet midsemester so you can think about how to focus your project.

**Schedule**

**Week 1: Introduction to Class, Brief Introduction to Key Terms and Concepts, CRT, and a History of Counterstory**
- Delgado and Stefancic, "I. Introduction"
- Discussion, writing prompt(s)

**Week 2: CRT and Counterstory, a History**
- Delgado and Stefancic, "II. Hallmark Critical Race Theory Themes"
- Discussion, writing prompt(s)

**Week 3: CRT and Counterstory, a History**
- Delgado and Stefancic, "III. Legal Storytelling and Narrative Analysis"
- Delgado and Stefancic, "IV. Looking Inward"
- Cook, "Blurring the Boundaries: The Mechanics of Creating Composite Characters"
- Discussion, writing prompt(s)

**Week 4: Counterstory Genre, Part 1: Allegory and the Fantastic**
- Bell, "Introduction" from *And We Are Not Saved*
- Bell, "Prologue to Part I" from *And We Are Not Saved*
- Bell, "The Real Status of Blacks Today" from *And We Are Not Saved*
- Discussion, writing prompt(s)

**Week 5: Counterstory Genre, Part 1: Allegory and the Fantastic, cont.**
- Bell, "The Space Traders" from *And We Are Not Saved*
- Martinez, "Critical Race Theory Counterstory as Allegory: A Rhetorical Trope to Raise Awareness about Arizona's Ban on Ethnic Studies"
- "Men against Fire," from *Black Mirror*, Season 3, Episode 5 (available on Netflix)
- Discussion, writing prompt(s)

**Week 6: Counterstory Genre, Part 1: Allegory and the Fantastic, cont.**
- Prepare your CRT allegory draft for in-class workshop
- Prepare your CRT allegory draft for writing read-arounds

**Week 7: Counterstory Genre, Part 1: Allegory and the Fantastic, cont.**
- CRT allegory read-arounds and peer discussion/feedback
- CRT allegory final counterstory due

## Week 8: CRT and Counterstory, a History
- Delgado and Stefancic, "V. Power and the Shape of Knowledge"
- Delgado and Stefancic, "VI. Critiques and Responses to Criticism"
- Discussion, writing prompt(s)

## Week 9: Counterstory Genre, Part 2: Dialogue
- Delgado, "Storytelling for Oppositionists and Others: A Plea for Narrative"
- Martinez, "A Plea for Critical Race Theory Counterstory: Stock Story versus Counterstory Dialogues concerning Alejandra's 'Fit' in the Academy"
- Discussion, writing prompt(s)

## Week 10: Counterstory Genre, Part 2: Dialogue
- Prepare your CRT dialogue draft for in-class workshop
- Prepare your CRT dialogue draft for writing read-arounds

## Week 11: Counterstory Genre, Part 2: Dialogue, cont.
- CRT dialogue read-arounds and peer discussion/feedback
- CRT Dialogue final counterstory due

## Week 12: Thanksgiving Break

## Week 13: Counterstory Genre, Part 3: Narration and Chronicle
- Williams, "Excluding Voices: A Necklace of Thoughts on the Ideology of Style" from *The Alchemy of Race and Rights*
- Martinez, "Alejandra Writes a Book: A Critical Race Counterstory about Writing, Identity, and Being Chicanx in the Academy"

## Week 14: Counterstory Genre, Part 2: Narration and Chronicle, cont.
- Gonzalez, "21 Miles of Scenic Beauty . . . and Then Oxnard"
- Gonzalez, "Boxnard"
- Gonzalez, "Forget Microsoft Word"
- Gonzalez, "35¢ Sodas"
- Discussion, writing prompt(s)
- Prepare your CRT narrative/chronicle draft for in-class workshop

## Week 15: Counterstory Genre, Part 3: Narration and Chronicle, cont.
- Prepare your CRT narrative/chronicle draft for writing read-arounds
- CRT narrative/chronicle read-arounds and peer discussion/feedback

## Week 16
- CRT narrative/chronicle final counterstory due

## APPENDIX C: HISTORIES AND THEORIES OF RHETORIC(S)—OR, WHOSE TRUTH IS TRUE? SYLLABUS

**Course Description**
This course will interrogate rhetorical studies' central concept of "truth," through surveys of contextually situated topics such as histories of rhetoric, literacy, social turns, and activism. Considering social constructs created by rhetoric(s), as they exist in cultural, historic, economic, and political contexts, students will engage the production of knowledge as a raced, gendered, ableist and contested process with material consequences that has served to normalize and legitimize some while delegitimizing and even dehumanizing others. In all, this course examines difference and power as rhetoric is practiced across time, cultures, and publics.

Students will have the opportunity to practice rhetorical criticism, analytical and creative thinking, multimodal writing, and oral communication skills. This course is reading- and writing-intensive, and class participation is required.

**Required Materials**
Bizzell, Patricia, and Bruce Herzberg, editors. *The Rhetorical Tradition: Readings from Classical Times to the Present*, 2nd ed. Bedford/St. Martin's, 2001.
Foss, Sonja K. *Rhetorical Criticism: Exploration and Practice*, 5th ed. Waveland Press, 2017.

Online materials can be found on our course site and are due to be read as indicated on our daily course schedule.

**Course Requirements**
Required work [Assignment sheets, if any, will be located on our course website.]

### Reader Responses (R&Rs)

This assignment will be due at the beginning of each class period from Week 2 through Week 13. Each week you will submit one typed question and two typed quotations from the assigned readings. You should pose open-ended questions that generate conversation and cannot be answered with "yes" or "no." Your question can address a specific reading or a theme running through several readings. Quotations may be anything from the readings that resonate with you. Along with the quotation, write a paragraph or two explaining why you find the quotation significant. Personal reflections that are connected with the readings/discussions are perfectly appropriate for this assignment.

### Rhetorical Criticism

Due at the end of Week 6 and the beginning of Week 12 is a 5- to 6-page short essay of rhetorical criticism that will build toward your multimodal seminar project. Each essay will undergo a writing process in which you will submit a first draft to me on the course site for feedback, in addition to a draft for in-class peer review. Final papers will not be accepted without documented submission of first drafts, and grades are determined based on evidence of significant revision between first draft and final paper.

### Multimodal Seminar Project

At the conclusion of the semester, you will present a project which you build on your arguments and writing from your R&Rs, rhetorical criticism assignments, and other social media and media-oriented forms of documentation used throughout the course. In this assignment you will weave references to our readings, your own writing and documenting, and class discussions together to form an argument that you will also present in class. Additional details forthcoming.

### Schedule

#### Week 1: Whose Rhetoric?
- Heinrichs, "Introduction: Open Your Eyes"
- Booth, "How Many 'Rhetorics'?"
- Foss, "Introduction," and "The Nature of Rhetorical Criticism: Rhetoric"
- Bizzell and Herzberg, "General Introduction"
- Kennedy, "Traditional and Conceptual Rhetoric"

**Week 2: The Rhetorical Tradition or the *Euro-Western* Rhetorical Tradition?**
- Chávez, "Beyond Inclusion: Rethinking Rhetoric's Historical Narrative"
- Glenn, "Mapping the Silences, or Remapping Rhetorical Territory"
- Dolmage, "Disability Studies of Rhetoric"
- Baca, "Preface" and *'te-ixtli:* The 'Other Face' of the Americas"
- Gilyard, "Introduction: Aspects of African American Rhetoric as a Field"
- Mao and Young, "Performing Asian American Rhetoric into the American Imaginary"

**Week 3: Practicing Rhetorical Criticism, an Introduction**
- Foss, "The Nature of Rhetorical Criticism: Rhetorical Criticism"
- Foss, "Doing Rhetorical Criticism"
- Foss, "Neo-Aristotelian Criticism: Genesis of Rhetorical Criticism"

**Week 4: Whose Truth? Or, It's All Sophistry!**
- Bizzell and Herzberg, "Classical Rhetoric: Introduction"
- Anonymous, "Dissoi Logoi"
- Plato, "Phaedrus"
- Foss, "Ideological Criticism"
- Gorgias, "Encomium of Helen"
- Isocrates, "Against the Sophists"

**Week 5: Rhetorical Women, Interstices of Rhetoric**
- Foss, "Feminist Criticism"
- Glenn, "Classical Rhetoric Conceptualized, or Vocal Men and Muted Women"
- Bizzell and Herzberg, "Aspasia"
- Christine de Pizan, from *The Book of the City of Ladies*
- Margaret Fell, "Women's Speaking Justified, Proved, and Allowed by the Scriptures"
- Sor Juana Inés de la Cruz, "The Poet's Answer to the Most Illustrious Sister Filotea de la Cruz"

**Week 6: Rhetorical Criticism 1 Due**

**Week 7: The Enlightenment Era: An Imperative for Racial Rhetorical Criticism**
- Flores, "Between Abundance and Marginalization: The Imperative of Racial Rhetorical Criticism"
- Bizzell and Herzberg, "Enlightenment Rhetoric: Introduction"
- West, "A Genealogy of Modern Racism"
- Jefferson, from "Notes on the State of Virginia"

- Locke, from "An Essay Concerning Human Understanding"
- Hume, "Of the Standard of Taste"

**Week 8: Rhetorics, Literacies, and Access**
- Foss, "Generative Criticism"
- Bizzell and Herzberg, "The Rhetorics of Men of Color"
- Jackson, "When Will We All Matter: A Frank Discussion of Progressive Pedagogy"
- Du Bois, "Double Consciousness"
- Smitherman, "From Africa to the New World and into the Space Age: Introduction and History of Black English Structure"
- Pritchard, "Yearning to Be What We Might Have Been: Queering Black Male Feminism"

**Week 9: Spring Break**

**Week 10: Through the Lens of Survivance—Cultural Rhetorics**
- Villanueva, "Rhetoric of the First 'Indians': The Taínos of the Second Voyage of Columbus"
- Driskill, "Decolonial Skillshares: Indigenous Rhetorics as Radical Practice"
- Castillo, from "Massacre of the Dreamers"
- Anzaldúa, "Borderlands/La Frontera"
- The Cultural Rhetorics Theory Lab, "Our Story Begins Here: Constellating Cultural Rhetorics"
- Cobos et al., "Interfacing Cultural Rhetorics: A History and a Call"

**Week 11: Cultural Rhetorics in Practice**
- Foss, "Narrative Criticism"
- Sano-Franchini, "Cultural Rhetorics and the Digital Humanities: Toward Cultural Reflexivity in Digital Making"
- Haas, "Wampum as Hypertext: An American Indian Intellectual Tradition of Multimedia Theory and Practice"
- Faris, "How to Be Gay with Locative Media: The Rhetorical Work of Grindr as a Platform"
- Banks, "Groove: Synchronizing African American Rhetoric and Multimedia Writing through the Digital Griot"
- Kennedy, "Designing for Human-Machine Collaboration: Smart Hearing Aids as Wearable Technologies"

**Week 12: Rhetorical Criticism 2 due**

**Week 13: Cultural Rhetorics in Practice**
- Pandey, "Departures and Returns: Literacy Practices across Borders"
- Ong, "Transnational Asian American Rhetoric as a Diasporic Practice"

- Alvarez, "Brokering the Immigrant Bargain: Second-Generation Immigrant Youth Negotiating Transnational Orientations to Literacy"
- Kynard, "Stayin Woke: Race-Radical Literacies in the Makings of a Higher Education"
- Ore, "Whiteness as Racialized Space: Obama and the Rhetorical Constraints of Phenotypical Blackness"
- Martinez, "The Responsibility of Privilege"

**Week 14: Historical Rhetorics in Action and Practice**
- Truth, "Ain't I a Woman?"
- Malcolm X, "The Ballot or the Bullet"
- Carmichael, "Black Power"
- "The Black Panthers' Ten-Point Plan"
- Combahee River Collective, "A Black Feminist Statement"
- Davis, "Rape, Racism and the Myth of the Black Rapist"
- Alexander, "The New Jim Crow"

**Week 15: Seminar Project Draft 1 Due**
**Week 16: Seminar Project Final Paper Due**

# APPENDIX D: CONTEMPORARY RHETORICS—CULTURAL RHETORICS SYLLABUS

**Course Description**
Drawing primarily from ethnic studies, disability studies, queer theory, and feminist rhetorical theories, we will interrogate rhetorical studies' central concept of "truth," through a survey of situated histories and theories of contemporary (1960s–present day) rhetorical studies. Considering social constructs created by rhetoric(s), as they exist in cultural, historic, economic, and political contexts, we will engage the production of knowledge as a raced, gendered, ableist and contested process with material consequences that has served to normalize and legitimize some while de-legitimizing and even dehumanizing others. In all, this course examines difference and power as rhetoric is practiced across cultures and publics.

**Course Materials**
We will read excerpted journal articles or book chapters/essays located on our online course site.

**Recommended Books**
Dolmage, Jay Timothy. *Disabled upon Arrival: Eugenics, Immigration, and the Construction of Race and Disability.* Ohio State UP, 2018.
Foss, Sonja K. *Rhetorical Criticism: Exploration and Practice*, 5th ed. Waveland Press, 2017.

**Course Requirements**
Required work [Assignment sheets, if any, will be located on our course website.]

**Reader Response (R&Rs)**
This assignment will be due at the beginning of each class period from Week 2 through Week 14. Each week you will submit one question and one quotation from each of the assigned readings (i.e., if three texts were assigned, you will have, at minimum, three quotations—one from each text). You should pose open-ended questions that generate conversation and cannot be answered with a "yes" or "no." Your question can address a specific reading or a theme running through several readings. Quotations

may be anything from the readings that resonate with you. Along with the quotation you will discuss why you find the quotation significant. Personal reflections that are connected with the readings/discussions are perfectly appropriate for this assignment.

**Rhetorical Précis and Discussion Facilitation of Assigned Reading**
You are each expected to facilitate class discussion once in the semester. Signup will be during Week 2. I will provide a detailed assignment sheet on the course website. You are required to meet with me in my office five days prior to your scheduled facilitation in order to discuss the approaches you are considering and any questions you may have. By the time of your scheduled facilitation you should have carefully and critically read through the week's readings. Before the day of your facilitation, you will submit to the course website a handout that includes rhetorical précis for the assigned readings/authors and an accompanying list of discussion questions. Finally, you should feel free to suggest up to twenty pages of additional readings for the class in anticipation of your own facilitation.

**Facilitation Pedagogical Reflection Paper**
A day or two after your facilitation, you will submit a 2-page reflection paper about your experience, focusing specifically on pedagogy. Include a short summary of the discussion, including the ways it did and did not go according to your plan. Again, I will provide a detailed assignment sheet for this assignment on our course website.

**Seminar Project**
You will have two options for the seminar project: (1) A literature review of a rhetorical studies narrative of your choosing, or (2) a syllabus, with an accompanying theoretical framework, for a rhetorical studies core course. Details forthcoming.

**Schedule**

**Week 1: The Politics of Historiography**
- "The Politics of Historiography"
- "Octalog II"
- Brooks, "Reviewing and Redescribing 'The Politics of Historiography': Octalog I 1988"
- "Octalog III"
- "Rhetorical Historiography and the Octalogs"

**Week 2: Defining Terms, Constructing Analytic Frameworks, Part 1**
- Dolmage, "Introduction: Immigration Has Never Been about Immigration"
- Perez, "Sexing the Colonial Imaginary"
- Combahee River Collective, "A Black Feminist Statement"
- Flores, "Between Abundance and Marginalization"
- Foss, "The Nature of Rhetorical Criticism"
- Foss, "Doing Rhetorical Criticism"

**Week 3: Defining Terms, Constructing Analytic Frameworks, Part 2**
- Booth, "How Many Rhetorics"
- Ratcliffe, "Rhetorical Listening: A Trope for Interpretive Invention and a 'Code of Cross-Cultural Conduct'"
- Gilyard, "Introduction: Aspects of African American Rhetoric as a Field"
- Driskill, "Decolonial Skillshares: Indigenous Rhetorics as Radical Practice"
- Baca, *"te-ixtli:* The 'Other Face' of the Americas"
- Mao and Young, "Performing Asian American Rhetoric into the American Imaginary"
- Dolmage, "Disability Studies of Rhetoric"

**Week 4: Rhetorics of Queer World-Making**
- Cox and Faris, "An Annotated Bibliography of LGBTQ Rhetorics," pp. 1–11
- Chávez, "The Differential Visions of Queer Migration Manifestos"
- Chávez, "Homonormativity and Violence against Immigrants"
- Pritchard, "Yearning to Be What We Might Have Been: Queering Black Male Feminism"
- Pritchard, "Black Girls Queer (Re)Dress: Fashion as Literacy Performance in *Pariah*"
- Craig, "Courting the Abject: A Taxonomy of Black Queer Rhetoric"

Suggested Readings:
- Pritchard, "Grace Jones, Afro Punk, and Other Fierce Provocations: An Introduction to 'Sartorial Politics, Intersectionality, and Queer Worldmaking'"
- Pritchard, "Black Supernovas: Black Gay Designers as Critical Resource for Contemporary Black Fashion Studies"

**Week 5: Rhetorics of Access and Embodiment**
- Ribero, "Citizenship" from *Decolonizing Rhetoric and Composition Studies*

- Chávez, "The Body: An Abstract and Actual Rhetorical Concept"
- Dolmage, "Ellis Island and the Inventions of Race and Disability"
- Licona, "Borderland Rhetorics and Third-Space Sites"
- Licona, "Embodied Intersections: Reconsidering Subject Formation and Binary Bodies"
- Licona and Luibhéid, "The Regime of Destruction: Separating Families and Caging Children"

Suggested Readings:
- Maldonado, Licona, and Hendricks, "Latin@ Immobilities and Altermobilities within the US Deportability Regime"

**Week 6: Digital Rhetorics, Technologies, and New Media**
- Haas, "Wampum as Hypertext: An American Indian Intellectual Tradition of Multimedia Theory and Practice"
- Banks, "Scratch: Two Turntables and a Storytelling Tradition" and "Groove: Synchronizing African American Rhetoric and Multimedia Writing Through the Digital Griot" from *Digital Griots*
- Faris, "How to Be Gay with Locative Media: The Rhetorical Work of Grindr as a Platform"
- Kennedy, "Designing for Human-Machine Collaboration: Smart Hearing Aids as Wearable Technologies"
- Dolmage, "Technologies of Immigration Restriction"
- Boyle, "Introduction: Questions Concerning the Practice of Rhetoric" from *Rhetoric as Posthuman Practice*

**Week 7: Rhetorical Literacies: Rhetorical Situations for Learning**
- Alvarez, "Literacy" from *Decolonizing Rhetoric and Composition Studies*
- Alvarez, "Brokering the Immigrant Bargain: Second-Generation Immigrant Youth Negotiating Transnational Orientations to Literacy"
- Pandey, "Departures and Returns: Literacy Practices across Borders" from *South Asian in the Mid-South: Migrations of Literacies*
- Nordquist, Introduction and "Literacy in Place and Motion" from *Literacy and Mobility*
- Winn, "Building a 'Lifetime Circle': English Education in the Age of #BlackLivesMatter"
- Kynard, "Stayin Woke: Race-Radical Literacies in the Makings of a Higher Education"

Suggested Readings:
- Winn, "Toward a Restorative English Education"
- Winn and Behizadeh, "The Right to Be Literate: Literacy, Education, and the School-to-Prison Pipeline"

**Week 8: Rhetorics of Race, Racism, and Whiteness**
- Villanueva, "On the Rhetoric and Precedents of Racism"
- Schell, "Racialized Rhetorics of Food Politics: Black Farmers, the Case of Shirley Sherrod, and Struggle for Land Equity and Access"
- Ore, "Whiteness as Racialized Space: Obama and the Rhetorical Constraints of Phenotypical Blackness" from *Rhetorics of Whiteness*
- Engles, "Racialized Slacktivism: Social Media Performances of White Antiracism"
- Martinez, "The Responsibility of Privilege" from *Rhetorics of Whiteness*
- Sanchez, "Trump, the KKK, and the Versatility of White Supremacy Rhetoric"

**Week 9: Spring Break**

**Week 10: Decolonial Rhetorics, Cultural Rhetorics**
- Ruiz and Sánchez, "Introduction: Delinking" from *Decolonizing Rhetoric and Composition Studies*
- Cultural Rhetorics Theory Lab, "Our Story Begins Here: Constellating Cultural Rhetorics"
- Villanueva, "Rhetoric of the First 'Indians': The Taínos of the Second Voyage of Columbus" from *Rhetorics of the Americas*
- Ong, "Transnational Asian American Rhetoric as a Diasporic Practice"
- Sano-Franchini, "Cultural Rhetorics and the Digital Humanities: Toward Cultural Reflexivity in Digital Making"
- Cobos et al., "Interfacing Cultural Rhetorics: A History and a Call"

**Week 11: Rhetorics of Access and "Diversity"**
- Ahmed, "The Language of Diversity"
- Kerschbaum, "The Market for Diversity in Higher Education"
- Dolmage, "Eating Rhetorical Bodies"
- Wood, "Rhetorical Disclosures: The Stakes of Disability Identity in Higher Education"
- Walters, "Defining a Rhetoric of Touch"
- Hitt, "Rhetorical Identification across Difference and Disability"

**Week 12: The Future of Contemporary Rhetorics: Looking Back toward Looking Forward, Part 1**
- Burke, "Traditional Principles of Rhetoric" from *A Rhetoric of Motives*
- Berlin, "Revisionary Histories of Rhetoric: Politics, Power, and Plurality"
- Vitanza, "Taking A-Count of a (Future Anterior) History of Rhetoric as 'Libidinalized Marxism' (A PM Pastiche)"

- Borrowman et al., "Introduction: At the Conjunction of Rhetoric and Composition—the Contributions of Theresa J. Enos"
- Miller, "The Impossible Rhetoric: The Impossible Composition"
- Crowley, "Pure Rhetoric"

**Week 13: The Future of Contemporary Rhetorics: Looking Back toward Looking Forward, Part 2**

- Cortez, "History" from *Decolonizing Rhetoric and Composition Studies*
- Chávez, "Beyond Inclusion: Rethinking Rhetoric's Historical Narrative"
- Martinez, "Core-Coursing Counterstory: On Master Narrative Histories of Rhetorical Studies Curricula"
- Wetherbee Phelps, "Traveling Time's Arrow in Rhetoric and Composition: The Janus Face of Doctoral Education"
- Vitanza, "An After/Word: Preparing to Meet the Faces That 'We' Will Have Met"

**Week 14: Seminar Project/Paper Workshops**
**Week 15: Writing Day**
**Week 16: Seminar Project/Final Paper Due**

# NOTES

**Prologue: Encomium of a Storyteller**
1. *Prieto* translates to "dark" or "dark-skinned." As a surname for my composite character, I refer to my grandfather's beautiful chocolate-brown skin—skin he jokes arrived at this hue from "drinking lots of coffee" as a child.
2. There's even a hot sauce by this name!
3. The details here are fuzzy in my family's collective memory. Depending on which tía or tío you ask, Nana Ignacia was either stolen/kidnapped by Victoriano and the Leyva family, or she was given to Victoriano as settlement of a gambling debt. Either way, she was treated like property.

**Chapter 1. A Case for Counterstory**
1. Publishing reader reviews of counterstory is a practice of CRT. Notably, in *The Alchemy of Race and Rights* Patricia J. Williams has composed a composite reader review letter from a journal in which she "carefully crafted and paraphrased . . . rejection after rejection after rejection" (214). If anything, the public sharing of reader reviews/rejections of counterstory maps an interdisciplinary academic tradition of resistance to this methodology.
2. Specific to rhetoric, writing, and literacy studies, Kynard has written and taught extensively about critical race theory and often deploys the methodology of counterstory in her own writing and as assignments for her students' writing. See, particularly, her meticulous websites, *Education, Liberation and Black Radical Traditions for the Twenty-First Century: Carmen Kynard's Teaching and Research Site on Race, Writing, and the Classroom* and *Real Writing: Writing Courses with Dr. Carmen Kynard, PhD.*
3. In "Blind: Talking about the New Racism," Victor Villanueva discusses Kenneth Burke's four master tropes that frame analysis of rhetoric's epistemological "truths" (5). Extending Villanueva's ap-

plication of Burke's tropes toward analysis of color-blind racist language, I have defined and discussed Bonilla-Silva's frames of abstract liberalism, naturalization of race, cultural racism, and minimization of racism as tropes in application to an analysis of color-blind writing produced by Chicanx FYW students ("The American Way"). See also Asao B. Inoue's *Antiracist Writing Assessment Ecologies* for a discussion concerning tropes of color blindness and white habitus particularly as applied to writing assessment practices.

4. Cornel West in his "A Genealogy of Modern Racism" traces the emergence of "the idea of white supremacy within the modern discourse in the West," and asserts that "it is important to note that the idea of white supremacy not only was accepted by [prominent Enlightenment figures such as Montesquieu, Voltaire, Kant, Jefferson, and Hume], but, more important, it was accepted by them *without their having to put forward their own arguments to justify it*" (105; emphasis in original).

5. See also Bonilla-Silva's trope of "minimization of racism" (77).

6. Many race theorists would cite W. E. B. Du Bois's articulation of double consciousness as perhaps the earliest expression of intersecting identity categories; however, I contend Truth's description not only predates Du Bois's conception but is inherently critical race feminist.

7. See Delgado and Stefancic's *Critical Race Theory: An Introduction*. This text is in its third edition and is integral to my own undergraduate writing/rhetoric/research methods course, "Writing Critical Race Counterstory." (See Appendix B for a course syllabus.)

8. For a recent rhetoric and writing studies example see the WPA listserv.

9. By *major* I mean loudest, most readily cited, and most prominently containing a general thematic of critique categories. For parties interested in critiques beyond Kennedy's and Farber and Sherry's, Delgado and Stefancic dedicate an entire chapter of their textbook *Critical Race Theory: An Introduction* to additional critiques of CRT. Included at the conclusion of their "Chapter VI: Critiques and Responses to Criticism" is a cited list of additional critiques and CRT responses. Prendergast also discusses critiques of counterstory—particular of Williams's, which I'll expand upon in Chapter 4—in which these narratives are accused of being self-indulgent, paranoid, methodologically nonchalant, and inclusive of personal irrelevancies that invite readers to dismiss authors and their scholarship (53).

10. As Yosso notes, composite counterstories integrate at least four data sources: (1) empirical research data (e.g., findings from surveys, focus groups, etc.); (2) existing social science, humanities, legal, or other literature on the topic(s) evidenced in the research; (3) judicial records (court filings, rulings, oral arguments); and (4) author's professional and personal experiences (*Critical Race Counterstories* 11).
11. See Martinez, "Critical Race Counterstory as Allegory," "A Plea for Critical Race Theory Counterstory," "Alejandra Writes a Book," and "Core-Coursing Counterstory."
12. With particular importance to rhetoric and writing studies, Frankie Condon has explored this genre of antiracist epistolary or "a series of letters to tell a story" (Solórzano, "Critical Race Theory's Intellectual Roots" 48) in an exchange with Vershawn Ashanti Young as the final chapter in her book *I Hope I Join the Band: Narrative, Affiliation, and Antiracist Rhetoric.*

## Chapter 2. Richard Delgado and Counterstory as Narrated Dialogue

1. In the dedication of their *Handbook of Critical Race Theory in Education*, Marvin Lynn and Adrienne D. Dixson name Bell the "Father of Critical Race Theory."
2. Concerning the importance of perspective, Derrick Bell has remarked, "Indeed, even a critical race theory critic finds that the 'clearest unifying theme' of the writing is 'a call for a change of perspective, specifically, a demand that racial problems be viewed from the perspective of minority groups, rather than a white perspective'" ("Who's Afraid" 907–8).

## Chapter 3. Derrick Bell and Counterstory as Allegory/Fantasy

1. According to Delgado and Stefancic in their introduction to *The Derrick Bell Reader*, "Bell resigned his position as dean when he and his faculty found themselves in fundamental disagreement over the hiring of a young Asian American teaching candidate, whom the appointments committee had listed *third* in a list of over one hundred candidates for an open teaching position. When the top two candidates declined, instead of offering the position to the Asian woman, the committee convinced a majority of faculty to reopen the search. Knowing she was fully qualified and convinced that hiring the school's first Asian American law professor was the right thing to do, Bell announced his resignation effective at the end of the school year" (10; emphasis mine).

2. The website of the late white supremacist conservative activist Andrew Breitbart.
3. In the preface to *Faces at the Bottom of the Well,* Bell says he learned and adopted this motto from Mrs. Biona MacDonald, an elder and civil rights organizer in Mississippi. Bell met and worked with Mrs. MacDonald during his years with the NAACP Legal Defense Fund (xxiv–xxv). See also Carmen Kynard's discussion of Bell and Mrs. MacDonald in "Remembering Nelson Mandela and Racial Realism."
4. Even if you've not read Alexander's book (which you should), you may have otherwise encountered Alexander and her book's argument, both prominently featured in the framing of Ava DuVernay's important and critically acclaimed film *13th*.
5. Introducing her in *And We Are Not Saved,* Bell describes Geneva Crenshaw as a "former civil rights lawyer who was injured while working in Mississippi during the late '60s and who has only recently recovered from a long coma. She awakens with tremendous insight." Continuing, Bell says, "Another question I get is why did I choose a black woman. The answer is that I couldn't imagine anybody else. Women, in particular, bring to life a very special strength and understanding about what this is all about. It just seemed very natural that Geneva, who is black, well over 6 feet tall and very striking, is the kind of individual who would be almost a modern-day prophet of the racial condition. In many stories, I'm the traditional, integration-oriented civil rights lawyer, and she's the one who's prodding me to get with it" (qtd. in Goldberg 58).
6. For more on the historically pedagogical nature of CRT and counterstory, and their implications within rhetoric and writing studies, see Chapter 5.
7. Further affirming the pedagogical significance of Bell's allegories and parables, Alexander relates her first encounter with counterstory as a Stanford Law student in 1992, when *Faces* was originally published: "I remember being confused when I first read Bell's short stories as a law student. I was stunned not only by the content but also by the simplicity of the parables. Why would a renowned constitutional law scholar choose to write bizarre fictional dialogues involving an imaginary alter ego? Why were the stories written in such a simple, straightforward fashion using language an eighth grader could understand? Weren't law professors supposed to write stuff that only other academics could comprehend? I will confess that I didn't fully appreciate the genius and power of these stories until I

began discussing and debating them with others inside and outside classrooms. For many of my law school classmates—especially those of us who were black and brown—the parables functioned like a key to a secret door that we did not know had been locked within us. Once the door was opened, we found ourselves sharing our own stories, personal experiences with race and racism, including generational pain and trauma many of which we had not had the courage to reveal before. And many of us began asking questions out loud that had been buried deep within us, locked away out of necessity or convenience or habit. . . . Back then, in 1992, when this book was originally released, the mere act of telling stories that challenged the assumption of neutrality in the law or that questioned the utility of law, litigation, or policy reform was deemed a radical, subversive act in many law schools . . . and I remember well the battles that raged among faculty members, as well as students, regarding whether and to what extent Bell's claims (and the entire field of critical race theory) ought to be taken seriously. . . . Here we are, twenty-five years later. Bell's commitment to storytelling is no longer controversial in the legal academy. Women, Latinx, and queer scholars have found their voice in legal scholarship in no small part because of the doors Derrick Bell threw wide open" (xi–xiii).
8. See Chapter 1, "A Caveat Concerning Composite Compositions."
9. Octalogs II (1997) and III (2011). Coincidentally, I was asked to participate in CCCC 2020's Octalog IV.
10. In many rhetorical studies/theories graduate courses.
11. Theresa Jarnagin Enos, as editor of *Rhetoric Review,* organized the 1988 Octalog and published the position statements, the conference panel proceedings, and reflective statements by the original eight in the journal.
12. Anthony Squiers, in "A Critical Response to Heidi M. Silcox's 'What's Wrong with Alienation?'" discusses epic theater as Brecht's proposal that a play should not cause the spectator to identify emotionally with the characters or action before them, but should instead provoke rational self-reflection and a critical view of the action on the stage. Brecht thought that the experience of a climactic catharsis of emotion left an audience complacent. Instead, he wanted his audiences to adopt a critical perspective in order to recognize social injustice and exploitation and be moved to go forth from the theater and effect change in the world outside. For this purpose, Brecht employed the use of techniques that remind the spectator that the play is a representation of reality and not reality itself,

techniques that lend themselves well to an allegory/fantasy counterstory.
13. This unseen audience, these shadowy figures, represent the audiences a writer cannot possibly know. Unless I am cited or someone emails or approaches me about my work, I continuously wonder who will read my work, who will engage it—but you never quite know. Who is your audience? There is the intended audience, but then there's the reach audience. And then there's the audience of those you teach, and how you craft your course may not be the course any of the Eight might teach on the same question of rhetorical histories and theories. Thus, the audience is a shape, but a shadow as well.
14. Extending the concept of Self as a metaphor, I find the Cultural Rhetoric Theory Lab's (CRTL) description of their composite character "Niij" helpful in explaining the potential of such characters: "A collective interlocutor who brings the real questions we've experienced from a disciplinary community into the performance into this story in a respectful way . . . we don't see Niij as an adversary; on the contrary, the questions that s/he asks have helped us think more deeply, more persistently, and more broadly about our collective work and its relationship to the discipline of rhetoric and composition." Building a character like Self, as informed by Brechtian techniques and the CRTL's "Niij," this allegorical/fantasy character can hold space for and play a role of interlocutor for anyone (or any collective) to step into. In using such a rhetorical strategy within this Bell-inspired form of counterstory, my hope is that those reading this narrative, especially students, can imagine stepping into the role of Self and crafting a similar exchange with the Eight. I believe this technique helps readers/students engage the text beyond reading comprehension toward a deeper understanding of the text through a demonstration of their role within it (i.e., how and where they locate themselves in this argument).
15. The tenets of CRT. See Chapter 1.
16. See Appendixes C and D.
17. See Alejandra's first chronicle: Martinez, "A Plea for Critical Race Theory Counterstory: Stock Story versus Counterstory Dialogues concerning Alejandra's 'Fit' in the Academy."
18. See Appendixes C and D for examples of this.

# Chapter 4. Patricia J. Williams and Counterstory as Autobiographic Reflection

1. *Regents of the University of California v. Bakke* refers to the June 28, 1978, ruling in which the US Supreme Court declared affirmative action constitutional but invalidated the use of racial quotas.
2. Williams on crafting narratives in consideration of/inspired by her white great-great grandfather and her enslaved great-great grandmother: "I do think that the traumatic history of racism—I think of the white slave owner who molested the child who was my great-great grandmother, the violence and sexual assault that was such a common part of slavery's 'breeding' systems—is something that is largely invisible to those in the white community and that is rarely spoken of in black families. When I began to call my great-great grandfather 'my great-great grandfather' as opposed to 'the master' or 'the owner' of my great-great grandmother's people, I took it out of the language of commerce and put it into the language of the family and it startled my great aunts who were in their eighties and nineties. Putting it in terms of family relationships startled them and it startles many people who then ask when did your great-great grandmother and your great-great grandfather get married? No. A violent and illegitimate relationship, you know, illegitimate! And, so that's some part of what I'm trying to do and it's not a solution in the programmatic or legal sense but it is part of what I see as my ethical project, of uncovering an injury for which there has been so little consideration and so few words" (Mirza 123).
3. See Chapter 1 for my discussion of a ninth tenet: accessibility.
4. I could say I also serve in a third capacity as arranger—although the words of each scholar are their own, I cut and arranged these quotations into portions that best fit together so as to effect a conversation among these individual quotations from separate works.
5. "Arizona's SB 1070: The US Supreme Court has upheld the most hotly disputed part of Arizona's anti-immigrant law, SB 1070, which requires police to determine the immigration status of someone arrested or detained when there is 'reasonable suspicion' they are not in the US legally. After SB 1070 passed in 2010, two dozen copycat bills were introduced in state legislatures across the country; five passed[,] in Alabama, Georgia, Indiana, South Carolina and Utah. Laws inspired by Arizona's SB 1070 invite rampant racial profiling against Latinos, Asian-Americans and others presumed to be 'foreign' based on how they look or sound. They also authorize police to demand papers proving citizenship or immigration status from

anyone they stop and suspect of being in the country unlawfully" (ACLU of Arizona).
6. I am well aware of and reflect often on the irony of the Bahamian government hiring a team of researchers from the deserts of Arizona to travel—several times at that!—to Exuma (an enormously expensive endeavor) to speak with and gather the narratives of local Bahamian fishers. But here again, we, the anthropologists, represented the institution with its sanctioned methodologies for research. As a result, I *know* this experience was foundational to my pursuit of counterstory as a research methodology—a methodology that argues fervently for the rights and legitimacy of POC's narratives as researched data.
7. See Medina and Martinez and Martinez, Medina, and Howerton. In both cases the authors responded to our responses and employed either the "I'm sorry you were offended" or the "Now I'm offended that you were offended" rhetorical strategy.
8. See the NCTE/CCCC Latinx Caucus's bibliography for a comprehensive source (five-hundred-plus citations for some seventy-plus past and present caucus members) of scholarship concerning Latinx peoples navigating bordered spaces: https://tinyurl.com/latinxbib.
9. A growing number of scholars, particularly those in education, sociology, and legal studies, are in conversation concerning the socioeconomic and racial project of low-income schools that serve as "school-to-prison pipelines" for youth, particularly youth of color. David Simson offers a comprehensive and a CRT-framed approach in his 2014 *UCLA Law Review* comment: "Exclusion, Punishment, Racism and Our Schools: A Critical Race Theory Perspective on School Discipline." In this report, Simson offers "insights from the field of Critical Race Theory on the root causes for racial inequality in American society more broadly, and in the context of school discipline more specifically." Simson argues that "punitive school discipline procedures have increasingly taken hold in America's schools. While they are detrimental to the wellbeing and to the academic success of all students, they have proven to disproportionately punish minority students, especially African American youth. Such policies feed into wider social issues that, once more, disproportionately affect minority communities: the school-to-prison pipeline, high school dropout rates, the push-out phenomenon, and the criminalization of schools" (506).
10. See the ACLU report *Bullies in Blue: The Origin and Consequences of School Policing*, for a thorough study on armed law enforcement

presence in schools, particularly schools that are low-income with majority student of color populations.
11. See Note 5 above concerning Arizona's SB 1070.
12. See Note 5 above concerning Arizona's SB 1070.
13. In 2010, the Arizona legislature passed, and Governor Janet Brewer signed into law, House Bill 2281, effectively banning Mexican American Studies in Arizona schools, but particularly the renowned and successful RAZA Studies Program in the Tucson Unified School District. HB 2281 in part states the following:
    Public school pupils should be taught to treat and value each other as individuals and not be taught to resent or hate other races or classes of people[;] a school district or charter school in this state shall not include in its program of instruction any courses or classes that include any of the following:
    1. Promote the overthrow of the United States Government.
    2. Promote resentment toward a race or class of people.
    3. Are designed primarily for pupils of a particular ethnic group.
    4. Advocate ethnic solidarity instead of the treatment of pupils as individuals. (HB 2281 1)
14. Part of the fear felt by POC and migrant communities at the passing of SB 1070 was that this legislation vested law enforcement with the power to surveil and criminalize communities of color. The rubric stating that police officers could enact border protection and enforcement on "reasonably suspicious" individuals legally left open to interpretation the white supremacist racist imaginary that intensified an already (historically) precarious, violent, and mass-incarcerated/criminalized reality for POC in the borderlands. Undoubtedly, SB 1070's passing made way for other enforcement professionals, such as corporate security guards (oftentimes individuals who are former/retired police or who have unsuccessfully attempted acceptance to police academies), to surveil and criminalize those they deem "reasonably suspicious."
15. The forty-fifth president of the United States. I don't care to write his name in my book.
16. For those unfamiliar with the contextual specifics of this government form, it is the paperwork required of all legally documented workers in this country, and it is the direct result of the Immigration Reform and Control Act of 1986. This act requires that employers demand that all newly hired employees present what is termed *facially valid* documentation verifying the employee's identity and

legal authorization to work in the United States ("Statutes and Regulations").
17. See particularly Michelle Alexander's book *The New Jim Crow* and Ava DuVernay's film *13th* for excellent discussions of the United States' cultural and historic systems of privilege and oppression, with particular reference to mass incarceration.
18. See, for instance, social media pages such as www.facebook.com/DontTellMeWhatToWeartellThemNotToRape/.
19. See Martinez, "A Plea" and "Alejandra Writes a Book."
20. For more on "diverse" bodies in institutional spaces, see Sara Ahmed's excellent 2012 work *On Being Included: Racism and Diversity in Institutional Life*.
21. Think here of J. K. Rowling's description of Professor Dolores Umbridge's saccharine tone. Those of you who know, will *know*.

## 5. Counterstory in Education: Pedagogical Implications for CRT Methodology

1. Delgado and Stefancic have broken up *Critical Race Theory: An Introduction* into the following thematic sections: (1) an introduction to CRT, (2) hallmark CRT themes (the tenets), (3) legal storytelling and narrative analysis (counterstory), (4) looking inward (critical self-reflection), (5) power and the shape of knowledge (hegemonic whiteness), (6) critiques and responses, (7) CRT today, (8) forward-facing conclusion.
2. I myself teach with this text; see its application in my Writing Critical Race Counterstory syllabus, Appendix B.
3. I begin my classes each semester by introducing myself along with my pronouns—which I also include next to my name on syllabi. I invite students to share their names and pronouns too as I verify attendance on my roster.
4. This quotation is adapted from @the_bodylib_advocate account on Instagram.
5. I stand by my shameless *X-Files* plug.

## WORKS CITED

Agnew, Lois, et al. "Octalog III: The Politics of Historiography in 2010." *Rhetoric Review*, vol. 30, no. 2, 2011, pp. 109–34.

Ahmed, Sara. "Feminist Killjoys (and Other Willful Subjects)." *The Scholar and Feminist Online*, vol. 8, no. 3, 2010. sfonline.barnard.edu/polyphonic/ahmed_01.htm.

———. *On Being Included: Racism and Diversity in Institutional Life*. Duke UP, 2012.

Alexander, Michelle. Foreword. *Faces at the Bottom of the Well: The Permanence of Racism*, by Derrick Bell, 25th anniversary ed., Basic Books, 2018, pp. ix–xix.

———. *The New Jim Crow: Mass Incarceration in the Age of Colorblindness*. New Press, 2012.

Alvarez, Steven. *Brokering Tareas: Mexican Immigrant Families Translanguaging Homework Literacies*. State U of New York P, 2017.

American Civil Liberties Union. *Bullies in Blue: The Origins and Consequences of School Policing*, Apr. 2017, www.aclu.org/report/bullies-blue-origins-and-consequences-school-policing.

American Civil Liberties Union of Arizona. *United against SB 1070*, www.acluaz.org/en/campaigns/united-against-sb-1070.Accessed Feb. 2020.

Anzaldúa, Gloria. *Borderlands/La Frontera: The New Mestiza*, 2nd ed., Aunt Lute Books, 1999.

———. "To(o) Queer the Writer—Loca, Escritora y Chicana." *Living Chicana Theory*, edited by Carla Trujillo, Third Woman Press, 1998, pp. 263–76.

Arellano, Sonia C. *Quilting the Migrant Trail: Rhetorical Text(iles) and Rehumanizing Narratives*. 2017. U of Arizona, PhD dissertation. *ProQuest*, search-proquest-com.libezproxy2.syr.edu/docview/1925013596?accountid=14214.

Baca, Damián. *"te-ixtli:* The 'Other Face' of the Americas." Baca and Villanueva, pp. 1–13.

Baca, Damián, and Victor Villanueva, editors. *Rhetorics of the Americas: 3114 BCE to 2012 CE*. Palgrave Macmillan, 2010.

Baker, Houston A., Jr. *Afro-American Poetics: Revisions of Harlem and the Black Aesthetic*. U of Wisconsin P, 1988.

Banks, Adam J. *Race, Rhetoric, and Technology: Searching for Higher Ground*. Lawrence Erlbaum and National Council of Teachers of English, 2006.

*Barrio Historico Tucson*. Report by students of the College of Architecture, Fall 1971/72, U of Arizona. *U of Arizona Library*, www.library.arizona.edu/exhibits/swetc/barr/.

Bell, Derrick. *And We Are Not Saved: The Elusive Quest for Racial Justice*. Basic Books, 1987.

———. "An Epistolary Exploration for a Thurgood Marshall Biography." *Harvard BlackLetter Journal*, vol. 6, 1989, pp. 51–67.

———. *Faces at the Bottom of the Well: The Permanence of Racism*. Basic Books, 1992.

———. "The Final Report: Harvard's Affirmative Action Allegory." *Michigan Law Review*, vol. 87, no. 8, 1989, pp. 2382–410.

———. *Race, Racism, and American Law*. Little, Brown, 1973.

———. "Who's Afraid of Critical Race Theory?" *University of Illinois Law Review*, no. 4, 1995, pp. 893–910.

Bizzell, Patricia, and Bruce Herzberg, editors. *The Rhetorical Tradition: Readings from Classical Times to the Present*, 2nd ed., Bedford/St. Martin's, 2001.

Bonilla-Silva, Eduardo. *Racism without Racists: Color-Blind Racism and the Persistence of Racial Inequality in America*, 5th ed., Rowman & Littlefield, 2018.

Brown, Jane K. *The Persistence of Allegory: Drama and Neoclassicism from Shakespeare to Wagner*. U of Pennsylvania P, 2007.

Burke, Kenneth. *A Grammar of Motives*, U California P, 1969.

Butler, Octavia E. *Kindred*, Beacon Press, 1979.

———. *Kindred*, audiobook narrated by Kim Staunton. Audible, 2000.

Cabrera, Nolan L. "Where Is the Racial Theory in Critical Race Theory? A Constructive Criticism of the Crits." *The Review of Higher Education*, vol. 42, no. 1, 2018, pp. 209–33.

Castillo, Ana. *Massacre of the Dreamers: Essays in Xicanisma*. Plume Publishers, 1995.

Chávez, Karma R. *Queer Migration Politics: Activist Rhetoric and Coalitional Possibilities*, U of Illinois P, 2013.

Cohen, Tom. "Obama's Harvard Law Professor Challenged US Racism."

*CNN*, 9 Mar. 2012, www.cnn.com/2012/03/09/election/2012/derrick-bell-profile/index.html.
*Columbia University News*. "Professor Patricia Williams Named MacArthur Fellow." Columbia U, 21 June 2000, www.columbia.edu/cu/pr/00/06/williams.html.
Combahee River Collective. "A Black Feminist Statement." *This Bridge Called My Back: Writings by Radical Women of Color*, edited by Cherríe Moraga and Gloria E. Anzaldúa, 4th ed., State U of New York P, 2015, pp. 210–18.
Condon, Frankie. *I Hope I Join the Band: Narrative, Affiliation, and Antiracist Rhetoric*. Utah State UP, 2012.
Connerly, Ward. *Creating Equal: My Fight against Race Preferences*. Encounter Books, 2000.
Cook, Daniella Ann. "Blurring the Boundaries: The Mechanics of Creating Composite Characters." Lynn and Dixson, pp. 181–94.
Cook, Daniella Ann, and Adrienne D. Dixson. "Writing Critical Race Theory and Method: A Composite Counterstory on the Experiences of Black Teachers in New Orleans Post-Katrina." *International Journal of Qualitative Studies in Education*, vol. 26, no. 10, 2013, pp. 1238–58.
Crenshaw, Kimberlé. "Demarginalizing the Intersection of Race and Sex: A Black Feminist Critique of Antidiscrimination Doctrine, Feminist Theory and Antiracist Politics." *University of Chicago Legal Forum*, vol. 1989, 1989, article 8, pp. 139–67.
Crenshaw, Kimberlé, Neil Gotanda, Gary Peller, and Kendall Thomas. Introduction. *Critical Race Theory: The Key Writings That Formed the Movement*, edited by Crenshaw et al., New Press, 1995, pp. xiii–xxxii.
crunkadelic. "Get Your People." *The Crunk Feminist Collective*, 10 Nov. 2016, www.crunkfeministcollective.com/2016/11/09/get-your-people/.
Cultural Rhetorics Theory Lab. "Our Story Begins Here: Constellating Cultural Rhetorics." *Enculturation: A Journal of Rhetoric, Writing, and Culture*, vol. 18, 2014.
Cushman, Ellen. "Translingual and Decolonial Approaches to Meaning Making." *College English*, vol. 78, no. 3, 2016, pp. 234–42.
Davis, Angela Y. *Women, Race, and Class*. Random House, 1981.
Delgado, Richard. "Locating Latinos in the Field of Civil Rights: Assessing the Neoliberal Case for Radical Exclusion." *Texas Law Review*, vol. 83, no. 2, 2004, pp. 489–523.
———. *The Rodrigo Chronicles: Conversations about America and Race*. New York UP, 1995.

———. "Rodrigo's Roadmap: Is the Marketplace Theory for Eradicating Discrimination a Blind Alley?" *Northwestern University Law Review*, vol. 93, no. 1, 1998, pp. 215–45.

———. "Storytelling for Oppositionists and Others: A Plea for Narrative." *Michigan Law Review*, vol. 87, no. 8, 1989, pp. 2411–41.

Delgado, Richard, and Jean Stefancic. *Critical Race Theory: An Introduction*, 3rd ed. New York UP, 2017.

———, editors. *Critical Race Theory: The Cutting Edge*, 3rd ed. Temple UP, 2013.

———. Introduction. Delgado and Stefancic, *Critical Race Theory: The Cutting Edge*, pp. 1–5.

———, editors. *The Derrick Bell Reader*. New York UP, 2005.

Delgado Bernal, Dolores. "Critical Race Theory, Latino Critical Theory, and Critical Raced-Gendered Epistemologies: Recognizing Students of Color as Holders and Creators of Knowledge." *Qualitative Inquiry*, vol. 8, no.1, 2002, pp. 105–26.

———. "Using a Chicana Feminist Epistemology in Educational Research." *Harvard Educational Review*, vol. 68, no. 4, 1998, pp. 555–83.

Delgado Bernal, Dolores, Rebeca Burciaga, and Judith Flores Carmona. "Chicana/Latina *Testimonios:* Mapping the Methodological, Pedagogical, and Political." *Equity and Excellence in Education*, vol. 45, no. 3, 2012, pp. 363–72.

Dixson, Adrienne D., and Celia K. Rousseau, editors. *Critical Race Theory in Education: All God's Children Got a Song*, Routledge, 2006.

———. Introduction. Dixson and Rousseau, pp. 1–8.

Dolmage, Jay Timothy. *Disabled upon Arrival: Eugenics, Immigration, and the Construction of Race and Disability*. Ohio State UP, 2018.

———. "The Circulation of Discourse through the Body." Agnew et al., pp. 113–15.

Driskill, Qwo-Li. "Decolonial Skillshares: Indigenous Rhetorics as Radical Practice." *Survivance, Sovereignty, and Story: Teaching American Indian Rhetorics*, edited by Lisa King, Rose Gubele, and Joyce Rain Anderson, UP of Colorado, 2015, pp. 57–78.

Du Bois, W. E .B. *The Souls of Black Folk*. Signet Classics, 1969.

DuVernay, Ava, director. *13th*. Kandoo Films, 2016.

Enoch, Jessica, and Cristina Devereaux Ramírez, editors. *Mestiza Rhetorics: An Anthology of Mexicana Activism in the Spanish-Language Press, 1887–1922*. Southern Illinois UP, 2019.

Enos, Richard Leo, et al. "Octalog II: The (Continuing) Politics of Historiography." *Rhetoric Review*, vol. 16, no. 1, 1997, pp. 22–44.

Farber, Daniel A., and Suzanna Sherry. "Telling Stories out of School: An Essay on Legal Narratives." *Stanford Law Review*, vol. 45, no. 4, 1993, pp. 807–55.
Fish, Stanley. "What Should Colleges Teach? Part 3." *New York Times*, 7 Sept. 2009, opinionator.blogs.nytimes.com/2009/09/07/what-should-colleges-teach-part 3/.
Flores, Lisa A. "Between Abundance and Marginalization: The Imperative of Racial Rhetorical Criticism." *Review of Communication*, vol. 16, no. 1, 2016, pp. 4–24.
Florido, Adrian. "Mass Deportation May Sound Unlikely, but It's Happened Before." *NPR Morning Edition*, 8 Sept. 2015.
Foss, Sonja K. *Rhetorical Criticism: Exploration and Practice*, 5th ed., Waveland Press, 2018.
García, Romeo. *On the Cusp of Invisibility: The Lower Rio Grande Valley, Marginalized Students, and Institutional Spaces*. 2017. Syracuse U, PhD dissertation. *ProQuest*, search-proquest-com.libezproxy2.syr.edu/docview/1926727560?accountid=14214.
García, Romeo, and Damián Baca, editors. *Rhetorics Elsewhere and Otherwise: Contested Modernities, Decolonial Visions*. Conference on College Composition and Communication and National Council of Teachers of English, 2019.
García de Müeller, Genevieve. *Shifting Dreams: Intersections of the Rhetorical Imagination of US Immigration Policy and the Writing Practices of DREAMers*. 2015. U of New Mexico, PhD dissertation. *ProQuest*, search-proquest-com.libezproxy2.syr.edu/docview/1765692868?accountid=14214.
Gates, Henry Louis, Jr. "Contract Killer." Review of *The Alchemy of Race and Rights*, by Patricia J. Williams. *The Nation*, 10 Jun. 1991, p. 766–70.
Gilyard, Keith. *Voices of the Self: A Study of Language Competence*. Wayne State UP, 1991.
Glenn, Cheryl. *Rhetoric Retold: Regendering the Tradition from Antiquity through the Renaissance*. Southern Illinois UP, 1997.
Goldberg, Stephanie B. "Who's Afraid of Derrick Bell? A Conversation on Harvard, Storytelling and the Meaning of Color." *ABA Journal*, vol. 78, no. 9, 1992, pp. 56–58.
Gonzales, Laura. *Sites of Translation: What Multilinguals Can Teach Us about Digital Writing and Rhetoric*. U of Michigan P, 2018.
Gonzalez, Martín Alberto. *21 Miles of Scenic Beauty . . . and then Oxnard: Counterstories and Testimonies*. Viva Chiques, 2017.

Gutiérrez-Jones, Carl. *Critical Race Narratives: A Study of Race, Rhetoric, and Injury.* New York UP, 2001.

Haas, Angela M. "Race, Rhetoric, and Technology: A Case Study of Decolonial Technical Communication Theory, Methodology, and Pedagogy." *Journal of Business and Technical Communication,* vol. 26, no. 3, 2012, pp. 277–310.

Haney López, Ian F. "White by Law." Delgado and Stefancic, *Critical Race Theory: The Cutting Edge,* pp. 775–82.

Harris, Angela. Foreword. Delgado and Stefancic, *Critical Race Theory: An Introduction,* pp. xiii–xvii.

Harris, Cheryl I., "Whiteness as Property." *Harvard Law Review,* vol. 106, no. 8, 1993, pp. 1707–91.

Harris, Joseph. "From Classroom to Program: Response." *Composition Studies in the New Millennium: Rereading the Past, Rewriting the Future,* edited by Lynn Z. Bloom, Donald A. Daiker, and Edward M. White, Southern Illinois UP, 2003, pp. 222–24.

hooks, bell. *Sisters of the Yam: Black Women and Self-Recovery.* South End Press, 1993.

Inoue, Asao B. *Antiracist Writing Assessment Ecologies: Teaching and Assessing Writing for a Socially Just Future.* WAC Clearinghouse/Parlor Press, 2015.

Jackson, Ronald L. "When Will We All Matter: A Frank Discussion of Progressive Pedagogy." Agnew et al., pp. 117–18.

Jacobs-Huey, Lanita. "The Natives are Gazing and Talking Back: Reviewing the Problematics of Positionality, Voice, and Accountability among 'Native' Anthropologists." *American Anthropologist,* vol. 104, no. 3, 2002, p. 791–804.

Jefferson, Thomas. "From *Notes on the State of Virginia.*" *Rereading America: Cultural Contexts for Critical Thinking and Writing,* edited by Gary Colombo, Robert Cullen, and Bonnie Lisle, 8th ed., Bedford/St. Martin's, 2010, pp. 378–83.

"Jesuit Missionaries in Arizona." *Native American Netroots,* 10 Nov. 2010, nativeamericannetroots.net/diary/769.

Jost, Kenneth. "Up Close and Personal." Review of *The Alchemy of Race and Rights,* by Patricia J. Williams. *ABA Journal,* vol. 77, no. 7, 1991, pp. 97–98.

Kennedy, Randall L. "Racial Critiques of Legal Academia." *Harvard Law Review,* vol. 102, no. 8, 1989, pp. 1745–1819.

Kraut, Richard. "Plato." *The Stanford Encyclopedia of Philosophy,* edited by Edward N. Zalta, Fall 2017, plato.stanford.edu/archives/fall2017/entries/plato.

Kynard, Carmen. *Education, Liberation and Black Radical Traditions for the Twenty-First Century: Carmen Kynard's Teaching and Research Site on Race, Writing, and the Classroom*, carmenkynard.org. Accessed 12 Oct. 2019.

———. *Real Writing: Writing Courses with Dr. Carmen Kynard, PhD*, realwriting.org. Accessed 11 Oct. 2019.

———. "Remembering Nelson Mandela and Racial Realism." *Education, Liberation and Black Radical Traditions*, carmenkynard.org/remembering-mandela. Accessed 12 Oct. 2019.

———. "Teaching While Black: Witnessing and Countering Disciplinary Whiteness, Racial Violence, and University Race-Management." *Literacy in Composition Studies*, no. 3, vol. 1, 2015, pp. 1–20.

———. *Vernacular Insurrections: Race, Black Protest, and the New Century in Composition-Literacies Studies*. State U of New York P, 2013.

Ladson-Billings, Gloria. "Critical Race Theory—What It Is Not!" Lynn and Dixson, pp. 34–47.

———. Foreword. Dixson and Rousseau, pp. v–xiii.

Ladson-Billings, Gloria, and William F. Tate. "Toward a Critical Race Theory of Education." *Teachers College Record*, vol. 97, no. 1, 1995, p. 47–68.

Latina Feminist Group. *Telling to Live: Latina Feminist Testimonios*. Duke UP, 2001.

Licona, Adela C. "(B)orderlands' Rhetorics and Representations: The Transformative Potential of Feminist Third-Space Scholarship and Zines." *National Women's Studies Association Journal*, vol. 17, no. 2, 2005, p. 104–29.

Lipson, Carol S., and Roberta A. Binkley. Introduction. *Rhetoric before and beyond the Greeks*, edited by Lipson and Binkley, State U of New York P, 2004, pp. 1–23.

Logan, Shirley Wilson. "'When and Where I Enter': Race, Gender, and Composition Studies." *Feminism and Composition: A Critical Sourcebook*, edited by Gesa E. Kirsch, et al., Bedford/St. Martin's in cooperation with the National Council of Teachers of English, 2003, pp. 425–35.

Lorde, Audre. "The Transformation of Silence into Language and Action." *Sister Outsider: Essays and Speeches*, rev. ed., Crossing Press, 2007, pp. 40–44.

Lynn, Marvin, and Adrienne D. Dixson. *Handbook of Critical Race Theory in Education*. Routledge, 2013.

Maldonado, Marta Maria, Adela C. Licona, and Sarah Hendricks. "Latin@ Immobilities and Altermobilities within the US Deportability Regime." *Annals of the American Association of Geographers*, vol. 106, no. 2, 2016, pp. 321–29.

Martinez, Aja Y. "Alejandra Writes a Book: A Critical Race Counterstory about Writing, Identity, and Being Chicanx in the Academy." *Access and Equity in Graduate Writing Support*, edited by Shannon Madden and Michele Eodice, spec. issue of *Praxis: A Writing Center Journal*, vol. 14, no. 1, 2016, pp. 56–61.

———. "'The American Way': Resisting the Empire of Force and Color-Blind Racism." *College English*, vol. 71, no. 6, 2009, pp. 584–95.

———. "Core-Coursing Counterstory: On Master Narrative Histories of Rhetorical Studies Curricula." *Rhetoric Review*, vol. 38, no. 4, 2019, pp. 402–16.

———. "Critical Race Theory Counterstory as Allegory: A Rhetorical Trope to Raise Awareness about Arizona's Ban on Ethnic Studies." *Anti-Racist Activism: Teaching Rhetoric and Writing*, edited by Frankie Condon and Vershawn Ashanti Young, spec. issue of *Across the Disciplines: A Journal of Language, Learning and Academic Writing*, vol. 10, no. 3, 2013.

———. "Critical Race Theory: Its Origins, History, and Importance to the Discourses and Rhetorics of Race." *Frame—Journal of Literary Studies*, vol. 27, no. 2, 2014, pp. 9–27.

———. "A Plea for Critical Race Theory Counterstory: Stock Story versus Counterstory Dialogues concerning Alejandra's 'Fit' in the Academy." *Composition Studies*, vol. 42, no. 2, 2014, pp. 33–55.

———. "The Responsibility of Privilege: A Critical Race Counterstory Conversation." *Peitho: Journal of the Coalition of Feminist Scholars in the History of Rhetoric and Composition*, vol. 21, no. 1, 2018, pp. 212–33.

Martinez, Aja Y., Cruz Nicholas Medina, and Gloria J. Howerton. "Requiem for an Autopsy: A Response to Kim Hensley Owens's '*In Lak'ech*, the Chicano Clap, and Fear: A Partial Rhetorical Autopsy of Tucson's Now-Illegal Ethnic Studies Classes.'" *College English*, vol. 80, no. 6, 2018, pp. 539–50.

*Masader*. www.masader.om/eds?search=y&query=%22Alchemy+of+Race+%26+Rights%C+The+%28Book%29%22&type=DE. Accessed 12 Oct. 2019.

Matsuda, Mari J. "Voices of America: Accent, Antidiscrimination Law, and a Jurisprudence for the Last Reconstruction." *Yale Law Journal*, vol. 100, no. 5, 1991, pp. 1329–1407.

McKissack, Patricia C., and Fredrick McKissack. *Sojourner Truth: Ain't I a Woman?* Scholastic, 1992.

Medina, Cruz, and Aja Y. Martinez. "Contexts of Lived Realities in SB 1070 Arizona: A Response to Asenas and Johnson's 'Economic Globalization and the "Given Situation."'" *Present Tense: A Journal of Rhetoric in Society*, vol. 4, no. 2, 2015, pp. 1–8.

Mejía, Jaime Armin. "Tejano Arts of the US-Mexico Contact Zone." *Exploring Borderlands: Postcolonial and Composition Studies*, edited by Andrea Lunsford and Lahoucine Ouzgane, spec. issue of *JAC*, vol. 18, no. 1, 1998, pp. 123–35.

Mirza, Qudsia. "Patricia Williams: Inflecting Critical Race Theory." *Feminist Legal Studies*, vol. 7, no. 2, 1999, pp. 111–32.

Mitchell, Margaret. *Gone with the Wind*. Scribner, 1936.

Moraga, Cherríe, and Gloria Anzaldúa. *This Bridge Called My Back: Writings by Radical Women of Color*, 2nd ed. Kitchen Table/Women of Color Press, 1983.

Murji, Karim, and John Solomos. *Racialization: Studies in Theory and Practice*. Oxford UP, 2005.

Murphy, James J., et al. "Octalog: The Politics of Historiography." *Rhetoric Review*, vol. 7, no. 1, 1988, pp. 5–49.

National Council of Teachers of English/Conference on College Composition and Communication Black Caucus, Latinx Caucus, American Indian Caucus, Queer, Asian/Asian American Caucus. "Letter." 4 Dec. 2018, docs.google.com/document/d/1fsD-D5Y-KyQ007lLiMDmuIv7QV2TJ07qMUxJqQZIzHk/edit.

Olson, Gary A. "Working with Difference: Critical Race Studies and the Teaching of Composition." *Composition Studies in the New Millennium: Rereading the Past, Rewriting the Future*, edited by Lynn Z. Bloom, Donald A. Daiker, and Edward M. White, Southern Illinois UP, 2003, pp. 208–21.

Omi, Michael, and Howard Winant. *Racial Formations in the United States: From the 1960s to the 1980s*. Routledge & Kegan Paul, 1986.

Post, Deborah Waire. "The Politics of Pedagogy: Confessions of a Black Woman Law Professor." A. K. Wing, pp. 131–39.

Prendergast, Catherine. *Literacy and Racial Justice: The Politics of Learning after Brown v. Board of Education*. Southern Illinois UP, 2003.

Pritchard, Eric Darnell. *Fashioning Lives: Black Queers and the Politics of Literacy*. Southern Illinois UP, 2017.

Ramírez, Cristina Devereaux. *Occupying Our Space: The Mestiza Rhetorics of Mexican Women Journalists and Activists, 1875–1942*. U of Arizona P, 2015.

Richardson, Elaine. Interview by Julia Oller. *The Columbus Dispatch*, 14 Jun. 2018, www.dispatch.com/entertainmentlife/20180614/local-music-limelight-elaine-richardson.

———. *PHD to PhD: How Education Saved My Life*, Kindle ed., New City Community Press, 2013.

———. "Thirteen Questions for Singer/Songwriter Dr. E." Interview by Taylor Carlington. *Flawless Brown*, 13 Apr. 2017, www.flawlessbrown.com/single-post/2017/04/14/13-Questions-for SingerSongwriter-Dr-E.

Rieder, Jonathan. "Tawana and the Professor." Review of *The Alchemy of Race and Rights*, by Patricia J. Williams. *The New Republic*, 21 Oct. 1991, pp. 39–42.

Ruiz, Iris D., and Raúl Sánchez, editors. *Decolonizing Rhetoric and Composition Studies: New Latinx Keywords for Theory and Pedagogy*. Palgrave Macmillan, 2016.

Simpson, David. "Exclusion, Punishment, Racism and Our Schools: A Critical Race Theory Perspective on School Discipline." *UCLA Law Review*, vol. 61, no. 2, 2014, pp. 506–63.

Solórzano, Daniel. "Critical Race Theory's Intellectual Roots: My Email Epistolary with Derrick Bell." Lynn and Dixson, pp. 48–68.

Solórzano, Daniel G., and Dolores Delgado Bernal. "Examining Transformational Resistance through a Critical Race and Latcrit Theory Framework: Chicana and Chicano Students in an Urban Context." *Urban Education*, vol. 36, no. 3, 2001, pp. 308–42.

Solórzano, Daniel G., and Tara J. Yosso. "Critical Race Methodology: Counter-Storytelling as an Analytical Framework for Education Research." *Qualitative Inquiry*, vol. 8, no. 1, 2002, pp. 23–44.

Squiers, Anthony. "A Critical Response to Heidi M. Silcox's 'What's Wrong with Alienation?'" *Philosophy and Literature*, vol. 39, no. 1, 2015, pp. 243–47.

"Statutes and Regulations." *US Citizenship and Immigration Services*, 9 May 2017, www.uscis.gov/i-9-central/about-form-i-9/statutes-and-regulations.

Taylor, Edward. "A Critical Race Analysis of the Achievement Gap in the United States: Politics, Reality, and Hope." *Leadership and Policy in Schools*, vol. 5, no. 1, 2006, pp. 71–87.

TLCP Editorial Board. "Living History Interview with Richard Delgado and Jean Stefancic." *Transnational Law and Contemporary Problems*, vol. 19, 2011, pp. 221–30.

Trimbur, John, et al. "Counterstatement: Responses to Maxine Hairston, 'Diversity, Ideology, and Teaching Writing.'" *College Composition and*

*Communication*, vol. 44, no. 2, 1993, pp. 248–49.

"The Vetting: Obama Embraces Racialist Harvard Prof." *Breitbart*, 7 Mar. 2012. https://www.breitbart.com/clips/2012/03/07/Obama%20 Video%20Harvard/.

Villanueva, Victor. "Blind: Talking about the New Racism." *The Writing Center Journal*, vol. 26, no. 1, 2006, pp. 3–19.

———. *Bootstraps: From an American Academic of Color*. National Council of Teachers of English, 1993.

———. "*Memoria* Is a Friend of Ours: On the Discourse of Color." *College English*, vol. 67, no. 1, 2004, pp. 9–19.

———. "On the Rhetoric and Precedents of Racism." *College Composition and Communication*, vol. 50, no. 4, 1999, pp. 645–61.

———. "Rhetoric of the First 'Indians': The Taínos of the Second Voyage of Columbus." Baca and Villanueva, pp. 15–20.

West, Cornel. "A Genealogy of Modern Racism." *Race Critical Theories*, edited by Philomena Essed and David Theo Goldberg, Blackwell, 2002, pp. 90–112.

———. *Prophesy Deliverance! An Afro-American Revolutionary Christianity*. Westminster Press, 1982.

Williams, Patricia J. *The Alchemy of Race and Rights: Diary of a Law Professor*. Harvard UP, 1991.

———. Interview with Joan Oleck. *Contemporary Black Biography*, vol. 8, 1995.

———. "An Ordinary Brilliance: Parting the Waters, Closing the Wounds." Lecture 5 of the Reith Lecture Series *The Genealogy of Race: 1997*, by Williams. BBC Radio 4, 15 Mar. 1997, London.

Williams, Robert A., Jr. Foreword. Delgado, *Rodrigo Chronicles*, pp. xi–xvi.

Wing, Adrien Katherine, editor. *Critical Race Feminism: A Reader*, 2nd ed. New York UP, 2003.

Wing, Nick. "When the Media Treat White Suspects and Killers Better than Black Victims." *Huffington Post*, 14 Aug. 2014, www.huffington post.com/2014/08/14/media black-victims_n_5673291.html.

Wynter, Sylvia. "'No Humans Involved': An Open Letter to My Colleagues." *Voices of the African Diaspora: The CAAS Research Review*, vol. 8, no. 2, 1992, p. 13–16.

Yosso, Tara J. *Critical Race Counterstories along the Chicana/Chicano Educational Pipeline*. Routledge, 2006.

———. "Toward a Critical Race Curriculum." *Equality and Excellence in Education*, vol. 35, no. 2, 2002, pp. 93–107.

Young, Vershawn Ashanti. "Should Writers Use They Own English?" *Iowa Journal of Cultural Studies*, vol. 12, 2010, pp. 110–17.

———. *Your Average Nigga: Performing Race, Literacy, and Masculinity*, Wayne State UP, 2007.

# INDEX

academy
  borders, 97
  disciplinary boundaries, 134
accessibility, 18, 99, 135
ACLU, 176–77n10
affirmative action, 5, 11, 54
*Afro-American Poetics* (Baker), 123
agency, xxix, 73
Ahmed, Sara, 84–85
*Alchemy of Race and Rights: Diary of a Law Professor* (Williams), 21, 82, 84–86, 115, 169n1
Alexander, Michelle, 56, 172n4, 172n7
  *The New Jim Crow,* 55
alignment, 112, 113
allegory, 53–79
  craft of, 58–64
  definition of, 60
  in writing workshop, 61–62
alternative narrative, xxix
  . *See also* counterstory
Alvarez, Steven, 97
American Educational Research Association, 111
ancestorship, 87–95
*And We Are Not Saved: The Elusive Question for Racial Justice* (Bell), xi, 21, 56, 62
anomaly thesis, 10–11
antiessentialism. *See* essentialism and antiessentialism
Anzaldúa, Gloria, 97
  *Borderlands/La Frontera,* 126

Arellano, Sonia, 97
Arizona
  Arizona's SB 1070, 175–76n5, 177n14
  Mexican American studies, 177n13
audience, xxiii, 35, 174n13
autobiographical reflection, 86–93

Baca, Damián, 122
Bacon, Francis, 125
Bahamas, 176n6
  narrative of marine biologists, 96
Baker, Ella, xiii
Baker, Houston, Jr.
  *Afro-American Poetics,* 123
Banks, Adam J., 26, 57
  *Race, Rhetoric, and Technology,* 56
Bell, Derrick A., vii, xi–xiv, 1, 2, 3, 6, 7, 10, 11, 15, 18, 19, 30, 32, 53–64, 114–15, 171n2
  *And We Are Not Saved: The Elusive Question for Racial Justice,* xi, 21, 56, 62
  career, 55–58, 110
  composite characters, 25
  *Derrick Bell Reader,* 171n1
  "An Epistolary Exploration for a Thurgood Marshall Biography," 30
  *Faces at the Bottom of the Well: The Permanence of Racism,* xi, 21, 55, 57, 172n2, 172n7
  personal background, 53–54
  *Race, Racism, and American Law,*

191

7, 110
"Racism Is Here to Stay: Now What?," xi
"Space Traders," 60–62
"Who's Afraid of CRT?," 18–20, 31
workshop methods, 98
Berlin, James, 63, 68–69, 73, 74, 116
Bizzell, Patricia, 34, 58, 122
"Blind: Talking about the New Racism" (Villanueva), 169–70n3
Bonilla-Silva, Eduardo, 4–5, 11, 132, 169–70n3
*Borderlands/La Frontera* (Anzaldúa), 126
borders, 95–109, 124–25, 176n8, 177n14
academy, 97–98
citizenship, 97
disciplinary boundaries, 134
immigrant law, 175–76n5
marine protected areas, 96
Mexican Repatriation, xxvii–xxviii
nation states, 96
people of color, 109
US and Mexico borderland, 97, 126, 175–76n5, 177n14
Brecht, Bertolt, 173n12
Breitbart, 55
Breitbart, Andrew, 172n2
Brewer, Janet, 177n13
Brown, Jane, 60
*Brown v. Board of Education*, 11–12
*Bullies in Blue: The Origin and Consequences of School Policing*, 176–77n10
Burke, Kenneth, 169–70n3
Butler, Octavia
*Kindred*, 38, 41–42, 43, 45, 49–51, 116

Cabrera, Nolan L., 9
Carmichael, Stokely, 104
Carruthers, Charlene, xiii
Castillo, Ana, 126

Chávez, Karma, 97
Civil Rights Movement (1960s), 5–6
Cold War era, 11–12
colonization. *See* decolonization
color blindness, 7, 17, 63, 169–70n3
Combahee River Collective, 12
composite characters, 25, 174n14
teacher-student composites, 35–36
composite counterstorytelling (CCS), 23–25, 36, 171n10, 174n14
Condon, Frankie, 23, 87, 89, 92, 171n12
Connerly, Ward, 23
Connors, Robert J., 63, 69, 70, 116
Cook, Daniella Ann, 2, 3, 21, 23–25, 111, 113
counterstory
allegory, 53–79
as autobiographic reflection, 86–95
belief systems, 114, 136
community and, 114, 136
composite counterstorytelling (CCS), 23–25, 36, 171n10, 174n14
crossing borders, 95–109
definition, 3, 16, 33, 34, 82
examples
"An Autobiographic Reflection Octalog," 87–95
"Diary of a Mad Border Crosser," 98–109
"Epistolary Email on Pedagogy and Master Narrative Curricula," 118–38
"Politics of Historiography," 64–79
"Road Trip," 38–53
familiarity with concept, 1
fantasy, 53–79
vs. marginalized narratives, 17
memory, 136
as method/methodology, 2, 3, 21–23, 26–31, 34, 77, 113, 114, 136, 169nn1–2

as narrated dialogue, 32–52
oppression and, 114, 136
vs. stock story, 33–38
as theory, 2
transformation and, 114, 136
*Counterstory: The Rhetoric and Writing of Critical Race Theory* (Martinez)
purpose of, 2–4, 144–45
Crenshaw, Geneva (character), 21, 56, 62, 172n4
Crenshaw, Kimberlé, 6, 8, 12, 32
"Demarginalizing the Intersection of Race and Sex," 13
critical legal studies (CLS), 6, 8, 86, 110–11, 143
Critical Legal Studies National Conference
silence and race, 8
*Critical Race Feminism: A Reader* (Wing), 8–9, 81
critical race theory (CRT), xi, 8, 143–45
affirmative action, 11
counterstory (*see* counterstory)
critics, 18–21, 169n1, 170n9
definition, 7
goal of, 113
as heuristic, 112, 113, 132–33
history of, 4–9
methodology
autoethnography, 3
biography, 3
*cuentos*, 3
family history, 3
*testimonios*, 3, 29–30
pedagogy and, 110–38
as praxis, 132–33, 136
tenets, 9–18, 37, 56
*Critical Race Theory: An Introduction* (Delgado and Stefancic), 10, 20–21, 115, 170n7, 178n1
*Critical Race Theory: Key Writings That Formed the Movement*, 6
*Critical Race Theory: The Cutting Edge* (Delgado and Stefancic), 8

"Critical Race Theory Counterstory as Allegory" (Martinez), 59–60
"Critical Race Theory's Intellectual Roots: My E-Mail Epistolary with Derrick Bell" (Solórzano) 1, 30
Crowley, Sharon, 63, 73, 74, 75–76, 116
Cuádrez, Gloria, 29
curricula, 27–28, 61, 110, 130
context in, 134
core curricula, 116, 117, 123, 137, 143
disciplinary boundaries, 134
elective, 117
"An Epistolary Email on Pedagogy and Master Narrative Curricula," 118–38
Mexican American studies, 177n13
RAZA Studies Program, 177n13
reframing, 137
syllabi, 147–67

Davis, Angela, 83
"Decolonial Skillshares: Indigenous Rhetorics as Radical Practice" (Driskill), 126
decolonization, 118–38 *passim*
monolingualism, 120
*Decolonizing Rhetoric and Composition Studies* (Ruiz and Sánchez), 97
Delgado, Richard, xiv, 2, 3, 7, 8, 10, 15, 18, 19, 20–21, 30, 32–38, 98, 114–15
awards, 33
composite characters, 25
*Critical Race Theory: The Cutting Edge*, 8
*Derrick Bell Reader*, 171n1
as intellectual *padrino*, 33
publications, 33
*Rodrigo Chronicles*, xxv, 21, 33, 36
"Storytelling of Oppositionists and Others: A Plea for Narrative," 21–22, 25

Delgado Bernal, Dolores, 2, 3, 11, 22, 28, 111
"Demarginalizing the Intersection of Race and Sex" (Crenshaw), 13
dialogue. *See* narrated dialogue
"Diary of a Mad Border Crosser" (Martinez), 98–109
disability theory, 9
discourse, 123, 170n4
discourses of transcendence, 23
transcendence, 23
Dixson, Adrienne, 2, 3, 9, 23–25, 111–12, 113
Dolmage, Jay, 74, 135
double consciousness, 170n6
Driskill, Qwo-Li, 126
DuBois, W. E. B., 170n6
DuVernay, Ava, 172n4

empowerment, 29
Enos, Richard Leo, 63, 70, 71, 78, 116
Enos, Theresa Jarnagin, 173n11
epistemology, 113, 169–70n3
epistolary, dialogic, 30, 118–38, 171n12
"Epistolary Exploration for a Thurgood Marshall Biography, An" (Bell), 30
equal opportunity, 5
essentialism and antiessentialism, 14, 38, 63, 99, 113
ethnic studies, 15, 101, 134
Latinx rhetorics, xxiii
. *See also* LatCrit (Latinx critical race theory); syllabi samples
ethnocentrism, 16
experiential knowledge, 14, 15–16, 19, 38, 63, 85, 99, 112
diversity, 135
Exuma, Bahamas, 96

*Faces at the Bottom of the Well: The Permanence of Racism* (Bell), xi, 21, 55, 57, 172n2, 172n7

fantasy, 53–79
craft of, 58–64
Farber, Daniel A., 20
"Telling Stories Out of School: An Essay on Legal Narratives," 20
*Fashioning Lives* (Pritchard), 93
feminist theory, 9, 81, 118
feminist killjoy, 84–85
feminist poetics, 82–86
Fish, Stanley, 124
Flores, Lisa, 97
Florido, Adrian, xxvii
Foss, Sonja, 118–38 *passim*
*Rhetorical Criticism*, 118

García, Romeo, 97
García de Müeller, Genevieve, 97
Gates, Henry Louis, Jr., 85, 95
"A Genealogy of Modern Racism" (West), 125, 170n4
genre-blurring/genre-bashing, 84–86
Gilyard, Keith, 26, 87, 88, 91, 92, 93
*Gone with the Wind* (Mitchell), 38, 42–43, 45, 50, 116
Gonzales, Laura, 97
Gonzalez, Martín Alberto, 98
Gotanda, Neil, 6
Great Depression, xxvii
Gutiérrez-Jones, Carl, 2, 4, 30, 82–83

Haas, Angela M., 26
*Handbook of Critical Race Theory in Education* (Lynn and Dixson), 9
harassment, 55
Harris, Angela P., 110, 115
Harris, Joseph, 27
*Harvard Law Journal*, xi
*Harvard Law Review*, 19
Harvard Law School, 7, 54–55, 110–11
The Alternative Course, 7, 110–11
hegemonic whiteness, 17
Hendricks, Sarah, 96
Herzberg, Bruce, 34, 58, 122
historiography, 125

Hochschild, Arlie, 10
Holmes, Oliver Wendell, 6
hooks, bell, 118
Huichol people, xxvi

ideology
   dominant, 14, 38, 63, 91, 99, 110, 112
   . *See also* racism
Immigration Reform and Control Act (1986), 177–78n16
individualism, 91
individual with choice, 5
ingroup, 34
interdisciplinarity, 14, 38, 112, 116
interest convergence theory, 11, 17, 63, 112
intersectionality, 12–14, 17, 22, 44, 46, 63, 99, 113
   vs. binaries, 12–13

Jackson, Mississippi, 54
Jackson, Ronald L., 74–75
Jacobs-Huey, LaNita, 131
Jarratt, Susan C., 63, 73, 75–76, 78, 116–17
Jefferson, Thomas, 4, 125
Johnson, Nan, 63, 71–72, 117

*kairos*, 34
Kennedy, Randall L., 19
*Kindred* (Butler), 38, 41–42, 43, 45, 49–51, 116
Kraut, Richard, 59
Kynard, Carmen, vii, xiv, 2, 4, 24, 26, 56, 76, 77, 87, 91, 92, 93, 123, 169n2

Ladson-Billings, Gloria, 2, 10, 14–15, 16, 111–12, 132
   "Toward a Critical Race Theory of Education," 111
LatCrit (Latinx critical race theory), 22, 27–28
   definition, 22
Latina Feminist Group, 29–30
law, 172–73n7
   status quo and, 6
   . *See also* critical legal studies (CLS)
Lawrence, Charles, 32
law schools. *See* Harvard Law School
Leyva, Alejandro Ayala, xiii, xiv, xxv–xxix
Leyva, Victoriano, xxvi
liberalism, 4–12, 20, 37, 76, 81, 91, 110–11, 169–70n3
   abstract liberalism, 5, 19, 91, 169–70n3
Licona, Adela, 96, 97
Linnaeus, Carolus, 125
literacy studies, 86–93, 116, 135
Logan, Shirley Wilson, 4
Lynn, Marvin, 111–12

MacDonald, Biona, xii–xiv, 55, 172n3
*MacNeil/Lehrer Report*, 55
majoritarian stories, 3, 22–23, 24, 26
Maldonado, Marta Maria, 96
Marshall, Thurgood, 54
Martinez, Aja, xiv
   composite characters, 25
   "Core-Coursing Counterstory," 117–18
   "Critical Race Theory Counterstory as Allegory," 59–60
   "Diary of a Mad Border Crosser," 98–109
   octalogs, 64–79, 87–95
Martinez, Olivia Isabel
   birth story, 139–42
*Massacre of the Dreamers* (Castillo), 126
Matsuda, Mari, 7, 19, 32
Medina, Cruz, 97
Mejía, Jaime Armin, 97, 145
memory, xxv, 29, 88–89, 114, 126, 129, 136, 169n1
Mexicans
   Mexican Repatriation, xxvii–xxviii

US and Mexico borderland, 97, 175–76n5, 177n14
minoritized viewpoint, 35, 112, 113, 135
Mitchell, Margaret
 *Gone with the Wind,* 38, 42–43, 45, 50, 116
monolingualism, 120
Moraga, Cherríe, 97
Morrison, Toni, 85
Moses, Bob, xiii
Murphy, James J., 63, 65–67, 69, 75, 79
Myrdal, Gunnar, 10

NAACP
 Legal Defense Fund, 54
narrated dialogue, 32–52
 dialogue as method, 34
narrative, 87–93, 92
 family relationships, 175n2
 master narrative, 117
  "An Epistolary Email on Pedagogy and Master Narrative Curricula," 118–38
 narrated dialogue, 32–52
 narrative performance, 94
 . *See also* counterstory
neo-Aristotelian rhetorics, 63
*New Jim Crow, The* (Alexander), 55
new studies, 134
Nogales, Arizona, xxvii
*Notes on the State of Virginia* (Jefferson), 125

octalogs, 52, 64–79, 87–95, 97, 173n9, 173n11
Olson, Gary, 27
Omi, Michael, 12
oppression, racial, 16, 114, 132, 136

*papelitos guardados,* 29–30, 85
paradigms, 20–21

pedagogy, 27–28, 30, 57, 116, 130–31, 133
 CRT methodology, 110–38
 "An Epistolary Email on Pedagogy and Master Narrative Curricula," 118–38
 graduate-level, 137
Peller, Gary, 6
performance, narrative, 94
perspective, 33–38, 46–48, 123, 171n2, 173n12
 centralized power, 123
 counterperspective, 35
 minoritized viewpoint, 35, 112, 113, 135
*Phaedrus,* 35–37
Plato, 34, 35, 59
Post, Deborah Waire, 84, 115
Post–Civil Rights era, 6, 7
Prendergast, Catherine, 18, 26, 57, 84, 170n9
Prieto, Alejandra (character), xxv, 30, 63–79, 99–109, 117–38, 169n1
Pritchard, Eric Darnell, 86, 87, 90, 93
 *Fashioning Lives,* 93
privilege, 17, 22–23, 26, 34, 44, 46, 68–70, 73, 77, 104–5, 106, 109, 133
 . *See also* white privilege

queer theory, 9

race
 biology vs. social construct, 8, 12
 bounding, 124–25
 hearing, 124, 125
 permanence of, 14, 38, 56, 63, 99, 112, 133, 134
 praxis, 113
 racial rhetorical criticism, 121–22
 seeing, 124, 125
 social construct, 14, 38, 112
 white passing, 44–45
*Race, Racism, and American Law*

(Bell), 7, 110
*Race, Rhetoric, and Technology* (Banks), 56
racial formation, 17
   definition, 12
racial oppression. *See* oppression
racial realism, 88
racism, 5, 44, 50, 60, 124, 169–70n3
   black man rapist stereotype, 83
   blaming the victim, 83
   borderland, 97
   ideology, 124
   ingroup, 34
   liberal democracy and, 10–11
   permanence of, 14, 38, 56, 63, 99, 112, 133, 134, 143
   promiscuous black woman stereotype, 83
   racial inequality, 176n9
   school-to-prison pipeline, 176n9
   . *See also* ideology; liberalism
"Racism Is Here to Stay: Now What?" (Bell), xi
railroad, xxvii
Ransby, Barbara, xiii
RAZA Studies Program, 177n13
reflection, 17, 23, 68, 69, 82, 89, 98, 108, 109, 115, 131, 173–74n12, 173n12, 178n1
   analytical gaze, 131
   autobiographical reflection, 86–93
*Regents of the University of California vs. Bakke*, 80, 175n1
resistance concept, 28
*Rhetorical Criticism* (Foss), 118
rhetorical research
   composite counterstorytelling (CCS), 36 (*see also* composite counterstorytelling [CCS])
   counterstory as methodology, 2, 3, 21–23, 26–31, 34, 77, 113, 114
   Latinx rhetorics, xxiii, 22
   narrated dialogue, 36
   New Rhetoric, 55–58

racial rhetorical criticism, 124
   rhetorical strategy, 26
*Rhetorical Tradition, The* (Bizzell and Herzberg), 58, 122
rhetoric and writing studies, 116, 143
   canon, 133
   contemporary rhetorics, 133
   disciplinary boundaries, 134
   Euro-Western rhetorics, 123
   neo-Aristotelian rhetorics, 63
   rhetorical strategy, 26
"Rhetoric of the First 'Indians'" (Villanueva), 126
*Rhetoric Review*, 173n11
*Rhetorics of the Americas* (Baca), 122
Richardson, Elaine, 87, 88, 90, 91
*Rodrigo Chronicles* (Delgado), xxv, 21, 23, 33, 36
Roosevelt, Franklin Delano, xxvii
Rousseau, Celia, 113
Rowling, J. K., 178n21
Ruiz, Iris D., 97
   *Decolonizing Rhetoric and Composition Studies*, 97

Sánchez, Raúl, 97
   *Decolonizing Rhetoric and Composition Studies*, 97
self, 23, 37
Self as metaphor, 65–67, 75, 78, 174n14
Shakespeare, William, 64
Sherry, Suzanna
   "Telling Stories Out of School: An Essay on Legal Narratives," 20
Simson, David, 176n9
*Sisters of the Yam* (Bell), 118
skin color, 169n1
social justice, 16, 63, 99
Socrates, 34, 35, 37
Solórzano, Daniel, 2, 3, 11, 17, 22, 28, 111
   "Critical Race Theory's Intellectual Roots: My E-Mail Epistolary

with Derrick Bell," 30
"Space Traders" (Bell), 60–62
Squiers, Anthony, 173n12
status quo, 7, 8, 35
Stefancic, Jean, 10, 20
   *Critical Race Theory: An Introduction*, 10, 20–21, 115, 170n7, 178n1
   *Critical Race Theory: The Cutting Edge*, 8
   *Derrick Bell Reader*, 171n1
stock story, 33–38
Stoffle, Richard, 96
storyteller and storytelling, xxv–xxix, 169n3
   . *See also* counterstory
"Storytelling of Oppositionists and Others: A Plea for Narrative" (Delgado), 21–22, 25
Swearingen, Jan, 63, 117
syllabi samples, 147–67
symbiosis thesis, 10–11, 17
Syracuse University, 98

Tate, William F., 132
"Toward a Critical Race Theory of Education," 111
Taylor, Edward, 10
"Telling Stories Out of School: An Essay on Legal Narratives" (Farber and Sherry), 20
*Telling to Live*, 29–30
*testimonios*, 3, 29–30
*13th* (film), 172n4
Thomas, Kendall, 6
"Toward a Critical Race Theory of Education" (Ladson-Billings and Tate), 111
Trimbur, John, 26
Truth, Sojourner, 12, 170n6
*21 Miles of Scenic Beauty . . . and Then Oxnard: Counterstories and Testimonies* (Gonzalez), 98

University of Arizona, 98
University of Oregon Law School, 7
University of Wisconsin (Madison), 32
US Justice Department, Civil Rights Division, 54

valorization, 16
*Vernacular Insurrections* (Kynard), 4, 76, 77
Villanueva, Victor, xxiii, 24, 26, 87, 88–89, 91, 92, 94–95, 97
   "Blind: Talking about the New Racism," 169–70n3
   "Rhetoric of the First 'Indians'," 126
   *Rhetorics of the Americas*, 122
Vitanza, Victor J., 63, 71, 116

West, Cornel, 125, 170n4
"When Media Treat White Suspects and Killers Better Than Black Victims" (Wing), 124
white privilege, 3, 10, 11, 22–23, 26, 44, 46, 129
white supremacy, xiv, 10, 24, 56, 67, 69, 89–90, 104, 113, 131, 170n4
"Who's Afraid of CRT?" (Bell), 18–20, 31
Williams, Patricia, xiv, 2, 3, 7, 15, 18, 30, 32, 80–109, 114–15, 170n9, 175n2
   *Alchemy of Race and Rights: Diary of a Law Professor*, 21, 82, 84–86, 115, 169n1
   autobiographical reflection, 86–93
   career, 80–82
   composite characters, 25
   critics of, 84–86, 169n1
   crossing borders, 95–109
   feminist poetics, 82–86
   legal theory, 86

personal background, 80–81
Williams, Robert A., Jr., xxv, 33
Winant, Howard, 12
Wing, Adrien Katherine, 8–9, 81
Wing, Nick, 124
Wixáritari people, xxvi
writing studies. *See* rhetoric and writing studies

writing workshop, 61–62, 97–98

Yosso, Tara J., 2, 3, 17, 21, 22, 111, 113–14, 136, 171n10
Young, Vershawn Ashanti, 87, 90, 92, 94, 124

## AUTHOR

**Aja Y. Martinez** is assistant professor of writing and rhetoric at the University of North Texas. Martinez conducts research on and teaches a range of courses concerning rhetorics of race and ethnicity, including the rhetorics of race within both Western and non-Euro-Western contexts, and beginning, professional, and advanced writing courses. Martinez's work argues specifically that counterstory provides opportunities for other(ed) perspectives to contribute to conversations about narrative, dominant ideology, and their intersecting influence on curricular standards and institutional practices. Voices from the margins can become voices of authority through the formation of counterstories—stories that examine, document, and expose the persistence of racial oppression and other forms of subordination. Counterstory serves as a natural extension of inquiry for theorists whose research recognizes and incorporates lived and embodied experiences of marginalized peoples both in the United States and abroad. Martinez's scholarship has appeared in *College English, Composition Studies, Peitho,* and *Rhetoric Review.*

## BOOKS IN THE CCCC STUDIES IN WRITING & RHETORIC SERIES

*Counterstory: The Rhetoric and Writing of Critical Race Theory*
Aja Y. Martinez

*Writing Programs, Veterans Studies, and the Post-9/11 University: A Field Guide*
D. Alexis Hart and Roger Thompson

*Beyond Progress in the Prison Classroom: Options and Opportunities*
Anna Plemons

*Rhetorics Elsewhere and Otherwise: Contested Modernities, Decolonial Visions*
Edited by Romeo García and Damián Baca

*Black Perspectives in Writing Program Administration: From the Margins to the Center*
Edited by Staci M. Perryman-Clark and Collin Lamont Craig

*Translanguaging outside the Academy: Negotiating Rhetoric and Healthcare in the Spanish Caribbean*
Rachel Bloom-Pojar

*Collaborative Learning as Democratic Practice: A History*
Mara Holt

*Reframing the Relational: A Pedagogical Ethic for Cross-Curricular Literacy Work*
Sandra L. Tarabochia

*Inside the Subject: A Theory of Identity for the Study of Writing*
Raúl Sánchez

*Genre of Power: Police Report Writers and Readers in the Justice System*
Leslie Seawright

*Assembling Composition*
Edited by Kathleen Blake Yancey and Stephen J. McElroy

*Public Pedagogy in Composition Studies*
Ashley J. Holmes

*From Boys to Men: Rhetorics of Emergent American Masculinity*
Leigh Ann Jones

*Freedom Writing: African American Civil Rights Literacy Activism, 1955–1967*
Rhea Estelle Lathan

*The Desire for Literacy: Writing in the Lives of Adult Learners*
Lauren Rosenberg

*On Multimodality: New Media in Composition Studies*
Jonathan Alexander and Jacqueline Rhodes

*Toward a New Rhetoric of Difference*
Stephanie L. Kerschbaum

*Rhetoric of Respect: Recognizing Change at a Community Writing Center*
Tiffany Rousculp

*After Pedagogy: The Experience of Teaching*
Paul Lynch

*Redesigning Composition for Multilingual Realities*
Jay Jordan

*Agency in the Age of Peer Production*
Quentin D. Vieregge, Kyle D. Stedman, Taylor Joy Mitchell, and Joseph M. Moxley

*Remixing Composition: A History of Multimodal Writing Pedagogy*
Jason Palmeri

*First Semester: Graduate Students, Teaching Writing, and the Challenge of Middle Ground*
Jessica Restaino

*Agents of Integration: Understanding Transfer as a Rhetorical Act*
Rebecca S. Nowacek

*Digital Griots: African American Rhetoric in a Multimedia Age*
Adam J. Banks

*The Managerial Unconscious in the History of Composition Studies*
Donna Strickland

*Everyday Genres: Writing Assignments across the Disciplines*
Mary Soliday

*The Community College Writer: Exceeding Expectations*
Howard Tinberg and Jean-Paul Nadeau

*A Taste for Language: Literacy, Class, and English Studies*
James Ray Watkins

*Before Shaughnessy: Basic Writing at Yale and Harvard, 1920–1960*
Kelly Ritter

*Writer's Block: The Cognitive Dimension*
Mike Rose

*Teaching/Writing in Thirdspaces: The Studio Approach*
Rhonda C. Grego and Nancy S. Thompson

*Rural Literacies*
Kim Donehower, Charlotte Hogg, and Eileen E. Schell

*Writing with Authority: Students' Roles as Writers in Cross-National Perspective*
David Foster

*Whistlin' and Crowin' Women of Appalachia: Literacy Practices since College*
Katherine Kelleher Sohn

*Sexuality and the Politics of Ethos in the Writing Classroom*
Zan Meyer Gonçalves

*African American Literacies Unleashed: Vernacular English and the Composition Classroom*
Arnetha F. Ball and Ted Lardner

*Revisionary Rhetoric, Feminist Pedagogy, and Multigenre Texts*
Julie Jung

*Archives of Instruction: Nineteenth-Century Rhetorics, Readers, and Composition Books in the United States*
Jean Ferguson Carr, Stephen L. Carr, and Lucille M. Schultz

*Response to Reform: Composition and the Professionalization of Teaching*
Margaret J. Marshall

*Multiliteracies for a Digital Age*
Stuart A. Selber

*Personally Speaking: Experience as Evidence in Academic Discourse*
Candace Spigelman

*Self-Development and College Writing*
Nick Tingle

*Minor Re/Visions: Asian American Literacy Narratives as a Rhetoric of Citizenship*
Morris Young

*A Communion of Friendship: Literacy, Spiritual Practice, and Women in Recovery*
Beth Daniell

*Embodied Literacies: Imageword and a Poetics of Teaching*
Kristie S. Fleckenstein

*Language Diversity in the Classroom: From Intention to Practice*
Edited by Geneva Smitherman and Victor Villanueva

*Rehearsing New Roles: How College Students Develop as Writers*
Lee Ann Carroll

*Across Property Lines: Textual Ownership in Writing Groups*
Candace Spigelman

*Mutuality in the Rhetoric and Composition Classroom*
David L. Wallace and Helen Rothschild Ewald

*The Young Composers: Composition's Beginnings in Nineteenth-Century Schools*
Lucille M. Schultz

*Technology and Literacy in the Twenty-First Century: The Importance of Paying Attention*
Cynthia L. Selfe

*Women Writing the Academy: Audience, Authority, and Transformation*
Gesa E. Kirsch

*Gender Influences: Reading Student Texts*
Donnalee Rubin

*Something Old, Something New: College Writing Teachers and Classroom Change*
Wendy Bishop

*Dialogue, Dialectic, and Conversation: A Social Perspective on the Function of Writing*
Gregory Clark

*Audience Expectations and Teacher Demands*
Robert Brooke and John Hendricks

*Toward a Grammar of Passages*
Richard M. Coe

*Rhetoric and Reality: Writing Instruction in American Colleges, 1900–1985*
James A. Berlin

*Writing Groups: History, Theory, and Implications*
Anne Ruggles Gere

*Teaching Writing as a Second Language*
Alice S. Horning

*Invention as a Social Act*
Karen Burke LeFevre

*The Variables of Composition: Process and Product in a Business Setting*
Glenn J. Broadhead and Richard C. Freed

*Writing Instruction in Nineteenth-Century American Colleges*
James A. Berlin

*Computers & Composing: How the New Technologies Are Changing Writing*
Jeanne W. Halpern and Sarah Liggett

*A New Perspective on Cohesion in Expository Paragraphs*
Robin Bell Markels

*Evaluating College Writing Programs*
Stephen P. Witte and Lester Faigley

This book was typeset in Garamond and Frutiger by Barbara Frazier.
Typefaces used on the cover include Garamond and News Gothic.
The book was printed on 50-lb. White Offset paper
by Seaway Printing Company, Inc.

Made in the USA
Las Vegas, NV
20 August 2025

26620649R00134